THE **RIPPER** OF
WATERLOO ROAD

THE RIPPER OF
WATERLOO ROAD

THE MURDER OF ELIZA GRIMWOOD IN 1838

JAN BONDESON

The
History
Press

First published 2017

The History Press
The Mill, Brimscombe Port
Stroud, Gloucestershire, GL5 2QG
www.thehistorypress.co.uk

British Library Cataloguing in Publication Data.
A catalogue record for this book is available from the British Library.

ISBN 978 0 7509 6779 2

Typesetting and origination by The History Press
Printed and bound in Great Britain by TJ International Ltd

CONTENTS

FOREWORD

Back in 2006, I purchased, through the medium of eBay, a handsomely leather-bound set of the *New Newgate Calendar*, a scarce 'penny dreadful' issued in weekly parts from October 1863 until March 1865.[1] Its two volumes are full of lurid accounts of celebrated criminals, like the mariticidal Catherine Hayes who ended her days being burnt at the stake, William Corder who murdered Maria Marten in the Red Barn, the gamblers Thurtell and Hunt who murdered William Weare at Gill's Hill Cottage, and Mother Brownrigg who tortured and killed her young apprentice girls. Each penny issue has a gory frontispiece depicting some unfortunate individual being stabbed, shot or disembowelled; women are ravished, flogged or thrown out of carriages, and the sadistic Mother Brownrigg advances on her helpless, half-naked victim, whip in hand.

Issues 53 to 61 of the *New Newgate Calendar* contain another thrilling tale: 'Eliza Grimwood, or the Mysteries of Crime', beginning with the highly charged words:

> Murder!
>   How the horrible sound rings in the night air.
>   Murder!
>   What a thrill of horror darts through the frame of the cry. What atrocity — what crime is conveyed in the sentence. The poor, ghastly, bleeding victim, with glazed eyes and livid features, launched into eternity with frightful suddenness … What horror, what agony must be endured by the victim of the assassin's knife.

Murder! Murder!

The horrible cry wakes up the stillness of the night with dreadful effect. Such a cry was taken up from mouth to mouth one bright summer night in July 1838, in the locality of the Waterloo Road ... On the night in question an awful and atrocious murder was committed on a weak, frail woman – a wretched creature of the town was cruelly and barbarously murdered with more than usual atrocity.

Although the account in the *New Newgate Calendar* is full of exaggerations and inaccuracies, it rightly states that the Ripper of Waterloo Road 'with fiendly [*sic*], devilish and horrible atrocity, had inflicted the most hideous and diabolical injuries to the body of the wretched girl, abusing it in a manner that dare not be described'.

I decided to investigate the unsolved 1838 murder of Eliza Grimwood further, spending ten years gathering material for this book.[2] For the researcher or genealogist, it will be a welcome reminder that even what may be perceived as a relatively insignificant historical episode has generated considerable amounts of contemporary and secondary documentation, making it possible to tell the dramatic and exciting murder story as if Eliza Grimwood had been done to death just a few years ago. Well-nigh uniquely for a crime of that period, the diary of the police officer leading the investigation has been preserved for posterity. This means that the murder of Eliza Grimwood can be viewed from a triple perspective: that of the police, that of the contemporary newspapers, and that of its impact on popular culture and tradition. Why did the murder of Eliza Grimwood arouse such intense feelings of revulsion and outrage at the time? What was it about the sexually sadistic murder of a beautiful young prostitute that fascinated people at the time? What was the ultimate fate of Eliza Grimwood's restless spirit, said to have haunted the Waterloo Road murder house for many decades? And what can be deduced about the identity of the perpetrator, and how many victims did this proto-Ripperine Victorian man of blood really claim?

1

THE STAGE IS SET: LONDON IN 1838

In the year 1838, London was the greatest city in the greatest empire on the globe, and its inhabitants were ruled by the benign presence of the youthful, virginal Queen Victoria.[1] Neither George IV nor William IV had been particularly popular monarchs, and there had been jubilation when the reactionary Duke of Cumberland had succeeded to the throne of Hanover and left Britain for good. To Londoners of all classes of society, Victoria's accession to the throne in June 1837, when she was just 18 years old, seemed to herald a new and more prosperous era in the country's history, free of the corruption, waste and excesses for which her wicked uncles had made themselves notorious. There was widespread sympathy for the queen, since she was young, not unattractive and politically innocent. Many books, pamphlets and poems heralded the beginning of her spring-like reign; they dwelt at length on Victoria's great wisdom, goodness and sense of philanthropy. Although her looks owed more to youth than to regularity of features or shapeliness of figure, the early prints of her all depicted her as a beauty.[2]

The youthful Queen Victoria was fond of her old governess, Baroness Lehzen, who maintained a benign influence over her young charge. Although this formidable German lady had no formal position at court, she enjoyed a good deal of influence in royal circles. Queen Victoria's relations with her mother, the intriguing and unpopular Duchess of Kent, had always been problematic. Although the duchess was allowed to keep her

The young Queen Victoria, from Vol. 2 of the *Gallery of Engravings*.

apartments at Buckingham Palace, Victoria dismissed her mother's private secretary (and probable lover), the Irish adventurer Sir John Conroy. Lord Melbourne, the Whig prime minister, was a father figure to the orphaned young queen. A clever, educated gentleman, he dazzled her with his sparkling conversation and delighted her with his flattery. This experienced statesman was instrumental in helping her break free from the unwholesome influence of her mother and Conroy, and he did his best to guide her steps in matters of state after her accession to the throne. Queen Victoria was fond of simple pursuits, like counting the Canalettos in the Buckingham Palace picture galleries together with Baroness Lehzen (there were forty-three of them), amusing herself with puzzles and jigsaws, putting dissected pictures back together with the assistance of Lord Melbourne and Lord Conyngham, or watching her beloved spaniel Dash frolic in the palace grounds.

H. M. Queen Victoria

from a portrait by Dalton, after F. Winterhalter.

Another engraving of the young Queen Victoria, from a portrait by Dalton after F. Winterhalter.

Queen Victoria's household at Buckingham Palace was run to medieval standards by a number of inert functionaries, who jealously protected their ancient privileges, and resented trespass into the customary preserves of their departments. The office of the Lord Chamberlain provided lamps, that of the Lord Steward cleaned and trimmed them, and that of the Master of the Horse made sure they were lit. The insides of the Buckingham Palace windows were cleaned by the Lord Chamberlain's department, the outsides by the Office of Woods and Forests; the cleaning was never performed simultaneously, meaning that Victoria had to gaze through windows that were translucent only. The average age of the royal servants was high; they had been employed through a corrupt 'grace and favour' system, and stayed in service until well past normal retirement age. No person took responsibility for royal security, since it was considered well-nigh unthinkable that any person would have intent to harm or injure the queen. It would take the depredations of Queen Victoria's persistent young stalker, Edward 'the Boy' Jones, who stole her underwear and spied on her in the dressing room, lying underneath a sofa, and the pistol-toting would-be royal assassin Edward Oxford, who fired at the queen in her carriage, for royal security to be upgraded at long last.[3]

★ ★ ★

The same police force that guarded Queen Victoria was also responsible for maintaining law and order among her humble citizens in London's slums and rookeries. For centuries, London's policing had been based on a voluntary system, with unpaid petty constables being selected for an annual term, elected by their fellow parishioners. Since acting as the local policeman was far from popular already in the mid 1700s, many people paid to hire a replacement; this would have been beneficial if these substitutes had been vigorous young men, but often they were just feeble old workhouse inmates. In addition to this system of voluntary petty constables, each parish employed a force of nightwatchmen. Led by their Night Beadle, these watchmen each had a beat to patrol, and were armed with a staff, a lantern, and a rattle with which to sound the alarm if they saw anything untoward. The nightwatchman's lot was a hard one: their status in society was low, their salary a meagre one, and their working hours singularly unappealing.

Many of them were elderly and infirm, and there were unkind jokes about the cracking sound of their rattles, their cracking arthritic joints, and their weather-cracked old voices calling out the time.

Already, in 1785, there was a debate whether this voluntary system of policing was adequate in a London full of vice and crime. It was suggested that the metropolis should be subdivided into nine police divisions, each with its own police office, magistrates, and a force of twenty-five fit and able policemen, properly armed and with far wider powers than the parish constables. This suggestion was turned down, however, and the only major difference in the policing of London between 1690 and 1790 was the addition of a small force of Bow Street Runners, tough and resilient thief-takers in plain clothes based at the Bow Street police office. The capital's indifferent policing was shown up by the London Monster's reign of terror in 1790. This serial stabber of women on the streets of the metropolis sparked an unprecedented mass hysteria, with the people of London seeing Monsters everywhere. Eventually, after the Monster had claimed at least fifty victims, a Welsh artificial flower maker named Rhynwick Williams was arrested and charged with the crimes; he was sentenced to six years in Newgate, although there have been doubts over his guilt. A 'Foot Patrol' and a 'Horse Patrol', both mainly intended to hunt down footpads and highwaymen around London, were added to the Bow Street force in the early 1790s, and 1798 saw the foundation of the Thames River Police. In December 1811, two families were wiped out in the East End of London by an unknown intruder. The Ratcliffe Highway murders caused widespread alarm, since seven respectable people had been slaughtered by the elusive murderer. After much uproar in the East End, a sailor named John Williams was arrested and charged with the murders, but he rather conveniently was found hanged in his cell before he faced trial. Doubts concerning his guilt and speculation regarding the possible existence of an accomplice have persisted, however.[4]

There was widespread criticism of the police after their failure to swiftly apprehend the Ratcliffe Highway murderer, and suggestions that a detective police should be set up according to the system in Paris, but in the debate that ensued, the traditionalists preferring the old voluntary system of policing once more prevailed. The young Tory politician Robert Peel, who became MP for an Irish rotten borough in 1809 at the age of just 21, was a firm proponent of police reform, however. This was not because he had concerns about unsolved murders or dangerous criminals on the loose in London, but because he was fearful of riot and civil unrest. In the Gordon Riots of 1780, a mob 60,000 strong had been at large, marching on Parliament, sacking prisons and burning down houses, wholly unimpeded by the feeble parish constables patrolling the streets. In the 1815 London Corn Law Riots, houses were looted and burned down by the mob, the police once more standing by uselessly. Calling in the army could be dangerous indeed when the rioters were at large. At the Peterloo Massacre in 1819, things got out of hand when cavalry charged a mob of 70,000 in Manchester, resulting in eighteen fatalities and many hundreds of wounded. At the London riots after Queen Caroline's funeral in 1821, the mob blocked the road in front of the funeral cortege. After cobblestones and bricks had been thrown, the troops opened fire, and cavalrymen forming the guard of honour charged the mob with their sabres drawn. This time there were two fatalities among the civilians, and many wounded. The Duke of Wellington was more worried about the risk of mutiny in the Guards after Queen Caroline's return. He wrote a strongly worded memorandum to the Cabinet that to prevent chaos and mob rule, London needed a professional police force.[5]

In 1822, Robert Peel became Home Secretary in Lord Liverpool's Tory government. He took the chair of a select committee on police in the metropolis, and worked tirelessly for police reform. Peel was no conventional and reactionary Tory squire; he identified himself with the prosperous industrial middle class. Not at all unreasonably, he felt that London society needed higher standards of social discipline, through the employment of a professional police force. Later in 1822, there was odium when a well-to-do London lady, Mrs Donatty, was found murdered by an intruder in her house. The police bungled the investigation badly, and the murder was never solved. In 1827, the elderly housekeeper Mrs Elizabeth Jeffs was found murdered in her house at No. 11 Montague Place, Bloomsbury. In spite of a multitude of leads – and a young ne'er-do-well named Bill Jones was arrested and tried for the crime but was found not guilty – the murder was never solved.[6] Although by 1828 the seven London police offices employed constables of their own, and although many parishes had watchmen acting as extra constables, the total number of daytime policemen was just 450, a small force

Painted by Sir Tho. Lawrence P. R.A. Engraved by J. Cochran

THE R.T HON.BLE SIR ROBERT PEEL, BAR.T

Robert Peel, the great Metropolitan law enforcement pioneer, from Vol. 4 of the *New Portrait Gallery*.

indeed for 1.5 million Londoners. In July 1829, Peel finally had success: his Police Bill received royal assent, and work started to build up the embryonic Metropolitan Police. London was subdivided into seventeen alphabetically named divisions, each of which would be led by a superintendent, and employ four inspectors, sixteen sergeants and 144 constables. The New Police was led by two commissioners, the Waterloo veteran Colonel Charles Rowan and the up-and-coming young Irish barrister Richard Mayne, from headquarters at No. 4 Whitehall Place, Westminster, in the front half of the 'A' Division station house, which opened into Great Scotland Yard.

There was a good deal of unemployment in 1829, and recruitment of all these police constables proved surprisingly easy: discharged soldiers and sailors, labouring men of every description, and former Bow Street foot patrols joined the New Police with enthusiasm, although the hours were long and the pay low. To be eligible, the recruits had to be able-bodied and at least 5ft 7in tall, under 35 years old, literate and of good character. Former army warrant officers and NCOs secured many of the appointments as inspectors and sergeants. The New Policemen, or 'Peelers' as they were commonly known, were dressed in a distinctive uniform that was selected to be civilian-looking and uncontroversial: a swallow-tailed blue coat with a single row of shiny buttons, a stiff collar and leather neck-stock, and a reinforced tall hat; their trousers were white in the summer and blue in the winter. In contrast to the Bow Street Runners and Horse Patrols, who were armed to the teeth since they were dealing with dangerous ruffians and highwaymen, each constable carried only a rattle and a short truncheon. In order to appease the opponents of the New Police, Peel and the two commissioners emphasised that their police force was there to prevent crime, not to harass the good people of London. Neither of these three worthies considered that London needed a force of specially trained and selected detectives, however, and thus the uniformed officers of the New Police were in charge of investigating crimes of every severity, from capital murder down to petty theft.[7]

★ ★ ★

Sir Charles Rowan and Richard Mayne, the two first commissioners of the New Police.

Old Scotland Yard, from Vol. 3 of Hargrave L. Adam's *Police Encyclopaedia*.

It would not be long before the detection skills of the New Police were tested. In August 1830, the middle-aged widow Mrs Jane Whillett was murdered in her house at No. 30 Upper Prince's Street, Lambeth. She had been running a small marine store on the premises, selling second-hand clothes, empty bottles, and other humble articles to various needy locals. She had several sons, one of whom was still living at home, as was her daughter who had married a man named Norris; there was also a lodger named John Witham, who worked as a journeyman barge builder. It was Witham who had found Mrs Whillett beaten to death in her kitchen, with marks of repeated heavy blows to her face and head. Since she had been as poor as the proverbial church mouse, robbery seemed an unlikely motive; the 'L' or Lambeth division of the New Police, who were 'using the greatest exertions to discover the actual murderer', rather suspected a 'family drama'. They knew, through the local gossip mill, that the lodger Witham had been more than friendly with Mrs Whillett. Since the remaining Bow Street Runners were unkind enough to make some snide remarks about the failure of the New Police to catch the murderer, the Union Hall magistrate Mr Chambers 'hoped that no jealousy would exist between the old and new police upon this occasion, and that they would co-operate, and by their united exertions be the means of bringing the perpetrator of the murder to justice'. The New Police maintained that John Witham was the main suspect, since they thought Mrs Whillett had taken tea with her killer before he struck her down. But although Witham was examined by the Union Hall magistrates, there was no conclusive evidence against him, and his employer thought him a very respectable and hard-working man. When Witham was eventually discharged, and the murder of Jane Whillett remained a mystery, an article in the *Morning Post* took the part of the New Police. Unlike the old-fashioned and ineffective watchmen, and the corrupt Bow Street thief-takers, Peel's system of policing aimed for crime prevention rather than punishment. Although the New Police had been 'condemned for their over-anxiety to discover the perpetrator of the late murder in Lambeth', the new system was honest, fair and free of corruption, the journalist asserted; his readers were reminded that under the old system of policing, the murderers of Mrs Donatty and Mrs Jeffs had escaped with impunity.[8]

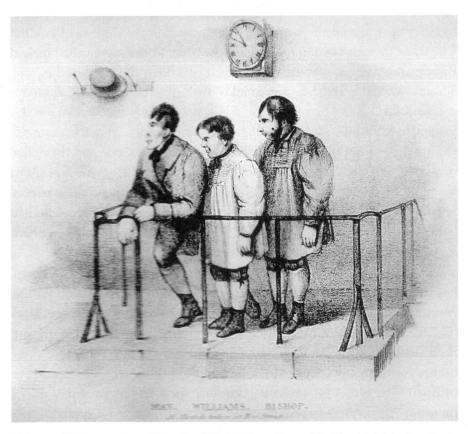

Bishop and Williams at Bow Street, from Vol. 2 of Percy Fitzgerald's *Chronicles of the Bow Street Police Office.*

In the 1820s and early 1830s, the medical faculties and anatomy schools of London had a considerable shortage of fresh bodies for detection. This opened the door for organised gangs of bodysnatchers, who would purchase the bodies of moribund people from the relatives, or rob newly dug graves in the churchyards. A good-quality cadaver could fetch £10 or even £20, meaning that, undeterred by the grisly fate of their Edinburgh colleagues Burke and Hare, these London ruffians could make a good living from their wholesale grave-robbing activities. On 5 November 1831, the two bodysnatchers John Bishop and James May delivered the corpse of a 14-year-old boy to the King's College anatomy school. They wanted 12 guineas, but were offered 9 guineas by the King's College porter. The cadaver seemed uncommonly fresh, however, and there were no signs that it had ever been buried; the face was strangely swollen and the eyes bloodshot. The 'F' or Covent Garden Division of the New Police were called in, and Bishop and May were arrested, along with two other members of the gang, Thomas Williams and Michael Shields. Bishop lived in a Bethnal Green cottage, No. 3 Nova Scotia Gardens, and when the police excavated the garden, they found items of clothing suggesting that the gang had committed multiple murders. The boy's identity remained a mystery, but the police suspected that he was Carlo Ferrari, an Italian who had made a perilous living by exhibiting a tortoise and some white mice in the London streets. Shields, who successfully argued that he had only been the porter who had helped to carry the boy's remains, was liberated, but the other three ruffians stood trial for murder.

The three London Burkers were found guilty and sentenced to death, but May was eventually reprieved and sentenced to transportation for life. Awaiting execution, Bishop and Williams confessed to their crimes. They had drugged two boys and a slum dweller with rum and laudanum, and then drowned them in a water butt in the rear garden, and sold their bodies for dissection. The police allowed the public access to the house of horrors at No. 3 Nova Scotia Gardens, for a fee of 5s, and many of the domestic fixtures were carried off by the curious, who wanted some souvenirs from the murderers' lair. Bishop and Williams were hanged at Newgate on 5 December 1831, in front of a crowd 30,000 strong. Rather suitably, considering the nature of their crimes, their bodies were dissected at the Theatre of Anatomy in Windmill Street, and the remains exhibited in public. The New Police were praised for the speedy arrest and conviction of the London Burkers.[9]

In December 1832, the 63-year-old clerk Henry Camp Shepherd was found murdered in the counting house of his employers, Messrs Williams & Sons, soap manufacturers, of Great Compton Street. His skull had been brutally bashed in with a poker. The counting house contained an unopened safe, for which Mr Shepherd held the keys. Although nothing had been stolen from the safe, Mr Shepherd's watch was missing, and the motive for the crime was supposed to have been robbery.

For undisclosed reasons, one of the remaining Bow Street Runners, Lloyd of Hatton Garden, took charge of the murder investigation.

A handbill on Bishop and Williams, from Vol. 2 of Percy Fitzgerald's *Chronicles of the Bow Street Police Office.*

THE TRIAL, SENTENCE, FULL CONFESSION, AND EXECUTION OF
BISHOP & WILLIAMS,
THE BURKERS.

BURKING AND BURKERS.

The month of November, 1831, will be recorded in the annals of crimes and cruelties as particularly pre-eminent, for it will prove to posterity that other wretches could be found base enough to follow the horrid example of Burke and his accomplice Hare, to entice the unprotected and friendless to the den of death for sordid gain.

The horrible crime of "Burking," or murdering the unwary with the intention of selling their bodies at a high price to the anatomical schools, for the purpose of dissection, has unfortunately obtained a notoriety which will not be soon or easily forgotten. It took its horrifying appellation from the circumstances which were disclosed on the trial of the inhuman wretch Burke, who was executed at Edinburgh in 1829, for having wilfully and deliberately murdered several persons for the sole purpose of profiting by the sale of their dead bodies.

APPREHENSION OF THE BURKERS.

On Tuesday, November 8th, four persons, viz., John

Bishop, Thomas Williams, James May, and Michael Shield, were examined at Bow Street Police Office on the charge of being concerned in the wilful murder of an unknown Italian boy. From the evidence adduced, it appeared that May, *alias* Jack Stirabout, a known resurrection-man, and Bishop, a body-snatcher, offered at King's College a subject for sale, Shield and Williams having charge of the body in a hamper, for which they demanded twelve guineas. Mr Partridge, demonstrator of anatomy, who, although not in absolute want of a subject, offered nine guineas, but being struck with its freshness sent a messenger to the police station, and the fellows were then taken into custody, examined before the magistrates, when Shield was discharged and the others ultimately committed for trial.

THE TRIAL.

Friday, December 2nd, having been fixed for the trial of the prisoners charged with the murder of the Italian boy, the Court was crowded to excess so early as eight o'clock in the morning.

At nine o'clock the Deputy Recorder, Mr Serjeant

The end of the London Burkers, from the *Curiosities of Street Literature* (London 1871), sheet 190.

Mr Shepherd is found murdered, from the
Illustrated Police News, 23 April 1904.

Mr Shepherd had complained that
when out on company business in
rural Hampstead and Highgate, he
had been followed by some ruffianly
fellows who had the appearance of
glaziers. Two men in similar attire had
been observed skulking about near the
soap factory. A young man named Samuel Newland was taken into custody
on suspicion of being involved in the murder, since he was employed at
the soap factory and had murmured against Mr Shepherd in the past, but
he could prove a solid alibi, and was discharged. Instead, another remaining
Runner, Lea of Lambeth Street, got a tip from a convict that Mr Shepherd
had been murdered by two previous associates of this convict, named Tom
Ainsley and Jem Martin. These two were promptly arrested and brought
before Mr Allen Laing, the Hatton Garden magistrate. It turned out that
Ainsley had no previous convictions, and since he seemed like a respectable man, he was released. Jem Martin, who had several convictions for
petty theft, and who looked most dejected at being accused of murder,
was several times examined by the magistrate. Runner Lea had discovered
that Martin's clothes had been stained with blood, and he took note of the
man's alibi for the time of the murder, which he hoped to be able to prove
false. But in the end, Jem Martin was also discharged by the magistrate, due

to the lack of evidence against him,
and in spite of a government reward of
£100, matched by another £100 from
Mr Williams the soap manufacturer,
the murder of Henry Camp Shepherd
was never solved.[10]

Catherine Elms is found murdered, from the
Illustrated Police News, 28 November 1903.

In May 1833, the New Police faced yet another challenge when the elderly spinster Catherine Elms was found murdered in her house at No. 17 Wellesley Street, Chelsea. She had been stabbed around the face and throat with some formidable instrument. In her younger days, Miss Elms had kept a school in Smith Lane, but now she was retired and let out rooms in her house to lodgers. A quiet, inoffensive old lady, she was not known to have any enemies. A young woman known as Mrs Mortimer, who lodged in the house, appeared very keen to get up to her own room and check her belongings; since this attracted suspicion, she was arrested by the police. Mrs Mortimer asserted her innocence, and went as far as to put her hand on the mangled body of Catherine Elms, exclaiming, 'So help me God, I am innocent of any participation in this murder!' This exhibition of the old superstition of 'touching the body' impressed the police greatly, and Mrs Mortimer was promptly released. At the coroner's inquest on Catherine Elms, it was revealed that before the murder she had gone to the Wellesley Arms to purchase half a pint of stout for her dinner. Since the jug she had brought for her stout was found to be empty, and since no remains of food were found in her kitchen, it was presumed that she had finished her frugal repast, before being surprised and murdered by some intruder or intruders. Two ruffianly fellows had been spotted lurking outside the pub when Miss Elms came to have her jug filled, and they were presumed to have been the murderers. There was no clue whatsoever to their identity, however, and the coroner's inquest returned a verdict of murder against some person or persons unknown. On 15 May, a man named John Sharpe came up to a police constable and confessed that he was one of the men who had murdered Miss Elms. He was a man of low repute, and a suspected coiner; he had previously given himself up for murdering his two children, but they turned out to have died from the measles. After being examined by the magistrate Mr White, at the Queen Square police office, Sharpe withdrew his confession, and he was eventually released since there was no convincing evidence against him. It aroused suspicions among the police, however, that he had spoken of the pump in Miss Elms' kitchen, since there was really such a pump – a fact that had not been made public. In spite of some late bruits that the nephew of Catherine Elms had returned to London from New York to murder her, due to some testamentary shenanigans from an uncle who had died in the West

James Greenacre dismembers Hannah Brown, from an old print.

Indies and left £7,500, the murder was never solved." As for the murder house at No. 17 Wellesley Street, which was later to become Upper Manor Street and today is Chelsea Manor Street, it no longer stands.

In late December 1836, a sack containing a woman's headless and limbless torso was found at a recently constructed terrace of houses in the Edgware Road, near the Pineapple Tollgate. A week later, a woman's severed head, with long grey hair, was found jamming a lock in the Regent's Canal. In early February, a Camberwell workman found a sack containing two legs, which fitted the torso perfectly. This was clearly a case of murder with dismemberment, and the first task for the New Police was to identify the Edgware Road murder victim.

The severed head was put in a jar of spirits and exhibited in a workhouse, but no person could recognise its bloated and battered features.

A washerwoman named Hannah Brown, the widow of a shoemaker, was reported missing by her relatives, and her brother Mr Gay recognised the severed head's mutilated ear, the result of an earring being pulled out by a fellow servant. A naïve and trusting woman, Hannah Brown had answered a newspaper advertisement from a certain James Greenacre, and agreed to supply her savings of £300 to support the commercial exploitation of a novel washing machine he had invented. These two had become very friendly, and just before she had disappeared on Christmas Eve, Hannah Brown had told her relatives that they were planning to get married.

Greenacre the Murderer of M.ʳˢ Brown.

James Greenacre on the frontispiece of a small provincial *Newgate Calendar*, printed in Derby 1844.

Inspector Feltham and Constable Pegler, of the 'T' or Kensington division of the New Police, found out that the 51-year-old James Greenacre was a businessman who dabbled as a grocer and tea merchant, and owned a number of slum houses. He claimed to hold an estate in Hudson Bay, something that had impressed Hannah Brown very much. Three of Greenacre's previous wives had died of disease, and he had left the fourth behind in America. After Christmas, Greenacre had told a friend that the marriage was off since Hannah Brown had unexpectedly got into debt and left London.

Instead, his mistress Sarah Gale had moved back into his house. The police suspected that Greenacre had murdered Hannah Brown on Christmas Eve 1836, dismembered the body and distributed its mutilated parts all over London, before getting on with his life as well as he could. Greenacre and Sarah Gale were both arrested by Inspector Feltham on 24 March, just as they were making preparations to sail for America, and they were committed to stand trial at the Old Bailey the following month. The sack containing Hannah Brown's remains could be traced to Greenacre, and her earrings had been found in Sarah Gale's possession. Greenacre asserted that Hannah Brown had died accidentally when her chair had tipped over backwards, but he was not believed, since she had clearly been hit hard with a stick or bludgeon, putting her eye out. Both James Greenacre and Sarah Gale were found guilty and sentenced to death, although Gale received a reprieve and was transported to Australia, where she lived on for another fifty years, not expiring until 1888. The public execution of Greenacre in front of Newgate was a fairground event, attracting 20,000 spectators. The New Police could exult that they had been able to bring a cunning and premeditating murderer to justice.[12] Greenacre's head was shaved after death, for phrenological examination, and his death mask was exhibited at the Black Museum for many years. In his poem 'A Lay of St Gengulphus', Richard Harris Barham included a topical reference to the sanguineous career of the Edgware Road murderer:

They contrived to pack up the trunk in a sack,
Which they hid in an osier-bed outside the town,
The clerk bearing arms, legs and all on his back,
As that vile Mr Greenacre served Mrs Brown.

LIFE, TRIAL, CONFESSION, & EXECUTION

OF

JAMES GREENACRE,

FOR THE

EDGEWARE ROAD MURDER.

On the 22nd of April, James Greenacre was found guilty of the wilful murder of Hannah Brown, and Sarah Gale with being accessary after the fact. A long and connected chain of evidence was produced, which showed, that the sack in which the body was found was the property of Mr. Ward; that it was usually deposited in a part of the premises which led to the workshop, and could without observation have been carried away by him; that the said sack contained several fragments of shavings of mahogany, such as were made in the course of business by Ward; and that it contained some pieces of linen cloth, which had been patched with nankeen; that this linen cloth matched exactly with a frock which was found on Greenacre's premises, and which belonged to the female prisoner. Feltham, a police-officer, deposed, that on the 25th of March he apprehended the prisoners at the lodgings of Greenacre; that on searching the trowsers pockets of that person, he took therefrom a pawnbroker's duplicate for two silk gowns, and from the fingers of the female prisoner two rings, and also a similar duplicate for two veils, and an old-fashioned silver watch, which she was endeavouring to conceal; and it was further proved that these articles were pledged by the prisoners, and that they had been the property of the deceased woman.—Two surgeons were examined, whose evidence was most important, and whose depositions were of the greatest consequence in throwing a clear light on the manner in which the female, Hannah Brown, met with her death. Mr. Birtwhistle deposed, that he had carefully examined the head; that the right eye had been knocked out by a blow inflicted while the person was living; there was also a cut on the check, and the jaw was fractured, these two last wounds were, in his opinion, produced after death; there was also a bruise on the head, which had occurred after death; the head had been separated by cutting, and the *bone sawed nearly through*, and then broken off; there were the marks of a saw, which fitted with a saw which was found in Greenacre's box. Mr. Girdwood, a surgeon, very minutely and skilfully described the appearances presented on the head, and showed incontestibly, that the head had been severed from the body *while the person was yet alive;* that this was proved by the retraction, or drawing back, of the muscles at the parts where they were separated by the knife, and further, by the blood-vessels being empty, the body was drained of blood. This part of the evidence produced a thrill of horror throughout the court, but Greenacre remained quite unmoved.

After a most impressive and impartial summing up by the learned Judge, the jury retired, and, after the absence of a quarter of an hour, returned into court, and pronounced a verdict of "Guilty" against both the prisoners.

The prisoners heard the verdict without evincing the least emotion, or the slightest change of countenance. After an awful silence of a few minutes, the Lord Chief Justice said they might retire, as they would be remanded until the end of the session.

They were then conducted from the bar, and on going down the steps, the unfortunate female prisoner kissed Greenacre with every mark of tenderness and affection.

The crowd outside the court on this day was even greater than on either of the preceding; and when the result of the trial was made known in the street, a sudden and general shout succeeded, and continued huzzas were heard for several minutes.

THE EXECUTION.

At half past seven the sheriff arrived in his carriage, and in a short time the press-yard was thronged with gentlemen who had been admitted by tickets. The unhappy convict was now led from his cell. When he arrived in the press-yard, his whole appearance pourtrayed the utmost misery and spirit-broken dejection; his countenance haggard, and his whole frame agitated; all that self-possession and fortitude which he displayed in the early part of his imprisonment, had utterly forsaken him, and had left him a victim of hopelessness and despair. He requested the executioner to give him as little pain as posible in the process of pinioning his arms and wrists; he uttered not a word in allusion to his crime; neither did he make any dying request, except that his spectacles might be given to Sarah Gale; he exhibited no sign of hope; he showed no symptom of reconciliation with his offended God! When the venerable ordinary preceded him in the solemn procession through the vaulted passage to the fatal drop, he was so overcome and unmanned, that he could not support himself without the aid of the assistant executioner. At the moment he ascended the faithless floor, from which he was to be launched into eternity, the most terrific yells, groans, and cheers were vociferated by the immense multitude surrounding the place of execution. Greenacre bowed to the sheriff, and begged he might not be allowed to remain long in the concourse; and almost immediately the fatal bolt was withdrawn, and, without a struggle, he became a lifeless corse.—Thus ended the days of Greenacre, a man endowed with more than ordinary talents, respectably connected, and desirably placed in society; but a want of probity, an absolute dearth of principle, led him on from one crime to another, until at length he perpetrated the sanguinary deed which brought his career to an awful and disgraceful period, and which has enrolled his name among the most notorious of those who have expiated their crime on the gallows.

On hearing the death-bell toll, Gale became dreadfully agitated; and when she heard the brutal shouts of the crowd of spectators, she fainted, and remained in a state of alternate mental agony and insensibility throughout the whole day.

After having been suspended the usual time, his body was cut down, and buried in a hole dug in one of the passages of the prison, near the spot where Thistlewood and his associates were deposited.

T. Catnach, Printer, 2 and 3, Monmouth Court.

The end of James Greenacre, from the *Curiosities of Street Literature* (London 1871), sheet 192.

★ ★ ★

Prostitution was a subject that both repelled and fascinated the Londoners of the 1820s and 1830s.[13] According to the conventional morals of the time, prostitution was the Great Social Evil, a cancer in the midst of society that could not be cut out. Moralist authors emphasised the harm done by the prostitute, corrupting the minds of young men and infecting them with venereal disease, and described the brothels as hellholes full of every vice and debauchery. Respectable men should pass the harlot flaunting herself in the street with downcast eyes, and decent women should not even have knowledge of what she was doing. A woman falling into prostitution was supposed to be an accursed creature who could not live long in her sin and shame. Debauched, drunken and disease-ridden, the prostitute was wont to destroy herself in a fit of anguish and remorse, and leap headlong into the Thames.

The slums of London were more symmetrically distributed in 1838 than they are today. Whereas Kensington, Chelsea and Bloomsbury were respectable middle-class suburbs, parts of Westminster and most of St Giles were notorious slum rookeries. The East End was quite a black spot already in the 1830s. The 1837 *Return of the number of Brothels and Prostitutes within the Metropolitan Police District* lists 3,325 brothels and an estimated 9,409 prostitutes throughout the metropolis; of these, 209 brothels and 1,803 prostitutes were based in the 'H' police division, incorporating Spitalfields, Whitechapel and Ratcliffe, some of the most deprived slums of London.[14] Similarly, an academic study of the first point of contact between prostitute and client, estimated from the Old Bailey proceedings from 1820 until 1829, shows a sinister cluster in the East End, where brothels were plentiful and street-walking prostitutes a common sight. There is a second cluster in the Covent Garden area, the traditional headquarters of London vice in Georgian times, with many theatres, coffee houses, taverns and brothels. Quite a few prostitutes were active in various parts of the City of London, fewer in Westminster, and very few in Kensington and Chelsea.[15]

Several early authors on prostitution made attempts to estimate the number of prostitutes in the metropolis. As early as 1791, the police magistrate Patrick Colquhoun claimed that the capital was home to 50,000 prostitutes, half of them 'kept women', the other half common street prostitutes. In 1839, Dr Michael Ryan, another anti-prostitution campaigner, claimed that London had between 80,000 and 100,000 prostitutes. This vast army of fallen women, a veritable scourge on decent society, each had a 'bully' or protector: vicious men capable of murder, or any other crime. Although he was a respectable medical lecturer and editor, Dr Ryan seems to have had a bee in his bonnet about prostitution and its vices, and his figure is not based on practical experience but on extrapolation alone.[16] The 1837 estimate of about 9,000 London prostitutes is likely to be closer to the truth.

An impediment for any attempt to estimate the number of prostitutes in London is how to define a 'prostitute', since the profession was heterogeneous enough. At the bottom of the social scale, there were the East End wretches inhabiting the slum brothels: poor, drunken, prematurely aged and riddled with venereal disease, and resembling the victims of Jack the Ripper although living fifty years earlier. Some of the more ambitious streetwalking prostitutes wanted to escape the brothels, rather understandably so, since the brothel-keepers took much of their earnings, and employed 'bullies' who beat them up if they complained. These independent prostitutes often had boyfriends of their own, who doubled as pimps who protected them from perverts and violent drunks, and made sure the customers paid their fee. The better class of prostitutes had houses or lodgings of their own, and mostly saw 'regulars' – either jolly young rakes or respectable gentlemen who wanted some extramarital 'fun'. They could choose their customers rather than accept all takers, and prostitute themselves if and when they wanted to, leading a normal life most of the time; they did not walk the streets, but might occasionally pick up customers in the West End theatres. It sometimes happened that one of these 'regulars' wanted to 'keep' their favourite to have her for himself; all over London, there were 'kept women' supported by wealthy Lotharios, who might have a wife at home and a different mistress for every day in the week. Nor was it unknown for the better class of prostitute to retire at the age of 30, and buy a nice coffee house or lodgings for the earnings she had accumulated, to lead a humdrum and respectable life for the remainder of her days. At the very top of the social scale of London prostitutes were the courtesans of high society, 'kept' by noblemen and wealthy magnates.

In Georgian times, there was little sympathy for the London streetwalking prostitutes. Immoral, sinful and disease-ridden, they were viewed as common street pests. The police made the occasional raid, arresting a number of prostitutes, but they were not kept in custody for very long, returning to work the streets after just a few days in prison. But in the 1820s and 1830s, there was finally some compassion for London's downtrodden fallen women. They were known as 'unfortunates', seduced and let down by some village rake, and forced into prostitution as a result. Efforts were made to close down the brothels, and to reform their inhabitants by various stratagems.[17] As for the brothel-keepers and 'bullies' who lived on the earnings of the unfortunates, they were viewed as the scum of the earth, scoundrels capable of any atrocity.

★ ★ ★

In 1838, London extended north as far as Camden Town and Islington, east as far as the West India Docks, south as far as Lambeth, Kennington and Walworth, and west as far as Chelsea and Kensington. From west to east, the Battersea, Vauxhall, Westminster, Waterloo, Blackfriars, Southwark and London bridges crossed the Thames. Peckham, Clapham and Tooting remained small villages situated just south of London.

In 1806, the Strand Building Company had decided to construct another bridge across the Thames. The Strand Bridge, as they initially decided to call it, would be situated midway between the Westminster and Blackfriars bridges, and the company hoped to recoup its investments through the income from bridge tolls. North Lambeth, on the southern side of the proposed bridge, was still very rural in the early 1800s. It contained a number of woollen cloth manufactories and breweries, as well as several small farms. On the southern bank of the Thames were a number of shipyards and timber yards. The Strand Building Company purchased 3 acres of land from Jesus College for the southern approach to the bridge. They decided on an attractive bridge design by John Rennie, with nine semi-elliptical river arches made of Cornish granite.

Following the Battle of Waterloo, the Strand Building Company became the Waterloo Bridge Company, and Rennie's bridge became Waterloo Bridge. The bridge and its approaches cost in excess of £937,000 to con-

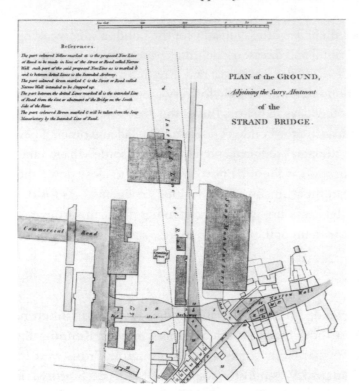

A drawing showing the plan for the new Strand Bridge.

Waterloo Bridge and Somerset House. An engraving from an aquatint by T.S. Roberts.

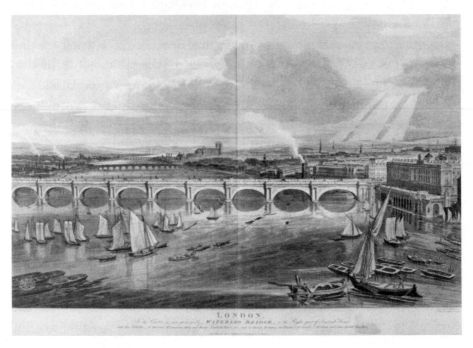

struct. It was opened by the Prince Regent and the Duke of Wellington on 18 June 1817, with much pomp, on the second anniversary of the Battle of Waterloo.[18] The artist John Constable was present at the opening of Waterloo Bridge, and made several sketches, which he made use of to paint a monumental canvas of the opening ceremony, exhibited at the Royal Academy in 1832. The great Italian neoclassical sculptor Antonio Canova was deeply impressed with Waterloo Bridge, calling it the noblest bridge in the world, and declaring that, for a foreigner, it was worth going to London solely to see it. A French art lover named M. Dupin called Waterloo Bridge a colossal monument, comparable with the efforts of the Pharaoh Sesostris and the Caesars. But in spite of these plaudits from the Continental aesthetes, there were soon worrying signs that Waterloo Bridge would not become a commercial success. The bridge did not lead to anywhere particularly interesting, since the Lambeth side was still largely undeveloped in 1817. Furthermore, impecunious Londoners could save their halfpenny toll by crossing the river on the nearby Westminster or Blackfriars bridges instead, since they were both toll-free.

When Waterloo Bridge was opened in 1817, work was already under way to transform North Lambeth into another London suburb south of the river. Waterloo Bridge Road, later called Waterloo Road, would run in a straight line from the new bridge to the junction with Westminster Bridge Road, Blackfriars Road and Borough Road at St George's Circus. By 1838, Lambeth had been fully 'developed' and incorporated with London. The old farms, fields and rustic cottages were all gone, although a few of the factories, and many of the riverside shipyards and timber yards, had been allowed to remain.[19] Not far away from Waterloo Bridge was a curious Thames-side edifice known as the Shot Tower or the Lambeth Lead Works, a tall and distinctive tower constructed in 1826 for the manufacture of lead shot through dropping molten lead from a great height.

The southern approaches to Waterloo Bridge were carried on a series of brick arches, along which was a terrace of houses and shops on each side: Wellington Terrace to the east and Southampton Terrace to the west. In the 1830s, rows of terraced houses in a main street were often given names of their own, and numbered independently; this was the case for 'Wellington Terrace, Waterloo Road'. Wellington Terrace was first mentioned

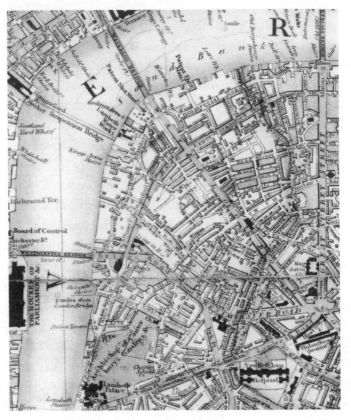

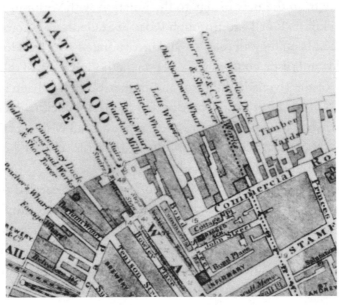

in the newspapers in May 1826. It consisted of twenty-five terraced houses, numbered from south to north. It may well have been constructed in 1823, since an authority on old London street tablets makes mention of a tablet inscribed 'Wellington Terrace, 1823' situated between what had become No. 35 and No. 37 Waterloo Road.[20]

The Feathers tavern, situated at the northern extremity of Wellington Terrace at No. 25, was really two public houses, the upper one in Waterloo Road itself, the lower in Commercial Street, far below the arches of the bridge. A forgotten Victorian novel, Albert Smith's *Christopher Tadpole*, gives a lurid description of this strange part of London, a street above a street. The houses were all cellars, storeys under storeys of cellars, the lowest of which no one could fathom. From these subterraneous regions, inhabited only by dray horses and coal heavers, the wind rushed up frightful chasms from the unknown depths below, through the iron gratings in Waterloo Road. According to Smith, the neighbourhood was a seedy one, and prostitution abounded: 'The streets adjoining are nearly all tenanted by the same fallen fair ones of creation; or, more properly, by persons who live on them, and with whom they live and lodge.'

Opposite Page:

Top: North Lambeth in 1844, from Laurie's *Map of London*.

Bottom: The area around Waterloo Road in 1876, from McIntosh's *Plan of the Parish of Lambeth*. This is the only London map to show the situation of Wellington Terrace.

The Feathers public house and Wellington Terrace, from Vol. 6 of Walter Thornbury and Edward Walford's *Old and New London* (London ND).

A LEAP FROM WATERLOO BRIDGE.

Intent on self-destruction, a desperate woman leaps from Waterloo Bridge, from the *Illustrated Police News*, 13 June 1885.

Opposite: Busy traffic on Waterloo Bridge, from a postcard stamped and posted in 1912.

A look at the relevant Post Office directories tends to put the lie to Smith's statement, however, since most of the Wellington Terrace householders are listed as respectable tradesmen: bakers, cheesemongers, plumbers, tailors and fruiterers. Many, but not all, of the houses had shops on the ground floors. Albert Smith was right, however, that the area south of Waterloo Bridge was a seedy one: many of the streets leading into Waterloo Road were infested with prostitutes, bullies and brothels, Granby Street and the New Cut in particular. It was not for nothing that Waterloo Bridge became known as a 'suicide bridge' where desperate women jumped into the Thames to destroy themselves, inspiring Thomas Hood's poem 'The Bridge of Sighs'.

The Frenchwoman Flora Tristan, who wrote a book after visiting London in the 1820s and 1830s, went across Waterloo Bridge one evening to titillate her Paris readers about this London black spot of vice, accompanied by two sturdy Frenchmen armed with canes. She was appalled to see that:

The neighbourhood is almost entirely inhabited by prostitutes and people who live off prostitution: it is courting danger to go there alone at night. It was a hot summer evening; in every window and doorway women were laughing and joking with their protectors. Half-dressed, some of them naked to the waist, they were a revolting sight, and the criminal, cynical expressions of their companions filled me with apprehension.[21]

The London lecher 'Walter', author of the pornographic book *My Secret Life*, went to Granby Street to meet a prostitute in 1845, and was equally impressed by the amount of vice going on in the streets leading off Waterloo Road.[22]

But enough of 'Peelers', enough of prostitutes, enough of bridges and Lambeth topography; the stage has been set, the acting company is waiting in the wings; let the Waterloo Road tragedy commence! There will be blood, there will be murder, there will be suspense – let us investigate one of the great mysteries of old London: the unsolved murder of the beautiful Eliza Grimwood back in 1838.

2

THE WATERLOO ROAD HORROR

It is the evening of Friday 26 May 1838.[1] We are at the Strand Theatre, a fashionable establishment managed by the celebrated playwright Douglas William Jerrold, and situated at Nos 168–9 Strand. In spite of its narrow façade to the Strand, the theatre boasts a dress circle, a first circle, twelve private boxes and a capacious pit, giving it a capacity of not less than 1,500 souls. The theatre had been constructed as recently as 1832 and handsomely decorated in white, silver and gold. It was considerably enlarged in 1836. A reviewer called it an elegant little theatre, and admired the performances laid on by Douglas Jerrold and his partner William John Hammond: plays based on the early novels of Charles Dickens, and various popular burlesques, melodramas and extravaganzas.[2]

It is not known what performance was playing at the Strand Theatre on 26 May 1838, but we know that on the night, the theatre was quite crowded.

Among the throng of people in the pits is our beautiful young heroine Eliza Grimwood, elegantly attired in a fawn-coloured dress, a dark shawl and a blue bonnet with a flower in it. She speaks to some female friends belonging to the better class of prostitute, just like herself. Many of them are at the theatre for prearranged meetings with various regular customers. About fifteen minutes before the play is to end, Eliza spies a dapperly dressed, foreign-looking young man, whom she was obviously planning to meet at the theatre; she taps her friend on the shoulder with her fan, and

A rather grainy photograph of the Strand Theatre, taken before its demolition in 1905. *In the Soup* is playing.

says something that sounds like, 'I am going out with … He is here.' After the performance has ended, Eliza goes to meet her gentleman friend, and they leave the theatre together. In spite of his foreign looks, the man speaks good English; he is well dressed in dark clothes and a wide-brimmed hat, and although it is a warm and dry summer evening, he is carrying a mackintosh across his arm. At the cab rank opposite the Spotted Dog public house, Eliza and the Foreigner take a cab across the bridge to her home at No. 12 Wellington Terrace, Waterloo Road; as he takes her hand, she gaily steps into the chariot of death. The Devil had beguiled her, and she did eat!

As the old-fashioned hansom cab is slowly progressing across Hood's Bridge of Sighs, Eliza and her young friend are speaking and laughing together; the cabman thinks them very jolly, as if they were old friends. The young man calls her 'Lizzy' and seems quite cheeky and familiar. The cabman hands over half a penny to the Waterloo Bridge toll-keeper – *Date obolum Belisario!* – and the vehicle proceeds across to the Lambeth side of the bridge. The passenger is the Devil, the driver a man without a face, the horse snorts sulphur and brimstone, and sinister sparks fly from the cab wheels. Yet Eliza seems to suspect nothing, keeping up a cheerful conversation with her companion as the cab rolls past the Feathers public house, and pulls to a halt outside No. 12 Wellington Terrace.

The Foreigner hastily walks out, as if perhaps he was keen to hide his face, but Eliza lingers for a while as she pays the cab fare. She strokes the cabman's horse on the nose and says, 'You have a nice horse,' before rejoining her companion like she hasn't a single worry or concern in the world.

Eliza Grimwood entering the cab with the Foreigner. A fanciful drawing from *Famous Crimes Past and Present*, Vol. V, No. 61.

Waterloo Bridge and the Shot Tower, from an old postcard.

Waterloo Bridge in 1827. An engraving from a drawing by Thomas Shepherd.

As Eliza and her companion enter No. 12 Wellington Terrace, a three-storey terraced house not far from Waterloo Bridge, we lose sight of them for a while, as they withdraw to Eliza's bedroom to enjoy their guilty embrace. In the manner of an old-fashioned horror film, we are only allowed short glimpses of them inside the house; shadows flit around in the empty rooms, and they appear and disappear in a short and sinister *danse macabre*, as if Nosferatu had been at his fell work in Wellington Terrace that grim evening. The sum of 8 florins changes hands, and the Foreigner dons his mackintosh as if he is ready to leave, but just as Eliza is about to put her wages of sin away in an elegant cabinet, he suddenly and wordlessly pulls out a short bayonet and stabs her violently in the back of the neck.

She pitches forward, blood gushing from the wound, but the man grasps her round the neck from behind, preventing her from crying out. Avoiding her flailing arms, he cuts her throat with dreadful force, severing the windpipe and gullet, and making the blood spurt out from the carotid arteries. He holds on to her body for a minute or so, before carefully lowering it to the ground. He listens carefully for a while, to make sure he has not been detected. But all is silence, except that the murdered woman's little spaniel dog, whose hearing is more acute than that of the other residents in the

A postcard stamped and posted in 1906, showing the terrace from No. 93 to No. 105 Waterloo Road, situated on the eastern side of the street, a few blocks south of Wellington Terrace.

Eliza Grimwood is murdered, from the *New Newgate Chronicle* (London 1863).

house, gives one or two barks before settling down. The murderer stands for a while, gloating at what he has just accomplished. He can see that Eliza's dressing gown has been swept aside, exposing her stays and underskirts, as well as some naked flesh. His perverted bloodlust is reawakened by this sight, and he stabs her hard in the abdomen with his formidable weapon, ripping her hard one, two, three times.

At long last, the diabolical surgery is over. After standing for a while look-ing at the murdered, mutilated woman in the blood-spattered room, as if he wants to remember every detail of this still life in blood, this masterpiece of horror, the murderer takes out a canvas bag from his pocket. He removes his bloody mackintosh, gloves and gaiters, wipes his face with a cloth, and puts all these garments in the bag, along with the bayonet. Admiring himself in the mirror, he is pleased to see that although the room is deluged in blood, not even his collar or cuffs are bloodstained. He makes a move to look at the murdered woman's cabinet, planning to take back the eight florins he had given her for her company for the night. But as he is about to do so, he can see an elegant, well-filled little purse in another drawer. He opens it and sees that it is well stocked with gold guineas. It suits his sense of humour to take the purse and leave the eight large silver coins behind. Carefully side-stepping the large pool of blood on the floor, he opens the door to the hallway and noiselessly walks out. He opens the front door, closes it gingerly behind him, and then he is gone.

As the darkness of night envelops the murder house at No. 12 Wellington Terrace, and hides the horror within from the eyes of men, an invisible vortex of evil still envelops the rather mean-looking terraced house. Eliza's little dog, the only creature awake on the premises, must have been able to smell the blood, and sense the disaster, but since the timid canine is locked inside the back kitchen, it is unable to make its presence known. The time measured by the ticking of the clock in Eliza's parlour, and by the slow drip of her blood onto the floor, the night passes slowly in the house of horrors, the little dog in the back kitchen its sole inhabitant to sense the visitation of the grim spectre of Murder, and the hideous presence of Death.

3

THE LAMBETH MURDER

At six o'clock in the morning of Saturday 27 May 1838, the brick-layer William Hubbard, Eliza's boyfriend and the householder at No. 12 Wellington Terrace, reluctantly crawled out of his shabby bed in a small first-floor bedroom. Bracing himself for a long day's work at the building site, he donned his blue working jacket and a pair of rough corduroy trousers, grabbed his toolbox and trudged downstairs. Walking through the common hallway of the house, he was surprised to see a candlestick lying on the mat near the hall door. Hubbard walked up to the half-open door to the back parlour, which was used as a bedroom by Eliza. Since he was well aware that she was a prostitute, and unlikely to approve of him barging in when she was entertaining some customer, he called out 'Eliza!' but there was no response.

After waiting for a while, Hubbard walked into the room. Since it was still quite dark, it took some time for him to get his bearings. At first, he could only see what he thought was a bundle of clothes on the floor, inside which there was a small pinkish object like a crayfish. But as he bent down to touch it, he became aware that it was in fact part of Eliza's knee that was only just showing between two folds of her voluminous skirts. Eliza was lying still on the floor, and her face was covered with a counterpane. Hubbard had barely realised that there was clearly something very wrong, when he perceived something sticky under his feet and looked down, to find that he was standing in a huge pool of blood.

WILLIAM HUBBARD DISCOVERING THE BODY OF ELIZA GRIMWOOD.

Hubbard discovers Eliza Grimwood's body, from the *Illustrated Police News* of 18 November 1888.

Slipping and sliding in the blood, the distraught Hubbard made his way out of the room, staggered up to the front door and cried out, 'Murder!' But since there were very few people about this early on a Saturday morning, no person took any notice. Hubbard instead dashed upstairs and tore open the door of his lodger, the prostitute Mary Glover. She was in bed with her boyfriend, the commercial traveller William Best. As Hubbard came bursting into the room, Best hastily leapt out of bed, fearful that it was another boyfriend of Miss Glover's, who had come to beat him up. But as Best was searching for his trousers in the darkened room, he could see that it was Hubbard, from whom Mary Glover rented her room.

The agitated bricklayer blurted out: 'For God's sake, come downstairs!'

'What's the matter?' asked the bewildered Mr Best.

'Poor Eliza has been murdered!'

Having recovered from this shock to the senses, Mr Best got dressed, grasped a candlestick and resolutely went downstairs. He entered Eliza's bedroom and could confirm that she was indeed dead, lying in an immense pool of blood. The room was very much bloodstained, even the ceiling.

HUBBARD,
THE MAN IN CUSTODY FOR THE MURDER IN THE
WATERLOO-ROAD.

ELIZA GRIMWOOD,
WHO WAS MURDERED IN THE
WATERLOO-ROAD.

The celebrities of the day: Hubbard and Eliza, from the *Penny Satirist* of 16 June 1838. It may be questioned whether these are real portrait drawings, however. 'Eliza' looks rather like a stock image of a ballet dancer, including the dancing shoes.

As Best was examining the lifeless body, Hubbard, who was fearful of burglars, distractedly ran about the house to see if anything had been stolen. As he came lurching into the candlelit murder room and saw the state of it, he nearly had a fit, and Best 'was fearful that he intended to lay violent hands on himself'.

Hubbard's hysterics were accompanied by those of the young servant Mary Fisher, who had waited on Hubbard and Eliza for the last two years, and the piteous crying of poor Mary Glover, who had known Eliza well. How could some person have murdered her friend in the room just underneath her own, without the slightest noise being heard by any person in the house?[1]

★ ★ ★

Having managed to calm down Hubbard and the two women, the cool-headed Mr Best went outside to give the alarm. Soon, a crowd of curious neighbours and passers-by congregated on the pavement outside No. 12 Wellington Terrace. One of them went to the old watch-house in Waterloo Road, where a watchman alerted Constable Charles Burgess Goff from his beat near the toll gate on Waterloo Bridge. Constable Goff, a young and alert policeman, immediately went to the murder house, where Best told him what had happened.[2]

The distraught Hubbard had gone to No. 88 York Road to get the local surgeon, who probably did not appreciate being woken up that early on a Saturday morning. The bleary-eyed Surgeon William Henry Cooke reluctantly got dressed and trudged after Hubbard the short distance to Wellington Terrace.

He had a brief look round before asking Hubbard what he thought had happened. Hubbard said, 'I believe somebody has …' and pulled his hand across his throat to indicate that Eliza had been murdered. But Mr Cooke pooh-poohed this notion. It was of common occurrence that unfortunate young women destroyed themselves, he said, and he had no doubt this was yet another suicide.

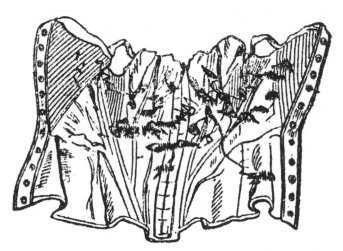

Appearance of the Stays worn by the unfortunate Woman when assassinated.

Eliza Grimwood's stays, from the *Weekly Chronicle* of 10 June 1838.

The trembling, almost hysterical Hubbard, who kept exclaiming, 'Oh, my poor Eliza! Oh, my dear Eliza!' was led out into the kitchen by his brother and mother, who had come to the house, and given a tot of gin and his tobacco pipe to calm his nerves. Since Hubbard's cupboard was in a similar state to that of his elderly female namesake,[3] Mary Fisher was sent to the local grocer to purchase some eggs and cheese, so that his relatives could have a proper luncheon.

4

AN INSPECTOR CALLS

About an hour after the surgeon had left the murder house, another visitor knocked on the front door, and was admitted. It was Inspector Charles Frederick Field, one of London's best-known police officers. Born in Chelsea in 1805, he had started a career as an amateur actor in various theatres. Charles Frederick Field joined the New Police on its formation in 1829, and since he stood out from the other applicants with regard to education and intelligence, he was immediately made a sergeant. He had several early successes, among them the capture of a notorious highway robber in a raid of a thieves' nest off St Giles's High Street. In 1833, he was promoted to inspector and posted to the 'L' or Lambeth division. This seedy part of London contained many rookeries, thieves' dens and brothels. The area around Waterloo Road was a favourite haunt for prostitutes, who used to cross Waterloo Bridge to pick up clients in the theatres and music halls near the Strand.

Inspector Charles Frederick Field, from the *Illustrated London News* of 1855. In 1838, of course, he looked a good deal fitter and more youthful than this.

Then as well as now, being a London police officer was a tough and haz-ardous job. Some contemporary newspaper notices provide details of some dramatic episodes from Inspector Field's career in Lambeth. In July 1835, two pugilists named March Barber and John Thibbert amused themselves by knocking some people down. When Inspector Field and some consta-bles gave chase, the boxers dodged them by leaping into the Thames and swimming to the north side. When the intrepid inspector caught up with them, he 'was ducked several times and nearly drowned'. Some weeks later, after the two pugilists had again made a riot, they once more escaped by swimming the Thames, with Inspector Field, Sergeant Powell and several constables in hot pursuit. But this time, the canny inspector had sent some constables to make a shortcut over Waterloo Bridge, and they caught the two miscreants, who were fined 20s each. In June 1836, when there was a fire at the rear of Astley's Amphitheatre, Inspector Field was quickly at the spot with a strong body of police, who were instrumental in preventing a full-scale fire. In April 1837, a rapist named Richard Jackson escaped from Newgate and disappeared without trace. Inspector Field tracked him down to some rooms in Queen Street, Lambeth, and valiantly went in to recapture him. The desperate criminal threatened him with a razor, but the inspector pulled up a pistol and held him at gunpoint. For the capture of Jackson, the inspector was highly complimented by the governors of Newgate.[1]

★ ★ ★

In the five years Inspector Field had served in the Lambeth area, he had made the acquaintance of many of its inhabitants. He had of course known Eliza Grimwood, who had commonly been called the Countess, because of her handsome appearance, elegant clothes and proud way of carrying herself. As he later told his friend Charles Dickens, 'when I saw the poor Countess (I had known her well enough to speak to), lying dead with her throat cut, on the floor of her bedroom, a variety of reflections calculated to make a man rather low in his spirits, came into my head'.[2] But when the inspector had a closer look at the body, his detective instincts took over. Could this really be a case of suicide? He thought the terrible cut that had severed the throat down to the vertebrae could hardly have been made by a suicide, let alone a woman. Inspector Field turned the body around, something the careless doctor had not bothered to do, and found another deep gash at the back of the neck. In his own words, this is what happened next:

> Ordered by Mr Superintendent Grimsall to make enquiries at the house [of the] deceased Eliza Grimwood, went there and on Examining the Head found a Cut at the back part, sent for Dr Cooke, who stated that he did not see that in the Morning when he first was called in.
>
> Said that she must have been murdered, commenced immediately to search the house. First examined Hubbard his clothes. Shut the Bed he slept in found a Card with a Blood between the Mattress and Bed, examined the Doors and passages, searched minutely all the Rooms and Cellar, ascertained that the Deceased came home the night before with a Gentleman.[3]

Horrible Murder in the Waterloo Road.

Apartment of the Murdered Female.

Eliza Grimwood's bedroom with the body; from the *Weekly Chronicle* of 3 June 1838.

It turned out that Eliza had lived in two large rooms on the ground floor, a parlour and a bedroom. The furniture in these rooms was of surprisingly good quality. On the first floor, Hubbard had a small room, while the larger front room was let to William Best and Mary Glover. There were also two small and bleak-looking attic rooms, both rather understandably without a tenant. The servant girl Mary Fisher, who waited on Hubbard and Eliza, slept in a small room adjoining the kitchen, which was situated at the back of the house, down half a flight of stairs from the ground floor. The house also had a large cellar, but this was too cold, dark and damp to be fit for human habitation. The curious layout of the terrace of houses meant that a flight of stairs down from this cellar led into another, even deeper cellar, and then into a small yard, from which there was a door to the dry arches of Waterloo Bridge, facing Commercial Street. Inspector Field found it unlikely that the murderer could have escaped through this tortuous route, had he not known the house intimately.

Having pondered the known facts, Inspector Field made some important early deductions. He had formed a low opinion of the truculent Hubbard, who could not deny that he had been partly supported by Eliza's earnings. It did not seem at all unlikely that this unsavoury prostitute's bully had killed Eliza in a fit of rage or jealousy. But there was no blood on Hubbard's clothes, except what had splashed onto his trousers in his mad dash to get out of the murder room, nor was there any trace of the murder weapon. And could Hubbard, who was clearly a creature of modest intellect and dissipated habits, really have committed the murder without alerting any other person in the house, or leaving any worthwhile clue? Like the experienced policeman he was, Inspector Field reserved his judgement. Since it was important to keep Hubbard under close observation, he posted Constable Goff to stay in the murder house, where he would guard the crime scene and keep out the curious onlookers who had already begun to gather in the street outside the house.

★ ★ ★

Inspector Field spent all Sunday looking for Eliza's elusive Friday night customer. Surely, if this man was found and could give a good account of himself, the net tightened around Hubbard. On the other hand, if this mystery man did not come forward, he would himself become the main suspect. Knowing, from the evidence of the servant Mary Fisher, that Eliza had travelled home from the Strand Theatre by cab, the inspector walked down to Waterloo Bridge and began questioning the cabmen at the ranks there. Tracking down a specific cab driver in London today would be like finding a needle in a haystack, but London was of course much smaller back in 1838, the cabs plied a limited area, and the cabmen all knew each other. It did not take long for Inspector Field to have 'traced out the Cab Man who brought Deceased home from the Strand Theatre', as he expressed it, and this individual had some very interesting things to say. Joseph Spicknell, driver of cab No. 949, said that a lady and a gentleman had hailed him near the Strand Theatre the evening of the murder. They seemed to know each other and the gentleman addressed his com-

panion as 'Lizzy', the name under which Eliza Grimwood was known to her friends. The lady was very good-looking, wearing a dark dress and a fawn-coloured bonnet. The man was 5ft 7in or 8in tall, young and foreign-looking, with dark hair and whiskers but no mustachios. He looked like a gentleman in an elegant waistcoat, a dark dress-coat and a dark, wide-brimmed hat. Although the weather was fine, he carried a mackintosh on his arm. The cabman drove them to the Hero of Waterloo public house near Wellington Terrace. After the woman had paid him his fare, she smiled at him, stroked the nose of his horse and said, 'You have a nice horse', before walking towards Wellington Terrace with her friend.

Eliza Grimwood, from the *Weekly Chronicle* of 10 June 1838.

Portrait of Eliza Grimwood.

It was fortunate for Inspector Field that, due to her attractive looks and fashionable dress, Eliza Grimwood was just the kind of person to get noticed. Outside the Strand Theatre, a certain John Rockall, waterman to the rank of cabs nearby, could well remember her entering one of these cabs along with a gentleman. When the waterman had opened the door for them, he heard Eliza say that she wanted to go across Waterloo Bridge. Inside the theatre, the inspector made further progress. The waitress Charlotte Parker, who had known Eliza for some time, could well remember that on the evening of the murder Eliza had come up to the refreshments stall and ordered a glass of wine, which she sat down and drank. As usual, she was quite elegant in her fawn-coloured dress, and her dark shawl and a blue bonnet. A foreign-looking young man in a broad-brimmed hat had paid 6*d* for the glass of wine; she got the impression he was a Frenchman. When she gave him his change, he said, 'Did I not give you half a sovereign?' but she was wise to this old trick and showed him the sixpence coin. The man was 5ft 8in tall, with dark hair and whiskers, but no mustachios. He was smartly dressed, rather like a respectable gentleman's servant, and spoke good English.

Inspector Field also found a jolly young prostitute who called herself Catherine Edwin. Although she looked very much like a teenager, she claimed to be 24 years old. Yes, she had known Eliza Grimwood; and yes, she had seen her the evening before, with a foreign-looking man. She had seen this individual with Eliza a few times before. He was always neatly dressed, with black whiskers and dark brown hair; he sometimes wore green-tinted spectacles like if he wanted to disguise himself. She did not know if this man was French or Italian, but he was definitely a foreigner, although he spoke fluent English. Rather overwhelmed by this unexpected torrent of information, the inspector asked her how she could be so certain about his nationality. She answered, with a merry giggle, that she had

The Murder in the Waterloo Road.

Portrait of Hubbard.

Subterraneous Communication between Hubbard's House and the Dry Arches.

The cellar of No. 12 Wellington Terrace, from the *Weekly Chronicle* of 10 June 1838.

heard him speak French once or twice. He had probably spoken Italian when he had taken her, Eliza and another young lady to have coffee in Mrs Rosedale's pastry-cook's shop near Piccadilly just a few days ago. Miss Edwin had to admit, however, that she herself could not speak a single word of either French or Italian. She seemed to think the entire situation exceedingly funny, giggling excessively and making various flippant remarks, until the inspector gruffly remarked that if she had really been such a close friend of Eliza Grimwood, she had a very strange way of mourning her death. At this well-deserved rebuff, Miss Edwin began to cry theatrically. One of her friends brought the smelling salts as she seemed totally overcome with grief. Disgusted with these histrionics, the inspector stood up to leave. Catherine Edwin's hysterical sobbing suddenly ceased when the inspector summoned her to give evidence at the coroner's inquest, like he previously had the cabman, the waterman and the waitress.

As the inspector angrily walked out of the theatre, he kept pondering the novel evidence about the Foreigner. Could this giddy young Catherine Edwin at all be relied upon? Unlike the other witnesses, she had been flippant and disrespectful, and wholly unimpressed by the dignity of an inspector of police. Inspector Field had heard many a lie in his day, and he thought it sounded like she was making up her story as she went along. But like the experienced policeman he was, the inspector immediately fastened on the one point in Catherine Edwin's story that could be proved or disproved. He went to Mrs Rosedale's shop and asked the relevant questions. She could well remember a foreign-looking young man, probably a Frenchman, treating three gaily-dressed young ladies to pastries and coffee. This rather unexpected corroboration of Catherine Edwin's story made the inspector thoughtful. Had the blasted little minx been telling the truth after all? He still pondered these matters as he travelled across Waterloo Bridge in a cab, reconstructing the final journey of Eliza Grimwood and the Foreigner.[4]

★ ★ ★

When the inspector returned to the murder house at No. 12 Wellington Terrace, he was pleased to see that Constable Goff had been joined by Sergeant Price, another keen young policeman with a talent for detective work. When making some inquiries locally during the day, the sergeant had found two further witnesses. Firstly, a woman named Mary Chambers, who lived at No. 6 Waterloo Road, had seen an old-fashioned cab, with a door opening backward, coming up to Wellington Terrace between midnight and 1 a.m. the night of the murder. A young woman fitting the description of Eliza Grimwood had alighted, followed by a man in dark clothes, about 5ft 8in tall. Secondly, a musician named Chapman had testified that as he had been walking across Waterloo Bridge the night of the murder, he had been passed by a box cab containing two people, one of whom was female. He had then walked on towards Wellington Terrace, where he saw Eliza Grimwood and the Foreigner, standing directly outside No. 12; he passed them not 6ft away. He observed that Eliza was gaily dressed; the man had large features, dark whiskers and a fashionable coat. Constable Goff could report that throughout the day, Hubbard had been in a state of prostration, drinking and smoking immoderately, and ranting and raving about his dear Eliza. When the inspector went to see Hubbard, the bricklayer looked much the worse for wear after these excesses. When he asked why he was kept under guard at the house, the inspector gruffly replied that it was for his own good, since throughout the day, large and rowdy crowds had gathered outside the murder house, baying for his blood.

The murder of Eliza Grimwood was headline news in every newspaper. The savage mutilation of the body, and the sheer mystery of the crime, put it in a class of its own among London murders. Not since James Greenacre had murdered Hannah Brown back in 1836 had there been a similar outrage in the metropolis. The alert London papers *The Observer, The Times, The Morning Post* and *Morning Chronicle* had already managed to tell the basic story of the murder already on Monday 28 May, although they got the victim's name wrong; 'Eliza Greenwood', described as a remarkably handsome young female aged around 25, had been brutally murdered through having her throat cut, and her room was deluged in blood. Hubbard, the man who slept in the house, had discovered the dreadful spectacle.[5]

According to *Bell's New Weekly Messenger*, 'The horrible transaction has caused a frightful sensation in the neighbourhood, and during the whole of Sunday crowds were collected in front of the house.' The *Globe* wrote that:

No occurrence of the kind that have taken place in the metropolis for years (not even the horrible atrocity perpetrated by Greenacre) has excited so much interest as this mysterious affair. During the whole of yesterday crowds collected in front of the house where the murder was committed; and at seven o'clock in the evening not fewer than a hundred and fifty persons had thus assembled, who were eagerly engaging in discussing the circumstances connected with the shocking occurrence. An individual who seemed to be a street-preacher attempted to 'improve' the event, but as no one appeared disposed to listen to him, he soon shifted his quarters. The toll-takers at Waterloo Bridge state that the receipts from foot passengers during the week have trebled the usual average, so great has been the crowd of curious gazers from all parts of the town.[6]

For those who could not afford to buy newspapers, there were handbills pasted up all over London to proclaim that a horrible murder had been committed. In Whitechapel Road, a man was parading with 'a show' representing, as his placard announced, 'the brutal murder of Eliza Grimwood'. The *Morning Herald* deplored that 'the recent horrible murder of Eliza Grimwood in the Waterloo-road has furnished subject for the pictorial talents of the penny showmen. This was too rich, too sanguinary, too disgusting, to be neglected by the itinerant caterers for the enjoyment of the rising generation ...'[7]

5

THE INQUEST BEGINS

On Monday 28 May, the coroner's inquest on Eliza Grimwood began at the York Hotel, a well-known local 'gin palace' situated at the crossing of York Road with the Waterloo Road.[1] Mr Richard Carter, the coroner for Sussex, first led the jury over to the murder house to see the corpse, which had been left in situ on the floor of the back parlour. A newspaper report says that the jurymen were much affected by the gory sight. Since the majority of them were ordinary shopkeepers and artisans, they had never seen a murdered woman before. After inspecting the body, the coroner said that it was obvious that she had been murdered. The dreadful wound in the neck nearly severed her head from the shoulders, and there were some deep cuts to the fingers of the left hand, as if the wretched woman had tried to grasp the murder weapon. Her face and hair were smeared with blood, as if she had been thrashing about with her hands in the agonies of death. Eliza's body was fully clothed, with the exception of her gown and bonnet.[2] There were still two visible impressions on the pillows on the bed, as if two people had been lying down, and the coroner suggested that Eliza had perhaps been murdered when she got out of bed. A *Weekly Chronicle* journalist invited to see the murdered woman was not the only person who found it 'extraordinary that, although there were several people sleeping under the same roof the night of the murder, none of them were awakened by the noise and scuffling which must have taken place during the perpetration of the murder'.[3] As the coroner and jury returned from the murder house, Inspector Field told Mr Carter about his promising clues from the Strand Theatre. He pointed

The York Hotel at No. 80 Waterloo Road, where the inquest was held. An 1826 watercolour reproduced by permission of the Trustees of the British Museum.

out that the testimony of Catherine Edwin seemed suspect and stated that he wanted more time to try to corroborate it. Mr Carter agreed to wait a few days before seeing the Strand Theatre witnesses; anyway, it seemed only reasonable to begin with Hubbard and the other residents of the murder house.

Indeed, Hubbard himself was the first witness. Looking calmer and more collected than previously, he said he had last seen Eliza alive at eight o'clock the evening before the murder; they had supped together before Eliza had gone off to the theatre to pick up her gentleman friend. He was well aware that 'she led a gay life, in spite of my entreaties to the contrary', and that she had done so for several years. Hubbard told the jury that he was a married man, although he had been separated from his wife for at least twelve years. He had been living with Eliza, who was actually his first cousin, for nearly ten years. She had drunk neither beer nor wine in the evening; indeed, he considered her as 'a young woman of remarkably sober habits'. Hubbard had heard nothing untoward during the night, except that Eliza's little spaniel dog had barked a few times. He described how he had found the body early on Saturday morning, adding that he had immediately suspected murder. Although extensively spattered with blood, the room had not been in disorder. The bed had looked as if two people had slept in it. Some drawers in Eliza's cabinet had been opened and he suspected that a purse full of gold guineas had been stolen, although Eliza's valuable gold watch and jewellery were still present. There were some knives in a kitchen drawer but none of them were bloodstained.

There were two razors in the murder house, one belonging to Hubbard himself and another he had given to Eliza to cut her corns with; both were still in the house. None of Hubbard's tools were missing from his toolbox, including his axe. He had never possessed a sharp instrument formidable enough to cause such extensive injuries. Hubbard said that he had often remonstrated with Eliza for bringing men home with her, although not recently. He had never struck her during these altercations. When asked by the coroner, Hubbard had to admit that they both received a benefit from her prostitution. There was a murmur of disgust among those present. When asked if he suspected any person for the murder, Hubbard said that the only person he suspected was an individual who had been standing in the street when he ran out to give the alarm. When asked the reason, Hubbard rather feebly replied that he had thought this man had seemed very eager to give assistance, something that must be interpreted as sinister. The coroner did not appear to share this view, since he curtly dismissed Hubbard and called the next witness.

William Best introduced himself as a commercial traveller, residing in Greenwich. He described how Hubbard had woken him up at six o'clock on Saturday morning in a dreadful state of agitation, and how he had gone downstairs and inspected the body. The evening before, when the servant Mary Fisher had let Eliza in at about midnight, he had heard a man's voice and concluded that she was bringing home a customer. Best had also heard the little dog barking once or twice. He agreed with Hubbard that the murder room had not been untidy. Although one of the drawers in the cabinet had been open, he had seen nothing missing. Hubbard had had some splashes of blood on his trousers, as if he had stepped in the pool of blood, but no bloodstains on the remainder of his clothing. He had heard Hubbard and Eliza quarrel more than once, but never violently; on the whole, they had seemed to be on quite good terms.

Young Mary Fisher next took the stand. She had been working as a servant to Hubbard and Eliza for two years. Hubbard and Eliza, she stated, had always got on very well together, and seldom quarrelled. The evening before the murder, Eliza had gone out in a cab after Hubbard had retired to his own room at about nine o'clock. At between midnight and one o'clock, she had heard a cab outside and correctly deduced that her mistress was returning home. When Mary opened the door, she could see that Eliza had brought a gentleman home with her. This individual seemed strangely reluctant to show his face, and swiftly walked into her bedroom. Shortly afterwards, Eliza herself came into the kitchen to get something to drink; she told Mary that she would not be needed any further this particular night. Mary then slept soundly all night, until she was woken up by the agitated Hubbard, and told that poor Eliza had been murdered. She could recall seeing the candlestick that she had put in Eliza's bedroom before going to sleep now standing on the hallway carpet, near the front door. When questioned, Mary Fisher said that she had no reason to believe that her master (Hubbard) had anything to do with the murder. Instead, she rather suspected that it had been committed by the stranger Eliza had brought home with her.

★ ★ ★

When the inquest continued, Inspector Field himself took the stand, to give a summary of the state of affairs with regard to the Grimwood murder investigation. He had found no recent bloodstains in Hubbard's room, apart from a few spots of blood on the undersheet of his bed. They did not seem to be recent. A newspaper reporter added that Hubbard 'accounted for the stains in a way that we cannot describe'.[4] Hubbard's trousers had been splashed with fresh blood, but not extensively. Their appearance was quite consistent with his own story that he had walked through the large pool of blood on the floor in Eliza's room. The inspector had also found a card with a bloodstain on each side of it; Hubbard had said that this was the membership card for a society of tradesmen that he belonged to, but he had been unable to explain the blood. Although the house had been carefully searched, no trace of the murder weapon had been found. Hubbard had been entirely distraught since the murder. His state of mind had been so desperate that the inspector had seen fit to have him watched by a constable to prevent him from doing himself any injury.

Inspector Field gave a brief summary of his activities the day before. It was now known that Eliza Grimwood had brought her customer, henceforth called the Foreigner, from the Strand Theatre. This individual had been seen by several reliable witnesses, who would hopefully be able to identify him when he was caught. The witness Mary Chambers was called to tell her story of Eliza and the Foreigner arriving at Wellington Terrace between twelve and one o'clock on Saturday morning. Then it was time for Mr Cooke the surgeon to give his findings after inspecting the body. In addition to the cut throat, there were several gashes on the back of the neck and injuries to the hands also, definitely indicating murder. He did not think a razor could have inflicted such terrible wounds, rather a heavier, very sharp knife or short sword. It was his opinion that Eliza had been dead for about four hours when he came to the house (this was between five and six in the morning). Hubbard's trousers were produced and the doctor was asked whether the bloodstaining on them was fresh. He replied in the affirmative, but added that judging from the blood spatter in the room, no person could have committed the murder without having his clothes extensively stained with blood. These important deductions from Mr Cooke all seemed reasonable to Inspector Field. He must have wondered how on earth such a brutal murder could have been committed with four people sleeping just a few thin walls away, and how a murderer who must have been almost covered in blood could have made his getaway without being noticed by anyone.

As the inquest was to be adjourned for the day, Superintendent Grimsall asked the coroner whether Hubbard should be detained. Mr Carter replied that the police might take whatever course of action they wanted, but he would make no order for Hubbard's arrest, since there was not enough evidence to warrant his detention.

★ ★ ★

Due to the number of witnesses still to come, the inquest was adjourned until Thursday, which left Inspector Field and his men two days to make some further inquiries. They wanted to begin with searching the murder house thoroughly, but when the inspector and Sergeant Price arrived there, they met with quite an emergency. Hubbard had greatly resented Eliza's brothers taking up residence in his house without permission. When Constable Goff had gone out to get some beer, Hubbard had sneaked out of the house and gone away in a cab! This unexpected development is unlikely to have earned the constable any praise from his superiors, particularly since Inspector Field 'had given him strict orders to watch Hubbard'.

But the canny inspector kept his calm. He hailed a cab and went round to various cab stands until he had found the cabman, who had taken Hubbard away. It turned out that the suspect had gone to a house in Mile End. The inspector and his men were relieved to find him still at the premises when they burst into the house, which belonged to Hubbard's mother. Suspecting that Hubbard had hidden the murder weapon on the premises, the policemen searched the house and privy but found nothing worthwhile. The houses of Hubbard's two brothers were treated in the same manner, but again with a negative result. The truculent Hubbard was taken back to the murder house, to be reunited with the equally cantankerous brothers Grimwood.

On Wednesday, Constable Goff searched the murder house as well as he could, while Sergeant Price guarded Hubbard. Although Hubbard had blamed his absconding on the rudeness of the Grimwood brothers, the inspector remained suspicious. Throughout the morning, he 'made Enquiries in the neighbourhood of Waterloo Road of Hubbard's mode of living'. It was no secret among the neighbours that Hubbard partially lived on the proceeds of Eliza's prostitution. He himself worked as a bricklayer on various building sites, but his income was insufficient to finance his dissipated habits, which included a fair amount of drinking. After finding out where Hubbard had been working, the inspector went there to inspect his tools and to find out what his workmates thought of him.[4]

In the afternoon, Inspector Field visited some former clients of Eliza's, who could tell him about her modus operandi. She belonged to the superior class of London prostitutes, charging at least half a guinea a night. She had mostly catered to established 'customers', many of whom she had known for years. Some of these customers were noblemen, barristers and wealthy tradesmen. Many of them had been genuinely fond of her and mourned her death. Eliza had really been a part-time prostitute, who for most of the time lived a quiet life at Wellington Terrace with Hubbard, her servant and her various friends. When her regular gentleman friends wanted her company, she was always ready to oblige, however. She often met them at the Strand Theatre. The wealthy customers took her to various hotels, or even to their own houses, but those who were more needy, or who had a wife waiting for them back home, preferred taking a cab across Waterloo Bridge to Wellington Terrace nearby. During her final evening alive, Eliza had seemed in good spirits, and perfectly sober; she had been looking forward to an excursion to the Epsom races with some of her friends.

★ ★ ★

Another of Inspector Field's duties was to find out more about Eliza Grimwood's background. The sullen, uncooperative Hubbard had little to tell: yes, Eliza was his first cousin; yes, he had left his wife to be with her; yes, he had known for a long time that she was prostituting herself, and had always resented it. Hubbard was a sturdy, muscular man, not unhandsome with his regular features and large bushy whiskers. Inspector Field must have wondered about his strange relationship with Eliza Grimwood. What kind of man would lie hidden in a tiny first-floor bedroom, listening to his mistress copulating with a man who had paid for her services?

London was buzzing with rumours about the Waterloo Road Horror, and there was great curiosity about the antecedents of the murder victim. The newspapers were full of confused suggestions about her life. One story told that Eliza Grimwood was the daughter of a respectable east country farmer named Rogers, and that she had turned to prostitution after being seduced by a customs officer. According to the one version, she had been seduced from home by an excise officer, whom she had deserted in favour of an actor at one of the minor theatres. Another newspaper rumour said that her family name was really Greenwood, and that her entire family had emigrated from England to Canada. According to a third version, she was the illegitimate daughter of a peer. An honest young man, who had wanted to 'save' this beautiful young girl from her life of shame and vice, had asked her to marry him, it was speculated, but the jealous Hubbard had intervened with deadly result. There were rumours that her sister had poisoned herself five years earlier under very distressing circumstances. Further spice was added by some enterprising journalist, who boldly claimed that in 1828 Eliza Grimwood had been on a visit to a friend's house in Polstead, and that it was she who had discovered 'the mangled corpse' of another famous female murder victim, Maria Marten, in the Red Barn.[5] This rumour ignores the fact that the murderer, Corder, had in fact buried the remains of his victim, which were dug up by Maria Marten's father several months after the murder.

Eliza's brother, the Brixton builder Thomas Grimwood, made things much clearer. He told Inspector Field that the Grimwoods had been respectable farmers in Stonham Aspal, Suffolk, for several generations. Samuel Grimwood, Eliza's grandfather, was born in 1727 and had four sons and two daughters. Samuel, the eldest son, carried on running the family farm, but John Grimwood, the fourth son, born in 1768 and Eliza's father, purchased another small farm in Stonham Aspal, where he settled down to a life of hard graft and honest toil in the manner of his forebears. In 1788, he married Frances Hubbard, and they had no fewer than nine children alive. Thomas, the eldest son, settled down as a builder. His brothers Francis and Charles also became respectable members of the lower middle classes. Eliza had probably been born in 1807, when Thomas was 18 years old.[6] A remarkably beautiful child, she became the pet of the family.

When Eliza was quite young, her father decided to go into business as a bricklayer in Ipswich, possibly joining forces with one of his sons, who had enjoyed a good deal of success. It is not known whether his wife and younger children came with him, or if they remained at the farm. The death of Eliza's father John Grimwood in 1813 meant that the younger children had to fend for themselves. Their widowed mother was unable to support them, and their elder brothers were unwilling to do so. At the age of 15, Eliza left school and went into service with a gentleman who occupied a large property near Stonham Aspal. She became the maid companion of a lame young daughter of this family, and seems to have carried out her duties satisfactorily. But it would not be long before the young lady's elder brother seduced her. When Eliza became pregnant, her seducer took her to London to have an abortion. This worthless young man gave her some money and left her behind in the metropolis, either because poor Eliza felt ashamed of returning to Stonham Aspal after her disgrace, or because he himself thought it would be good to be rid of her.

But it did not take long for Eliza to discover that London life was far more exciting than her rather humdrum existence back in the village, and that her youthful good looks gave her considerable advantages in the metropolitan demi-monde. She became the mistress of a fashionable actor, and then of an army captain. According to an unreliable source, she later became the mistress of a well-known burglar, even going as far as joining him for some late-night break-ins, just for the fun of it.[7] But after the Bow Street police once nearly caught the entire gang of burglars, Eliza decided to part company with her young hooligan friends.

★ ★ ★

After Eliza's elopement, the Grimwood family had made every effort to persuade her to return home, but without success. Her poor old mother, still living back in Ipswich, missed her very much. Although the four brothers Thomas, Francis, Charles and Samuel had become respectable citizens, the family had had its fair share of sorrow. One of Eliza's sisters had moved to London, where she had fallen into low company and finally 'destroyed herself, under the most painful circumstances' in the mid 1830s. Another sister had been a cripple since childhood, and the youngest brother, Richard, had become a drunken, miserable tramp.[8]

In 1828, Eliza met her first cousin, the bricklayer and labourer William Hubbard, who may once have been her childhood sweetheart. Hubbard was by then a married man, having wed Elizabeth Payne in Wiltshire the year before. Hubbard fell violently in love with Eliza, and lost no time before he evicted his wife from his house and installed Eliza in her place. Mrs Hubbard was most unwilling to go, but her caddish husband persuaded her using his fists. More than once, poor Mrs Hubbard came back to beg for money, but Hubbard and Eliza treated her with disdain. At the time of the murder, Hubbard had not seen his wife for at least six years.

Some time in the mid 1830s, another of Eliza's brothers – we do not know who – had come to London to take part in the proceedings before the House of Commons regarding the election at Ipswich. He stayed at Proctor's Hotel in Westminster Bridge Road, and either through chance or stratagem heard mention of his sister Eliza and her mode of living. It must have come as something of a shock to him that his sister had become a well-known London prostitute.

The brother managed to track Eliza down and asked her to return to Ipswich with him, to rejoin her elderly mother. Magnanimously, he assured her that 'not the slightest allusion would be made to her previous mode of life'. But far from showing her long-lost brother any gratitude, Eliza told him she was perfectly happy in her present situation; she had a well-furnished house to live in, and earned plentiful money by letting rooms to lodgers. Under no circumstance, she said haughtily, would she deign to live in a small house, since they were always situated in low neighbourhoods. Dismayed that his fallen sister was so 'exalted in her opinions', as he expressed it, the brother sadly returned home. He had left Eliza their mother's address, however, and Eliza sent her 73-year-old parent a pound of tea as a present, with the promise that she would come visiting in the summer. The news that Eliza had been murdered had a most injurious effect on Eliza's mother and crippled sister, and the latter had been in such a dangerous state ever since to leave little hope of her recovery.[9]

★ ★ ★

When the inquest was resumed at the York Hotel on Thursday 31 May, it was Mr Cooke the surgeon who again took centre stage. On Monday evening, he and five other surgeons had performed an autopsy on the murdered woman. After Eliza Grimwood's naked body had been washed and put on a shutter in the back parlour, it was closely inspected by the surgeons, who carved away with their knives to probe the various wounds. The cause of death was undoubtedly the terrible injury to the throat, which had severed both the left carotid artery and the windpipe. There was a wound to the left breast that had been deflected by one of the ribs, a second stab that had entered the thorax at the bottom of the sternum, and a 'ripping' stab to the abdomen about 3in lower. The stab to the back of the neck was also a most formidable one, completely separating the third and fourth cervical vertebrae and exposing the spinal cord. On the thumb and finger of the left hand were two small wounds, which appeared to have been sustained by the murdered woman raising her hand to protect her throat by grasping the murder weapon. According to a newspaper reporter, there was a murmur of horror among the jury and spectators when surgeon Cooke went through this gory list of injuries. Eliza's lips were very swollen and bruised, indicating that the murderer had held her mouth in a vice-like grip to prevent her from crying out as he went through this catalogue of butchery. The murder weapon was clearly neither a razor nor a stiletto, but a stronger and more formidable instrument.[10]

After his confident appearance at the inquest, the cocky young surgeon must have felt rather deflated when Inspector Field casually explained to the jury that it was actually *he himself* who had discovered that it was a case of murder in the first place, since the surgeon had not even bothered to turn the body around. Being asked some further questions about Hubbard's behaviour, Cooke conformed that the bricklayer had 'appeared to be in a state of great trepidation and excitement'. Hubbard had barely been able to explain the nature of his call to the surgery, nor had he made it clear whether he thought Eliza had been murdered or committed suicide. After touching the body and various utensils in the room, the surgeon's hands had become so bloody he had to wipe them on the corner of the bed sheets. When he looked round in the room, there were no signs of a person having washed himself, or even wiped his hands on any piece of fabric. This evidence was corroborated by the beadle Anderson, who had also searched the house that fateful morning. He added that there was no blood anywhere in the kitchen, nor any sign of a person having washed himself. There were a few tiny marks of blood in the hallway, possibly from Hubbard's shoes, but not even the slightest bloodstain on the candlestick that had been put down in the hallway, nor on the door handle. There was a bloody napkin underneath Eliza's head, but it was not clear to the beadle where it had come from.

The cabman Spicknell next told his story of driving Eliza and the Foreigner home, followed by the musician Chapman, who this time added that the Foreigner had worn a fashionable rough coat and that Chapman had been less than 6ft away from him. After him came a surprise witness, who had a most interesting story to tell. John Sharp, who introduced himself as a reporter for *The Times* newspaper, had been in the pits of the Strand Theatre the evening of the murder and had seen Eliza Grimwood three or four times. She had been in the company of another young female dressed in black, with whom she had spoken more than once. About fifteen minutes before the play ended, Eliza tapped her friend on the shoulder with her fan and said something that sounded like, 'I am going out with … He is here.' The reporter was of course asked to try to decipher this cryptic statement, but he replied that he had already been racking his brain over it all day. The theatre had been a very noisy place, and although he had been looking at the attractive Eliza Grimwood from time to time, he had not been actively trying to overhear her conversation. There might just have been a name after 'I am going out with …' but in that case, he had not heard it clearly. Inspector Field was probably grinding his teeth that this ideal opportunity of learning the name of the Foreigner had been lost in such a dismal fashion. Nor had Sharp seen the person Eliza had spoken about. When asked how he could be so certain the woman he had seen had been the murdered Eliza Grimwood, the enterprising reporter replied that he had already visited the murder house, where he had been readily admitted to see the body.

Thomas Grimwood, Eliza's eldest brother, next announced his presence. Having read about Eliza's death in the newspapers, he had decided to take up residence in the murder house, along with his two brothers. It must be suspected that the reason for their alacrity in moving into No. 12 Wellington Terrace was that they knew that Eliza had been in possession of a good deal of valuable property, which they feared Hubbard might be planning to steal away. Thomas Grimwood produced two letters recently delivered to the house, addressed to Eliza by her admirer the Birmingham sword cutler, which he handed over to the coroner.

The next witness was a certain John Francis Cubitt, residing in Wandsworth Road, who testified that on the night of the murder, he had been drinking hard at an establishment called the Coal-hole, before reluctantly walking home between five and six o'clock in the morning. On passing Waterloo Bridge, he had stopped to speak to the toll-keeper Lewis. Suddenly, a man had come running up to a policeman nearby and explained something to him before they took off together. Mystified, Cubitt lurched after them and saw them enter No. 12 Wellington Terrace. Cubitt believed this man to have been Hubbard. He had not seen him throw something from the bridge. Cubitt claimed that he had asked this man whether he could be of any assistance, and later accompanied him to the surgery. Inspector Field and the journalists present sagely noted that the drunken Cubitt must be identical to the man Hubbard had encountered standing outside the house, seemingly too ready to provide assistance.

A young lady named Emma Lewis next took the stand. She claimed that she had been met by Eliza Grimwood at the Strand Theatre at about ten o'clock on the evening of the murder. Eliza had been accompanied by another female, who was in mourning dress. Her name was either Julia Denman or Julia Seymour, and she lived in Crown Street, Westminster. Julia had told Emma that just before the play was to end, Eliza had tapped her on the shoulder and said, 'Julia, I am going out with my friend.' Emma Lewis claimed that she herself had again seen Eliza Grimwood about half an hour later. By then she was standing opposite the theatre door together with a tall gentleman who wore glasses and had a cloak on his arm. It looked like they were going away in a cab. Neither Emma Lewis nor her friend Julia knew the name of this gentleman.

Inspector Field, who must have found the testimony of Emma Lewis and the reporter Sharp most encouraging when it came to tracking down the Foreigner, next took the stand himself. When asked by the coroner why Julia Seymour was not in attendance, he had to reply that he had not known about the story of Emma Lewis until a few minutes ago, but that if the inquest was adjourned for a few days, he would track her down and summon her to attend. The coroner agreed, but the inspector was not yet done. He pointed out that this was a very formidable murder case, in which several lines of inquiry were required. Hubbard needed to be watched, the murder house guarded, and there was a need to search the house minutely, and to scour the area around Waterloo Road and Bridge for the murder weapon and for bloodstained garments. Since further witnesses kept turning up all the time, there was also a need to check their stories and to find others who might have seen the Foreigner the evening of the murder. All hotels and lodging houses catering for foreigners needed to be searched, and also all foreign ships. These steps needed to be taken quickly, since it was unlikely that the Foreigner would be tarrying long in London. It was of course impossible for just three policemen to accomplish all these tasks, and he would respectfully ask that some further constables were added to the Grimwood task force. This was quite a novel step at a time when even the most complex cases were investigated by just a few policemen, but both the coroner and Superintendent Grimsall willingly agreed to the inspector's request.

★ ★ ★

On Friday 1 June, Inspector Field and his troop of constables 'had the cesspool emptied, the water pipes taken down, the chimnies searched, and every part of the house minutely searched'. Nothing untoward was found. After supervising the search, the inspector 'proceeded to make inquiries about Hubbard's wife, and found that she was a Kept Woman'.[11]

It was decided that due to decomposition, Eliza Grimwood's remains should be buried on 1 June, in the churchyard of St John's Church in Waterloo Road. When Hubbard made it known that he wanted to attend as a mourner, Eliza's three brothers objected strongly. The Rev. Mr Irvine, minister of St John's Church, took it upon himself to go to see Hubbard to try to dissuade him from coming. After he had pointed out that there would be a large and rowdy mob present, and that Hubbard would be in danger of his life if he tried to attend, the clergyman succeeded in his purpose.

At four o'clock in the afternoon, the mourners followed Eliza Grimwood's hearse the short distance to the church in a row of coaches.[12] One of these contained the brothers Grimwood. Another carried Inspector Field, who may well have been surveying the crowd through the lattice blinds, like Bucket did at Tulkinghorn's funeral in Dickens's *Bleak House*. But the crowd of 'mourners' and interested onlookers following the procession on foot was immense. Notwithstanding that the rain was pouring down in torrents, the portion of the Waterloo Road from the bridge to the church was crowded with people. When the gates were opened after a short ceremony, a crowd of at least a thousand people, mainly women, rushed into the churchyard. A journalist from *The Globe* wrote, 'The prejudice existing against Hubbard is extensive and violent, and several of the women who were present at the funeral gave vent to loud and bitter imprecations against him. Had he followed the remains there is every reason to believe a serious disturbance would have taken place.'[13]

On Saturday 2 June, the Grimwood task force began making 'inquiries at the different docks, wharfs, and other places' to find out if any person fit-

NEW CHURCH, WATERLOO ROAD.

Published July.5. 1828. by Jones & C.º 3. Acton Place. Kingsland Road. London.

The church of St John, Waterloo Road, where Eliza Grimwood was buried. An engraving from a drawing by Thomas Shepherd.

ting the description of the Foreigner had left London by any of the Strand boats. The inspector went round to the passport office and began to work out which foreign ships were on the Thames at the time of the murder. The next day, the inspector 'had a long interview with the servant Mary Fisher respecting Hubbard and his living with the deceased'.[14]

A week after Eliza Grimwood had been murdered, the police seemed no closer to apprehending the culprit. The newspapers had initially been confident in the work of the police, but now they began to publish some critical letters. All the time, further spice was added to the proceedings by the bill-stickers, gangs of men who toured the slums and rookeries of London pasting up handbills about the latest murder. For those who could not afford to buy the newspapers, these bills were a prime source of news, although hardly unbiased. Sometimes, the bill-stickers acted as extra detectives and themselves proposed suspects for various notorious crimes. Many years later, a bill-sticker told Henry Mayhew that:

> We had, at the verry least, half-a-dozen coves pulled up in the slums that we printed for the murder of 'the Beautiful Eliza Grimwood, in the Waterloo Road'. I did best on Thomas Hopkins, being the guilty man – I think he was Thomas Hopkins – 'cause a strong case was made out against him.[15]

Very few of the original handbills on the Grimwood case have been kept for posterity, however, and no suspect named Hopkins was named either by the police or by the newspapers.[16]

THE STRANGE
WELSHMAN

On Friday 1 June, a short, bald-headed, furtive-looking man came into Mr Clayton's tailor's shop at No. 11 Wellington Terrace, next door to the murder house. He asked the assistant George Grant to fetch Mr Clayton, since he had something very important to communicate to this gentleman, who was one of the jurors in the Grimwood case. But Grant was not impressed with this scruffy-looking fellow and told him that unless he stated his business, there was no question of his master coming down. The mystery man, who refused to give his own name, then said that he knew who had murdered Eliza Grimwood!

Grant immediately ran upstairs to fetch his master, but when Mr Clayton came downstairs, the odd-looking little man seemed very reluctant to explain himself further. When asked why he had not already attended at Union Hall to give evidence before the coroner and jury, he said that he had a strong and decided objection to taking the oath, which he would have been obliged to do if he appeared as a witness. When Mr Clayton made a move to seize him by the arm, the man ran out of the shop, waving his arms about excitedly.

Mr Clayton acted with commendable resolution. He ordered young George Grant to follow the strange visitor at a distance and to watch his movements. The shop assistant, who had no objection to becoming an extra detective, could soon see the mystery man loping through the streets. From time to time he was looking furtively around him, as if he was fearful of

A constable in the Metropolitan Police, in the uniform of 1829.

being pursued. When it began to rain heavily, he did not take shelter but kept on hurrying along the streets, seemingly at random, taking many unnecessary turns. Finally, he purchased a sheet of paper in a stationer's shop in Rosemary Lane, near Tower Hill, and went into a coffee shop nearby. Grant could see him in there, swigging from his cup of coffee and scribbling furiously on the sheet of paper. Perceiving a police constable nearby, Grant ran up to him and explained the situation.

Having recovered from his initial surprise in finding himself a vital player in the hunt for London's most wanted murderer, Police Constable Leaman made quite a sensible plan. He himself was to keep watch at the window, to make sure the suspect did not escape, while Grant, in his civilian attire, entered the coffee shop to see what the mystery man was doing. Enthusiastic to do some more detective work, the shop assistant sneaked up behind the suspect, peering over his shoulder. He could see that the mystery man was clearly writing a letter. As he sealed and addressed it, Grant could see that it was addressed 'To either Mr Grimwood or Mr Best, 12 Wellington Terrace, Waterloo Road, Lambeth'. He went out to alert Constable Leaman, who resolutely walked into the shop and collared the suspect.

Seeing a large policeman standing just behind him seemed to give the mystery man a dreadful shock. He gabbled incoherently and seemed very reluctant to give the letter up, until Constable Leaman pulled it out of his pocket and read the following remarkable communication:

June 1st, half-past 2 o'clock in the afternoon.

Gentlemen – A friend of mine, this morning, has made to me a disclosure, in a particular way, that will, I have no doubt, lead to the detection of the villain that committed the atrocious murder. The man he suspects is a good-looking man, with dark or large whiskers, thin made, nearly about six feet. You will excuse me from writing his name and address, for many reasons. He is by profession a Baptist and member of Abstinence. He is considered by many a most singular character: a man that has been well educated. Formerly, in his first wife's time, in great prosperity; is now in great poverty and distress from two wicked rebellious children. I dare not, on any account, give you his name, but he lives not far from Granby Street, Waterloo Road; is by trade a cooper; served his time to Mr. George Davis, cooper, of Limehouse; was bound at

Cooper's-hall in the year 1800; can talk several languages. His father was nearly 50 years porter at Lyon's Inn, in the Strand. He would suffer anything, I believe, yea die sooner than take an oath.

Constable Leaman read and reread this curious missive. Did it describe one man or two, and was the singular Baptist cooper of Granby Street also the suspected murderer? The only way to resolve this matter, he decided, was to take the mystery man into custody.[1]

★ ★ ★

The very same afternoon, Constable Leaman brought his prisoner before the Lambeth Street magistrates. The constable had found his charge, who had steadfastly refused to give his name, very odd indeed. George Grant, who was also present, said that the only thing that had induced him to think the prisoner was not right in the head was that when the rain came down in torrents, he had still kept walking through the streets. The prisoner was sternly cautioned by the magistrate Mr Norton: the charge against him was a serious one, and he had better tell the whole truth of the matter, and stop his prevaricating. Reluctantly, the mystery man gave his name as John Owen, a jobbing cooper by trade, and a native of Wales. He was a poor, hard-working man, he said, a Baptist and a member of the Temperance Society. He resided at No. 5 Cottage Place, Granby Street near Waterloo Road. Although some people might consider him insane, he would assure the bench this was not the case, although his mind was very distressed owing to the conduct of two of his children. If he seemed confused or incoherent, it was because his sensitive nervous system had been so very badly rattled by the shock of being made a prisoner.

The prisoner was asked to restrict himself to the matter at hand. He admitted that the letter referred to himself as the witness who had seen the murderer: it was he who was the singular cooper with the rebellious children, and yes, he knew who had murdered Eliza Grimwood. But first there was the matter of possible reward he had seen mentioned in the newspapers …

The garrulous Welshman was again gruffly told to compose himself, and to explain what evidence he possessed.

Owen said that early in the morning of 27 May, he had been distressed in his mind about the misbehaviour of his wicked children. He could not sleep, and decided to take a walk in Waterloo Road nearby. When passing along Wellington Terrace, he had seen a man standing at one of the doors, wearing a pair of light pantaloons or drawers and a clean shirt with the arms tucked up to the elbows. He had some blood on his hands. Owen saw him raise his hands to the sky and exclaim, 'Oh! Oh! I have done the deed, how shall I acquit myself of it?!'

Perceiving Owen nearby, he closed the door. Mystified, Owen went up and put his ear to the door. Although fearful of being knocked down if some person decided to open the door in a hurry, he stood there listening for several minutes, but found it perfectly still inside. After three or four minutes, he continued his walk as far as the bridge; on his way back, he again put his ear to the door, but without hearing the slightest noise.

Mr Norton asked Owen when he had first heard of the murder of Eliza Grimwood.

'On Sunday or Monday morning,' he replied.

But then why did he not take action once he knew what had happened – did he not link the observation of the bloodstained man with this sensational murder?

No, certainly not, the odd-looking little man assured the magistrate, this had never even crossed his mind. But when he had mentioned what he had seen to his neighbour the day after the murder, this individual had urged him to go before the coroner and jury. Owen's great reluctance to take the oath meant that he had instead chosen this more contrived stratagem for making his observation known to the authorities. Mr Pelham, the solicitor employed by the brothers Grimwood, said that Owen's evidence was of considerable importance. Surely, he must have seen the murderer, and if he could identify Hubbard, then there would be a strong case against the bricklayer. But Mr Norton had formed a low opinion of the shifty-looking Welshman. Although there was no longer any suspicion that he was himself the murderer, he seemed far from sane, and his story too good to be true. Could the murderer of Eliza Grimwood, who had otherwise acted with such impressive cunning, really have stood in the doorway waving his bloodstained hands about and confessing his guilt to all and sundry like some demented ham actor? He ordered Constable Leaman to make sure Owen really lived at the address he had indicated; if that was the case, he should be released and bound over to return to give evidence when the inquest continued.[2]

★ ★ ★

Constable Leaman deposited Owen in Mr Clayton's house at No. 11 Wellington Terrace, next door to the murder house, before going off to find the Welshman's own house in Cottage Place. The door was opened by some miserable-looking children, who verified that Owen, whom they claimed as their father, really did live there. When the constable returned to Mr Clayton's house, he was shocked to find that Owen had sneaked out! Where had the prisoner gone? The constable stood on the pavement outside for a while, trying to gather his thoughts. Just at that time, there was a commotion in the doorway of the murder house, and the constable was relieved when he was reunited with his prisoner, who was led out by Inspector Field, gabbling volubly.

It turned out that the Welshman had entered the murder house clandestinely. His shifty behaviour had attracted the attention of Inspector Field, who had asked him to identify himself. Having been treated to a number of lengthy, incoherent harangues about sensitive nerves, wicked children and teetotalism, the inspector finally understood that Owen claimed to have seen the murderer. He resolutely took Owen with him to the kitchen, where Hubbard was sitting with a number of other people. Having been allowed to look around at those present, twenty people in all, Fields took Owen back into the hallway, where the Welshman said, 'Was that him, smoking a pipe?'

Owen wanted to go back and have a second look, but the inspector had had enough of his antics and led him out of the house, where he met his police colleague. When Constable Leaman upbraided the dismal Welshman for his audacity in arranging this unsolicited identification parade, Owen retorted that he objected very much to being shouted at, since it would do his sensitive nerves further injury. But when the constable explained who Owen really was and what he had testified at Union Hall, Inspector Field became thoughtful. Surely, it had seemed as if Owen had recognised Hubbard as the man he had seen the morning of the murder. If he could identify him again, before the coroner and jury, the murder of Eliza Grimwood might well be solved.

7

THE PROSTITUTE WHO KNEW TOO MUCH

When the inquest resumed on Monday 4 June, Inspector Field was looking forward to an important day. Catherine Edwin would tell her tale about the mysterious foreigner she had more than once seen with Eliza Grimwood, and face a searching questioning from the jury. Then it would be time for John Owen to perform. The inspector had arranged for Hubbard to be present, and for the Welshman to try to pick him out among the people present in court. Neither of these two potential star witnesses seemed particularly reliable, however, and Inspector Field must have been worried what antics these volatile, histrionic people would be up to when facing the coroner's jury.

And things would not start well for the unfortunate inspector. The first witness of the day was the elusive Julia Seymour, allegedly the companion of Eliza Grimwood the evening of the murder. After being tracked down by a police constable and summoned to the inquest, she introduced herself as a widow, living at No. 2 Newcastle Court off the Strand. But when asked, she denied knowing Eliza Grimwood, or being at the Strand Theatre the evening of the murder. Emma Lewis, who had confidently named Julia Seymour as Eliza's companion, now completely recanted, saying that she had only seen Eliza and her friend from behind and drawn her own conclusions when she heard the name 'Julia'. The jurymen 'expressed their astonishment at the prevarications of this witness'; she seemed to treat the proceedings with the greatest levity. Julia Seymour was not much better. When asked to prove that she was not at the theatre the evening of the murder, she first demanded that her word was taken in that respect, and then referred to the theatre doorkeeper, who would certainly have remembered her coming in and out of the theatre. The coroner, who did not share this belief, desired both these witnesses to retire.

The next witness was known to Inspector Field, although it was a surprise to him that she turned up in court. Harriet Chaplin introduced herself as a married woman living at No. 27 Great Russell Street and the niece of Eliza Grimwood. She had met with Eliza a couple of times each month, and had worked for her as a dressmaker on several occasions. She disliked Hubbard and had nothing good to say about him. About eight or nine months before, she had seen him strike Eliza with his hand after they had quarrelled about the management of the house. Some months later, Hubbard and Eliza had again been quarrelling, this time about her favourite gentleman friend, the Birmingham sword cutler. Hubbard ranted and raved, saying that if she was going out with the sword cutler, he would stab or shoot them both. When Harriet Chaplin said that he would look good in Newgate, Hubbard replied that he would not mind being hanged in Newgate for a just cause. Another time, when Eliza had told Harriet Chaplin that she wanted to leave Hubbard to be with her Birmingham friend, she also said that Hubbard had threatened her with the words that he would not mind shooting her. Harriet Chaplin here became so faint that water was sent for to refresh her.

When Harriet Chaplin had heard that Eliza was dead, she had exclaimed to her sister, 'Then she is murdered!' and the sister had replied, 'Then it is Hubbard!' Impressed by this anti-Hubbard farrago, one of the jurors suggested that he might ask the witness what kind of temper Hubbard possessed, but the stern coroner retorted that this would be a very improper question, since different people might entertain different notions about his temper. It was for the jury to judge the murder case, and the possible involvement of Hubbard, from the facts adduced before them.

There was a short recess, during which the knowledgeable Inspector Field approached the coroner. From the Grimwood brothers or some other source, he had obtained some information about the young lady in question. Ann Chapman, alias Harriet Chaplin, alias Caroline Chaplin, may once have been married to a man named Chaplin, but she was certainly not cohabiting with him any longer. She belonged to the better class of prostitute, operating from lodgings in Red Lion Square, Holborn. Giving a false name and false address is not a good start when you give evidence in court, and the inspector wanted to point out that she had for some time been shunned by her respectable relatives since she had led a very disreputable life. Although it was not unlikely that Eliza Grimwood had been employing her niece in making or altering her dresses, the rest of Harriet Chaplin's story would have to be treated with caution until it could be corroborated by other witnesses.

The next witness was none other than Eliza's old favourite, the Birmingham sword cutler William Osborne. He was no mere artisan, but a gentleman of considerable wealth and a kingpin in the Midlands sword cutlery trade. He had known Eliza for several years, always visiting her at some hotel when he was in London. They regularly wrote love letters to each other, and some of his amatory missives had been found in the murder room. During their last meeting, three weeks before the murder, nothing out of the ordinary had happened except that Eliza had given him a silver snuffbox as a keepsake. Osborne had visited the house in Wellington Terrace a few times, but he had never left a knife or swordstick behind.[1]

★ ★ ★

There was a hush in court when young Catherine Edwin took the stand. She confidently told the coroner and jury that the Wednesday before the murder, she had met her friend Eliza Grimwood in the Strand. As they stood talking, a young gentleman came up to them. He was dapperly dressed in a pair of dark green trousers striped in black, a primrose-coloured waistcoat and a dark frock coat. He wore dark green spectacles and a broad-brimmed hat. On perceiving him, Eliza said, 'Here comes my tormentor!' Catherine Edwin had seen Eliza with this man a number of times. He was an Italian but spoke fluent English and French. He was madly in love with Eliza and they had often been in company. Once, the Italian had invited Eliza and Catherine to a confectioner's shop, where they took their seats in a private room. The bushy-whiskered foreigner generously paid for all the refreshments. As Catherine tucked in, the Italian and Eliza discussed the opera, a subject where they were both knowledgeable. Boldly and unexpectedly, the Foreigner asked Eliza to marry him, but she turned him down. After this rebuff, the Italian angrily tore off his overcoat. As he did so, something metallic dropped to the floor. When Catherine picked it up, she saw that it was a large clasp knife! The Italian showed her how to open and shut the blade by means of two distinct springs. The coroner ordered Inspector Field to bring in Eliza Grimwood's stays, and to ask the witness if a knife like the one she had seen could produce similar cuts. When she saw the stays, which were completely saturated with blood, she became almost hysterical, before faltering that she thought it would. The coroner ordered that some water should be brought to her before she could face further questioning.

Inspector Field must have been listening open-mouthed at these amazing tales. Clearly, either Catherine Edwin's memory had improved greatly since he had first questioned her, or she was simply inventing her story as she went along. But the pert young witness had more sensations in store for him. When asked by the coroner whether she could recall the Italian's name, she replied that she had forgotten it, although it was very similar to that of one of the men who had shot at the King of France. Eliza Grimwood had always called him 'my crack-whiskered Antonio' or 'my crack-whiskered Don'. Then came the following remarkable exchange:

'Is the Italian a gentleman, or does he follow any profession or business?'

'No, I thought he was a thief!'

'Why did you think so?'

'Because he looked like one."

Again Inspector Field must have groaned, but Catherine Edwin's fun had not ended by any means. Once, when Catherine Edwin had visited Eliza at Wellington Terrace, the Italian had come in to see her. He then wore a valuable ring given to him by Eliza, on which was engraved 'Always faithful' on one side and 'Semper fidelis' on the other. Another time, the amorous foreigner had proposed to Eliza on Waterloo Bridge itself; when she gave him no answer, he threatened to throw her into the Thames. Catherine Edwin did not know where the Italian lived, although she thought he could be found near the Spread Eagle in the Regent Circus. He was always walking with his eyes down, wearing a cloak or a mackintosh to disguise himself, but if she saw him again she would recognise him immediately. The coroner sagely commented that Catherine Edwin's description of the Foreigner certainly corresponded with that given by the other witnesses. Such a remarkable character, striding along the Regent Circus in his green spectacles, broad-brimmed hat and long cloak, would surely not be difficult to pick out.

At this stage, Mary Glover asked to be recalled. Since she had been Eliza Grimwood's closest friend, she took strong exception to some of Catherine Edwin's statements. She had never met Catherine Edwin, nor heard Eliza speak of her. Eliza had often entertained various female friends in her parlour at Wellington Terrace, but Catherine Edwin had not been one of them. Nor had Eliza ever spoken of meeting any strange Italian with green spectacles, or being proposed to by such a person. Inspector Field, who still suspected that Catherine Edwin was lying, took good notice of this evidence.

Knowing that John Owen would soon be called, the coroner decided to ask Mary Glover some further questions. As staunchly as before, she claimed that Eliza had never complained of any ill usage from Hubbard. If any person had come downstairs and committed the murder, or opened the front door to exclaim, 'I have done the deed!' she would certainly have heard it. The inspector must once more have wondered who was lying and who was telling the truth in this extraordinary case.

★ ★ ★

After another short recess, it was time to introduce the star witness, John Owen. First, the coroner called the shopman Grant, who repeated his earlier testimony about the strange man coming to Mr Clayton's shop. Curiously, he added that Owen had first asked what day the murder had been committed; when told it was on the previous Saturday morning, he had sighed and exclaimed, 'Then I was right!' But Grant also testified that judging from Owen's manner and appearance, he was clearly not of sound mind. The vigilant shopman had either been ordered by the police to keep an eye on Owen, or assumed this task on his own accord. The previous day, he had seen Owen enter the murder house at No. 12 Wellington Terrace, where he offered a piece of iron in the shape of an anvil for sale, asking 2s for it. After this damning testimony, suggesting that Owen had once more been clandestinely trying to seek out Hubbard before the inquest, Constable Leaman described how he had arrested Owen in the coffee shop. When the strange letter was read aloud, several of the jurymen commented that if its contents were true, Owen could certainly identify the murderer.

There was a hush as Owen appeared in person. Described by the journalists as a scruffy, bald-headed man around 60 years old, Owen shuffled up to the coroner, asking to state something in private. When this was denied, he tried to avoid taking the oath, but at length was forced to do so. He made a long, rambling statement, displaying considerable agitation, about wicked children, teetotalism and his Baptist faith. He went on to claim, bending the truth somewhat, that Inspector Field had taken him into the murder house. In the kitchen, where twenty people were seated, he had pointed out the man he had seen the morning of the murder; he had been smoking a pipe at the time. But almost as if he deliberately wanted to devalue his evidence, the Welshman then began ranting again: some people might think him insane, but he was 'in competent senses' and could provide many respectable references. When asked about his second clandestine visit to the murder house, Owen did not deny it, saying that he was in dire financial straits and wanted to raise a little money.

When Hubbard was finally introduced into the room, the Welshman was told to look around and see if he could identify the man he had seen in Waterloo Road the morning of the murder. A hush went through the court-room as the bald-headed old fellow had a look round with his watery eyes.

'There he is!' he finally screamed out.

But Inspector Field's heart must have sunk within him as he saw that Owen was pointing at a well-dressed, respectable spectator! According to a newspaper reporter, 'Hubbard during this proceeding betrayed not the slightest agitation.' Perceiving that he had made a mistake, Owen tried to recant, saying that the man he had pointed out only resembled the murderer, and that he would like to try again. But Inspector Field made a sign to Constable Leaman and the voluble Welshman was summarily evicted from the inquest.

This dismal anticlimax virtually put an end to the day's proceedings. Owen's alleged daughter, a sluttish-looking young woman who had been expected to back up his statement about his early morning walk, did not do so; in fact, her 'father' had been in bed at nine o'clock. Inspector Field, still smarting over the Owen fiasco, testified that the dry vaults under

Wellington Terrace, the fields opposite, and the tops of the neighbouring houses, had all now been searched by the police, without anything resembling the murder weapon being found. Somewhat belatedly, he had also strip-searched Hubbard for any scratch or contusion that might indicate that he had been involved in a scuffle, but found none. Finally, the coroner tried to elucidate one of the many puzzling aspects of the murder, namely why Eliza's chamber pot had been found in the kitchen. The servant Mary Fisher said that there were three chamber utensils in the house. The evening before the murder, she had put these in the bedrooms of Eliza, Hubbard and Mary Glover. The morning after the murder, she had found Eliza's chamber pot underneath the kitchen sink. After Inspector Field had confirmed that no other witness could remember seeing the chamber pot in the murder room, Hubbard was again introduced into the room. With his usual coolness, he denied seeing any chamber utensil in Eliza's room, or any vessel contaminated with blood in any part of the house.

After this day of unmitigated disaster, Richard Carter and Charles Frederick Field must have been the two most low-spirited men in London. They had both had high hopes that the day would bring a vital breakthrough, but the result had been even more contradiction and confusion. The coroner and the inspector agreed that Owen was a worthless character, but Mr Carter still wanted to pursue the Catherine Edwin lead in spite of the inspector's misgivings. It was his wish that Inspector Field would take Catherine Edwin round all the places she had described to look for the Foreigner. The glum inspector reluctantly agreed. He 'afterwards followed one of the witnesses home, found that she was a gay woman living in Berkley Street West'.[2] This may well have been the mysterious Julia Seymour.

8

WILFUL MURDER AGAINST SOME PERSON OR PERSONS UNKNOWN

Tuesday 5 June 1838 must have been one of the most dismal days in the life of Charles Frederick Field. In his diary, the professional policeman tersely told that he:

> Went in company with Sgt Price to the residence of the witness Edwins. It being the coroner's wish that she should accompany me to the different places where she had met the Foreigner she stated in her evidence she was in the habit of meeting with the deceased. Went with her to Piccadilly, Regent Circus, Leicester Square, also to the pastry cooks she had mentioned in her evidence, and many places of public resort for Foreigners, in the evening went to the Opera House but saw no person answering to the description this witness gave of him.[1]

But in reality, the day was one of unceasing humiliation. As the exasperated inspector told a journalist from *The Globe*, Catherine Edwin was on her worst behaviour throughout. First they went to Mrs Rosedale's confectioner's shop, which Catherine Edwin confidently pointed out as the one where she and Eliza had met the Foreigner. But when Inspector Field asked her to come into the shop, she 'positively refused to go in with him, making use of some frivolous pretext for her conduct'. The inspector found that there was no private room, as Catherine Edwin had confidently stated at the inquest. They then proceeded to the Regent Circus, where the amusement started in earnest. Catherine Edwin pointed out one passer-by after another as the Foreigner, but when questioned by the inspector, they all turned out to be respectable people. After this kind of fun had been going on for more than three hours, Catherine Edwin finally declared that the Foreigner was not there.[2]

In the evening, Inspector Field took Catherine Edwin to the Opera House. This disreputable young woman tried her old tricks again, pointing out one man after another to the exasperated inspector, and then recanting, saying that he was not all that like Eliza Grimwood's sinister companion after all. When she began openly plying her trade as a prostitute, and even pointing out Field as her 'protector', he finally called it a day and quietly left the theatre. On his way home, he must have wondered why he ever left the stage to take up the precarious position as an inspector of police.

★ ★ ★

On Tuesday 6 June, the stalwart inspector did his best to rally his weary troops, who were still searching the dry docks under Waterloo Road and Bridge and the tops of houses nearby, trying to find the murder weapon. The drains in the neighbourhood were searched by a party of workmen under the direction of Mr Gwilt, surveyor to the commissions of sewers for Surrey and Kent.[3] Meanwhile, Inspector Field went to a building site in the Kent Road, where Hubbard used to work. Questioning the bricklayers at the site, he found out that Hubbard had not been held in high regard by his former workmates, and that he 'had treated his former wife with a great deal of ill usage when she lived with him'.

Inspector Field also had another good idea. With regard to the forensic evidence against Hubbard, a crucial question was how many shirts he had possessed prior to the murder and how many clean ones he could now produce. This inquiry should really have been made at a much earlier stage. Still, the inspector 'saw the laundress who washed for him, ascertained how many shirts he had, made Enquiries in the neighbourhood about him'.[4] It turned out that Hubbard had possessed seven shirts, in various states of repair. Mary

Glover told the inspector that Eliza had more than once complained of Hubbard's darned and worn shirts, and spoken of buying some linen to have some new shirts made for him, but this had never been acted upon. Mary Glover said that Eliza had not cared very much for household chores, leaving most of them to her servant Mary Fisher. It had in fact been Mary Glover herself who had taken care of Hubbard's shirts. She had numbered them from No. 1 to No. 7 and of these, No. 5 could not be found. Had this bloodstained shirt been discarded by Hubbard after the murder?

The next day, the police operation searching the neighbourhood for the murder weapon continued. Inspector Field also found time to investigate the claim of the man Cubitt, that Hubbard had been down to the toll gate on Waterloo Bridge early after the murder, but only to discover that it had probably been Mr Best who had approached the police constable standing there. Mary Glover had told the inspector that about a year ago, Hubbard had gone to work at a building site in Essex. Eliza had become 'uneasy about him forming a connection with another female. She went after him and fetched him back. They were very good friends after.'[5]

Finding this a worthwhile lead, Inspector Field went to investigate in person. Along with Edmond Champneys, the Epping local constable, he managed to find the cottage where Hubbard had lodged with a woman and her two daughters. A bricklayer told them that, indeed, Hubbard had presented himself as a single man, and paid particular attention to one of the daughters. One day, Eliza came to claim him as her husband. When confronting Hubbard in a public house, she had slapped his face hard, drawing blood. Hubbard had raised his hand but not struck her. Eliza and Hubbard had then made peace and he had agreed to return to London with her. When they went to the cottage to get Hubbard's effects, another angry altercation ensued between Eliza and Hubbard's paramour. Her sister tried to make peace between the infuriated females, but her intervention did not have the desired result, since Eliza sent her reeling with a bloody nose. As the thoughtful inspector was preparing to leave, the bricklayer handed him a dirty garment. Since he had read in the newspapers that the police were investigating Hubbard's shirts, he thought he ought to mention that his fellow bricklayer had left one of his shirts behind during his stay in Essex. Inspector Field could see that embroidered on the inside of the collar was the figure 5.

* * *

When the inquest continued on 8 June, Inspector Field and his men had devoted some further time to investigating the antecedents of John Owen, the former star witness. Mr George Francis, a leading member of the Philanthropic Society, took the oath to testify that in his opinion, Owen could not be relied upon at all. When the Welshman had applied for support from his society to feed his starving children, Francis had gone to his house and found a teenage girl and several young boys. The girl had been 'nearly naked, and in a wretched condition'. The place was a filthy, near-derelict hovel. Owen had received some money from the philanthropists and the promise of more to come. But when passing a public house a few days later, Mr Francis had seen the alleged teetotaller sitting at the bar, swigging heartily from a glass of beer! He became suspicious and made some inquiries in the neighbourhood, soon finding out that John Owen, alias Owen Owen, was a conniving liar and trickster. None of the 'children' he had shown the philanthropist were his own – the 'daughter' was a common prostitute who lodged in his house, and the 'sons' were street ragamuffins recruited by this Welsh Fagin for his elaborate charade. Mr Bryan, landlord of the Bell public house, corroborated the philanthropist's testimony with regard to Owen's drinking habits. Some spectators and jurors commented that they had themselves lent Owen money after hearing his pathetic stories about starving children, only to discover that it was all untrue.[6]

A young lad named William Clements had seen Owen walking through Granby Street the evening after his first appearance in court, followed by a crowd of people who were teasing him for his involvement in the Grimwood case. Clements was surprised when a well-dressed gentleman came up and gave Owen some silver coins, saying, 'Don't say too much,' and, 'Mind what you're about.' He suspected that this might be the murderer bribing the old man to perjure himself.

When Owen was recalled, he had to face many a jibe and jeer from the jury and spectators. Firstly, he was challenged with the evidence from the lad Clements. After having 'entered into a rambling statement as to the accuracy and inaccuracy of his memory', Owen admitted that a gentleman had approached him after the inquest at the York Hotel and spoken to him kindly. He had offered Owen a pint of porter but the stalwart teetotaller had refused. Instead, the kind gentleman had given him sixpence. Owen said that he did not like being laughed at in a public room, since it was painful to his feelings. The coroner retorted that he had a public duty to perform and that Owen had to answer his questions. The Welshman could not deny that he had applied for money from the Philanthropic Society. When asked whether he had a young woman living in his house, he truculently replied, 'I don't think I have a right to answer that question. It has nothing to do with the case, and I will not answer it.'

'Now, will you answer that question!' the coroner demanded.

'It is an indelicate question, and I won't answer it. I'll go to prison first. The newspapers have made use of my name in a very unwarrantable manner. Every person now says "There goes John Owen!"'

Finally, he had to admit that he slept in the same room as this girl. When asked whether they actually shared the same bed, he broke into incoherent exclamations about God and his soul, and pointed out that 'he bore an excellent private character'.

When the coroner asked, 'Was she a modest girl?' Owen guardedly answered, 'Yes, I believe so.' He then 'entered into an extraordinary lengthy statement in reference to his mother's death, and other circumstances not related to the inquiry, which called forth the hissing of those present'.

Inspector Field and his men had also found a neighbour of Owen's, with whom the Welshman had discussed the murder. Owen had said that he had seen a man he suspected to be the killer, but he had then asked, 'Supposing he is not the man, if the murderer is found out, what can they do with me afterwards?' The coroner indicated the spectator whom Owen had denounced as the murderer just a few days ago and asked if the Welshman still believed he was the man with the bloody hands standing in Waterloo Road the morning after the murder. Owen replied 'No, I do not' and declared himself ready to try again. There was loud hissing from the spectators as the jury formally pronounced that Owen was an impostor and that they would not take his word. The Welshman skulked out.

★ ★ ★

The humiliation of Owen must have acted as a tonic to the weary Inspector Field, who must have had enough of the Welshman's rantings about sensitive nerves, wicked children and teetotalism. But the inspector had another fish to fry. When he took the stand, he described his ludicrous day out with Catherine Edwin. There had been no private room at the pastry cook's, as she had confidently stated on oath. Her story or hearing of the murder from the doctor who was bleeding her was also untrue. The persistent inspector had tracked down the doctor in question and he had testified that it had in fact been Catherine Edwin herself who had been talking very much about the murder of Eliza Grimwood. The inspector had also found out that, although Catherine Edwin had represented herself to be 20 years old, she was in fact only 16. When questioned on 4 June, she had denied ever meeting Hubbard, but the inspector had evidence that the two had in fact met clandestinely at the murder house. When asked by the coroner whether Catherine Edwin was at all to be believed, the inspector replied, 'I should say not.'

The theatre waitress Charlotte Parker was then called to describe her meeting with Eliza and the Foreigner the evening of the murder. She added that Eliza had been a much better class of customer than the other 'ladies' who frequented the Strand Theatre: she had always been elegantly dressed, steady in her behaviour, and never the worse for drink. She still steadfastly denied that the Foreigner had spoken with a foreign accent. The pastry cook Mary Rosedale testified that she could indeed remember a foreign-looking gentleman and three young ladies coming into her shop and having refreshments in an adjoining room about a week before the murder, but she could not identify Catherine Edwin as one of them.

Constable Goff, who had been allowed to accompany Inspector Field to the inquest, next took the stand. He told the jury that last Monday, Hubbard had received an unexpected visitor at the murder house, namely Catherine Edwin. She had introduced herself as a great friend of Eliza's, who had once seen her with the supposed murderer. When confronted with this damning statement, Catherine Edwin responded that when giving evidence, she had forgotten all about her visit to the murder house; any way, she had spoken to Hubbard in the kitchen, not in the parlour as the policeman had said. It was none of their business how old she was, nor did it have any relevance to the proceedings. She made a rude gesture to some of the jurymen when they openly declared that there was not one word of truth in her various statements, and pulled a face at Inspector Field as Constable Goff escorted her out of the sessions room.

★ ★ ★

After the annoying Catherine Edwin had finally been removed, Constable Goff again took the stand. When asked by the coroner how Hubbard had behaved since the murder, Goff said that his prisoner had been very dejected. Once he had said, 'Oh, my dear Eliza, my dear Eliza! Would to God …' and then muttered something that Goff could not hear. He had once had a nightmare, during which he called out, 'Eliza! Oh, my dear Eliza!' in a loud voice. When Goff had come into his bedroom, Hubbard 'was looking very wild' and did not appear to recognise Goff. He said that he had been dreaming of his poor Eliza and asked for some beer to help him go back to sleep.

Constable Goff was also instrumental in solving another minor mystery. When he had been the first policeman on the scene the morning after the murder, he had asked the surgeon Cooke if this was really a case of suicide. The careless medical man had replied, 'No doubt of it!' At that time the chamber utensil was still present in the murder room. It might well be that the surgeon had washed his hands in the chamber pot and then taken it out to the kitchen.

The diligent Constable Goff had also found a new witness who had some interesting things to tell. Ann Sage lived with her married sister at No. 19 Bond Street. The night of the murder, the sister kept going up and down stairs because her husband was very ill. Since Ann Sage could not sleep, she diverted herself by looking out through the back window, which was facing the back of Wellington Terrace. At about a quarter to three, she could see a light in Hubbard's back parlour. Was this the murderer leaving the house? Ann Sage could not swear with certainty that the light was in Hubbard's house, however, since the houses in Wellington Terrace were much higher up than those in her own street.

A busybody named Ryman, who had previously been pestering Inspector Field with various theories about the murder, next made an appearance.

He said that he was living at No. 34 Waterloo Road and that seven o'clock the morning after the murder, he had seen the servant Mary Fisher walking past his house. Surely this was a mysterious circumstance that might imply that she was protecting Hubbard? But Inspector Field indicated that this might well have a perfectly natural explanation. When called, Mary Fisher readily explained that she had been out twice early in the morning, first to the Pear Tree public house to purchase some gin and brandy to calm the nerves of Hubbard and the other inhabitants of the murder house, and secondly to the cheesemongers at No. 35 Waterloo Road to buy some cheese and eggs. She had told the cheesemonger, 'Oh, sir, you will never see my mistress again, for she has been murdered!' When asked whether Hubbard had desired her to change her evidence after the murder, she indignantly replied, 'He has not, so help me God!'

★ ★ ★

After all the evidence had been heard, the coroner proceeded to sum up. He did not believe that any juryman would doubt 'that a murder of the most horrid and atrocious character has been committed'. Apart from that obvious fact, the case remained one of great mystery. Mr Carter emphasised that Hubbard had not been taken in a lie and that his story about what had happened the morning of the murder was backed up by other witnesses. The blood on his trousers had been satisfactorily accounted for. As for Owen's testimony, it seemed hardly credible that a murderer would lose all regard for his own safety and make use of loud exclamations at the front door, in full view of a stranger. Owen had seemed far from sane, and although he had allegedly picked Hubbard out during his clandestine visit to the murder house, he had failed to do so in court. Mr Carter did not attach much importance to evidence of the girl Chaplin that Hubbard had been threatening Eliza, since it was not corroborated by any other witness.

Many witnesses testified that the evening of the murder, Eliza had brought home a customer. According to the evidence of the servant girl Mary Fisher, this man had remained with Eliza for some time. From the surgeon Cooke's evidence, Eliza had been dead about four hours when he came to the house, and thus the murder had taken place between one and two in the morning.

Mr Carter suggested that after they had had intercourse, the customer had tried to 'depart without a gratuity'. When Eliza had tried to prevent his escape, or call Hubbard, the Foreigner had slashed at her neck with his knife and then cut her throat. Using the lit candlestick, he had then noiselessly let himself out, taking the murder weapon with him.

After enlightening the jury with these observations, the coroner left them to consider 'whether they think what they have received is fully sufficient to fix the guilt on any individual, or whether, from the mystery in which this case still remains involved, that you cannot form a just conclusion who is the guilty party'. After deliberating for half an hour, they unanimously found a verdict of 'Wilful murder against some person or persons unknown'.

THE CAVENDISH LETTER

On the evening of Sunday 10 June, Inspector Field was not in a particularly good mood. The coroner's inquest on Eliza Grimwood had produced few worthwhile leads and a multitude of annoying red herrings. The hunt for the Foreigner had been entirely devoid of success. All of Saturday, the inspector had led a troop of police constables 'visiting the different places and Hotels where foreigners are in the habit of going and ascertaining whether any of these had left their lodgings, also visited the different Gambling Houses in St James &c making the minute Enquiries at all foreign houses'.[1] By this time, every foreign ship, every seaman's hostel, every foreign hotel and lodging house, and every tavern or eating house where Frenchmen and Italians used to go had been searched by the Grimwood task force. But although this police operation had flushed out a number of dodgy foreigners, they could all give an account of themselves, and none of them answered the description of the young, dapperly dressed foreigner who had taken Eliza Grimwood home. It was scant consolation to the weary detective that the inhabitants of the Parish of St Mary, Lambeth, had held a public meeting and offered a reward of £50 for the apprehension of the murderer of Eliza Grimwood.[2]

For Inspector Field, it was also very important to maintain a good working relationship with the coroner and magistrates. But in the Grimwood murder investigation, there had more than once been clashes between the coroner's enthusiasm for new sensational leads and the inspector's reliance on good solid police work. It had greatly annoyed Field that at the inquest, the coroner and jury had openly sneered at the volatile, histrionic female witnesses he had presented. Something of a misogynist himself, he fully shared their low opinion of those flippant young harlots, but they were the best witnesses he had been able to find. Nor had the introduction of that pathetic perjurer John Owen done Field's prestige any good.

But as the gloomy inspector sat pondering the murder mystery, a caller was announced: it was Eliza's brother Thomas Grimwood, who had previously made himself useful in explaining her antecedents. By this time, there was no longer any police presence at No. 12 Wellington Terrace. Since Thomas Grimwood was still very worried that Hubbard would take off with Eliza's valuable property, he and his two brothers took it in turns to stay at the murder house. The Grimwoods did not get along with the volatile Hubbard, and angry altercations were the order of the day. This particular evening, something more momentous was afoot, however: Thomas Grimwood said that he had actually overheard Hubbard planning his escape from London.

★ ★ ★

Losing no time, Inspector Field got hold of a cab and went to Wellington Terrace, where he sat outside stealthily watching the murder house for several hours. Close to midnight, Hubbard sneaked out, hailed a cab and went across Waterloo Bridge, with the inspector following him. He went to a house in Doughty Square, where he stayed only a few minutes, and then to a house in Stafford Street. The inspector sat waiting outside, pondering what to do. Hubbard's behaviour was definitely suspicious, but he hardly seemed in a hurry to escape from London. Inspector Field thought he could recognise one of the people who received Hubbard as the suspect's brother Charles.[3] He decided to return to the station house to see what advice he could get from there. He was surprised to find the place in an uproar. Clearly there had been some important news. When the inspector told Superintendent Grimsall, who was directing operations in person in spite of the late hour, about his pursuit of Hubbard, he was ordered immediately to take him into custody. When Field asked why, the following letter, written on elegant black-edged paper, was thrust into his hands:

Goswell-street, June 8, 1838

Sir, - Though with the greatest reluctance, a sense of duty I owe to every fellow creature, and that justice may be obtained, compels me to break my silence touching the melancholy death of Eliza Grimwood. Ever since the horrid deed has been perpetrated I have had the public prints, and have attended the inquiry whenever I could obtain admittance, though in disguise, but have as yet remained silent. I am the person who accompanied Eliza Grimwood home on the night in question from the Strand Theatre ...'[4]

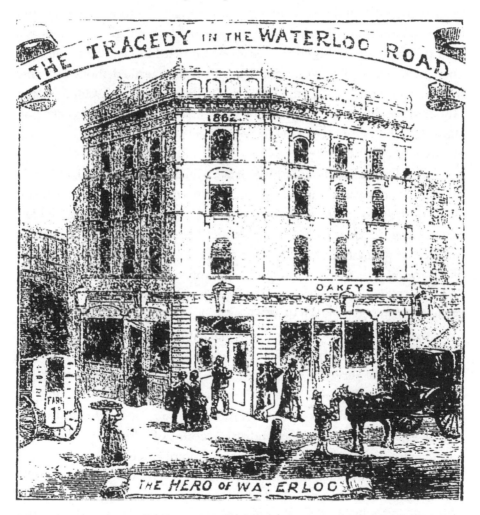

The Hero of Waterloo public house at No. 108 Waterloo Road, kept by Mr Okey to whom the Cavendish letter was delivered.

The letter writer, who signed his name 'John Walter Cavendish' and gave his address as Goswell Street, went on to declare that he had intended to remain with Eliza all night, but before going to bed, they 'had a few words'. The sound of their quarrel alerted the jealous Hubbard, who came charging downstairs. Fearful that he would be 'bullied' and robbed by Eliza's 'protector', Cavendish decided to escape. He took up the candlestick and made for the door, but Hubbard burst into the room in a fearful rage. After calling the nearly naked Eliza 'a bloody whore', he collared Cavendish and exclaimed, 'You bastard, I will do for you!' Cavendish managed to free himself and ran to the front door, leaving behind a pair of black kid gloves as well as a gold signet ring with his crest (a bear's head) that Hubbard had pulled off during the scuffle. The distraught Cavendish then walked about for some time, several times passing the house in Wellington Terrace. Once, he saw Hubbard standing with the front door ajar. His shirtsleeves were tucked up above his elbows, and when he perceived Cavendish he shut the door cautiously without slamming it.

At first, Cavendish thought little of what had happened. He had visited unfortunate females in various shady locations many times before, and was aware of the risks involved. He had twice been with Eliza at a hotel in Hart Street, Covent Garden. But after the murder had become known, he realised that he was sitting right in the middle of London's greatest mystery. He was by no means a foreigner, although his complexion was somewhat swarthy due to a seven-year residence in the West Indies. Fearful of being arrested as the Foreigner, Cavendish shaved his whiskers and disguised his dress. But realising that unless he came forth, the nefarious Hubbard would get away with murder, Cavendish reluctantly changed his mind and wrote his letter, declaring that to serve the course of justice he would appear in public and establish Hubbard's guilt.

This letter indeed looked very promising. Inspector Field could spot a few flaws, however. Firstly, Cavendish's account of a loud and vociferous scuffle, with violent threats being uttered, did not agree with the stories of the other people resident at No. 12 Wellington Terrace that night. Secondly, it was strange that although the letter writer gave his name and the name of the street he lived in, he did not provide the number of his house. But the inspector and superintendent knew one thing that had deliberately been kept from the public, namely that an unidentified pair of gloves had really been found in the murder room. It is true that they were lavender-coloured, not black, but there was no way the mysterious Cavendish could have known about them.

At three in the morning of Monday 11 June, Inspector Field and some constables returned to the house in Stafford Street. According to a journalist who had spoken to one of the constables involved, Hubbard 'did not appear as if taken by surprise nor betray much perceptible agitation when the policemen entered his bedroom'. The police brought Hubbard back with them, in handcuffs, to the Tower Street police station.[5]

★ ★ ★

On Monday morning, news soon spread about the arrest of Hubbard, and London was buzzing with rumours. In the morning, Inspector Field went to the Marlborough Street police office to see a suspect picked up as the Foreigner by Inspector Shamling. He was a Frenchman named Ernest Tondeur, a native of Bordeaux employed as a singer at one of the theatres, who had been arrested because he fitted Catherine Edwin's description of the killer almost exactly, even down to the whiskers, glasses and ability to speak French. But when this capricious young lady was called to identify him, she said that he did not in the slightest resemble the man she had seen with Eliza Grimwood! Despite the handicap of being a foreigner, Tondeur seemed a respectable man, and the magistrate concluded that he had been wrongfully apprehended.[6] The spectators seemed more concerned about what was happening to Hubbard. Several inquisitive journalists approached Inspector Field, but he told them nothing.

When the inspector went to the station house, where Hubbard was confined to one of the cells and closely watched by two constables, he was annoyed to find a large and unruly mob of people of both sexes waiting outside. They were cursing Hubbard as the murderer of Eliza Grimwood, and suggesting that he should be hanged there and then. The inspector began to fear for Hubbard's safety, since there was such immense prejudice against him. When Field left the police station in a cab, leaving Hubbard behind, there was a shout of 'There goes the murderer!' and some roughs leapt up

APPREHENSION OF HUBBARD ON MONDAY MORNING,
Examination at Union Hall, charged with the Wilful Murder of
ELIZA GRIMWOOD,
Who was Murdered at No. 12, Wellington Terrace, Waterloo Road, on Saturday May 26, 1838.

On Sunday afternoon Mr. Carter, the Coroner, received a letter at his house, signed "John Waters Cavendish," informing him that he, the writer, was the person who accompanied Eliza Grimwood to her lodgings on the night of the murder. That after he had been with the deceased a short time, Hubbard came down stairs, and entered the room where they were, and commenced assaulting both of them. A general scuffle ensued, during which he (the writer of the letter) succeeded in reaching the front door, and making his escape. The letter also stated, that in the scuffle the writer lost a pair of white kid gloves and a gold ring. The letter was dated from Goswell Street, and on enquiry the address was found to be correct. In consequence of this information, Hubbard was taken into custody at three o'clock on Monday morning, in Castle Street, Borough, (to which place he had removed on Sunday night,) and conveyed him to the station-house. At three o'clock he was examined at Union Hall, where the letter was read, and it was reported that the writer would attend at the examination, but he did not. The brother of the deceased stated, that when he first came to town he found a pair of gloves on the table in the room where the deceased was murdered, but no ring had been seen. The Magistrate stated, that this was a very strong fact, and in order that the Police might obtain further information, he would remand the prisoner till Tuesday next.

Hubbard when apprehended betrayed no sign of guilt, and continued so during the examination.

ON SATURDAY morning May 26, the inhabitants of the Waterloo Road, and the streets adjacent to it, were thrown into the greatest alarm, in consequence of the report that a female named Eliza Grimwood, residing at No. 12, Wellington Terrace, had been inhumanly murdered. The report of this murder was first given by a man named Hubbard, a bricklayer, who rents the above house, and under whose protection the unfortunate female had lived for some time. Hubbard stated in his evidence before the Coroner's Jury, that on Friday night, about ten o'clock, he supped with the deceased, after which she put on her things and went out, and he went to bed in a room on the second floor. At five o'clock on the Saturday morning he got up to go to his work, and on reaching the passage which leads to the house door, he felt some astonishment on observing a candlestick on the mat at the street door. On looking toward the back parlour, which is formed into a bed-room, he saw the door partly open, and by the side of the bed he thought he saw a bundle of clothes; he stooped to pick it up, and found it to be the knees of the deceased. He became greatly alarmed, and ran up stairs to alarm the lodgers in the first floor, and then went for medical assistance.

Mary Fisher stated, that she had lived servant to Hubbard for two years; that on the Friday evening her master and the deceased supped together, that her master went to bed at nine o'clock, and she did not see him again till the following morning. After this the deceased went out, and returned home again about one o'clock accompanied by a strange man. She (witness) opened the door for them, and the man, who was behind the deceased, on entering, shut the door after him, so that witness had not an opportunity of distinctly seeing who he was. The deceased went down stairs, but returned immediately and desired witness to go to bed, which she did, first hearing the deceased and the stranger go into the bed-room and lock the door. She heard no noise during the night, but on the Saturday morning she was awakened by Hubbard, who told her of the murder. On going into the bed-room, she saw the body of the deceased lying by the side of the bed, and the candlestick which witness had placed in the deceased's bed-room over night, she saw on the mat at the street-door.

Mr. William Best stated, that he was sleeping at the house on the night in question, in the first floor; at about five o'clock Hubbard opened his room door, looked in, and immediately closed it, and went down stairs. He came up a second time and said, "For God's sake come down, sir, poor Eliza is murdered." Witness immediately went down into the bed-room, and saw the body lying by the bed-side on the floor, with all the top clothes of the bed upon her, and her head quite visable. He saw her throat which was dreadfully cut, and the floor was stained with blood. She had all her clothes on except her frock. A policeman was immediately sent for, and Hubbard himself went for a medical man.

Mr. Cook, surgeon, of Waterloo Road, stated, that he examined the body of the deceased, which had been dead about four hours, and found two distinct gashes in her neck, one in front and one behind, commencing from near the right ear; there were wounds on her fingers also. There was also a wound which had penetrated the right cavity of the chest, and about three inches lower down, another wound had entered the abdomen. There was a wound two inches below the left nipple, and a slight wound on the forehead. The wound in the throat had completely severed the windpipe, & witness is of opinion that the wounds were inflicted not only by a heavy instrument, but by a most powerful arm.

From the length of the evidence, the Jury adjourned from Monday till Thursday, when they again met at the York Hotel. A gentleman connected with the public press stated, that the deceased sat behind him in the boxes of the Strand Theatre, on the Friday night, and that he heard her tell a female who was sitting by her, that she was going to meet a gentleman, and soon after she left the boxes.

A cabman came forward and stated, that at the close of the Theatre a lady and gentleman engaged him to carry them to Wellington Terrace, which he did, and saw them enter No. 12, but he should not know the gentleman again.

From the extent of the evidence the Jury sat on Monday, May the 28th; Thursday, May the 31st; on Monday, June the 4th; and again adjourned till Friday, the 8th of June, when hearing further evidence, the Jury returned a Verdict of—"Wilful Murder against some Person or Persons unknown." This Verdict will leave the case open for further investigation. No clue whatever is yet obtained of the murderer.

The unfortunate deceased is said to have been the daughter of a respectable farmer in one of the eastern counties, and that at a very early age she was seduced from home by a person in the Excise whom she in her turn deserted for the protection of an actor at one of the minor Theatres. At his death she formed various intimacies of a similar sort, and finally became a regular frequenter of the Theatres. On the evening of her death she had been seen by one of her acquaintances at ten o'clock, in good spirits, and making arrangements for an excursion to Epsom races. A remarkable fact is also related of her, that at the period of the murder of Maria Martin by Corder, the deceased was on a visit at a friends in the neighbourhood, and was the first person who entered the Red Barn where the murder was committed, and saw the mangled corpse of that ill-fated girl. The deceased is said to have had a sister, who about five years ago poisoned herself under very distressing circumstances.

ATTENTION give you parents dear,
Unto this dreadful tale,
To draw a tear from every eye,
It surely cannot fail
Eliza Grimwood on Friday night,
did meet a shocking fate,
By some monster in a human shape,
But who we cannot state.

In the country she was brought up,
And educated well.
But being handsome and of vice,
An early vic'im fell.
At thirteen many suiters strove,
Eliza's love to gain,
And one he was successful,
But her ruin was his aim.

To London he did her decoy,
Far from her native home.
And when she'd seen gay scenes of life,
She used the streets to roam.
Thus lost to all her friends at home,
She felt no shame or fear,
But pursued her wicked course of life,
Nor thought of parents dear.

Her beauty gain'd her many friends,
If so we may them call,
And often with them she would go
To the Play-house or a Ball.
In vice for years she onward toil'd,
Without any fear or dread.
But little did she think so soon
To be numbered with the dead.

On Friday night she left her home,
The gayest of the gay,
At night with some one did return,
Who took her life away.
Her throat was cut from ear to ear,
With a deep and ghastly wound.
And in a pool of crimson gore
Lay dead upon the ground.

Oh! such a horrid spectacle,
None saw in all their life.
Once handsome, now she sleeps in death.
By a base monster's knife.
Her murderer he may be conceal'd
Long from the public sight,
But Providence, whose ways are just,
Will bring this deed to light

Printed by T. BIRT, No. 39 Great St. Andrew Street, Seven Dials.

A handbill announcing the apprehension of Hubbard, reproduced by permission of the John Johnson collection of ephemera, Bodleian Library.

to look through its windows. All over town, rumours continued to fly that Hubbard would be examined later the same day. A large and rowdy crowd assembled opposite the front entrance of Union Hall. After seeing 'the vast assemblage surrounding the office, and the excited state of public feeling', the magistrate Mr Jeremy decided that it would be advisable to go through the day's other business before Hubbard was brought up.

At two o'clock in the afternoon, Hubbard was brought to Union Hall in a hackney coach, securely handcuffed and accompanied by Inspector Field and Sergeant Price. But they were recognised by the mob and 'a scene of almost undescribable confusion was the consequence; indeed, it was found necessary to appoint a number of the police to assist the officers of this establishment in preventing the mob from forcing their way into the justice-room'.[7] Shortly after half past two, Hubbard was placed within the felon's bar. He was dressed in a claret-coloured coat with a velvet colour, and a dark waistcoat and trousers, and a hat with a deep crepe band. A journalist noted that his appearance was very much altered since his attendance before the coroner: he was very pale, and obviously trying hard to maintain his self-possession.

Questioned by the magistrate Mr Jeremy, Inspector Field explained how he had followed Hubbard across Waterloo Bridge the previous evening. The inspector had probably made a deal with Thomas Grimwood that his name would not be mentioned, merely saying that he had acted on information received. Hubbard may well have visited the houses of his mother, brother and sister. Field then described how he had been shown the Cavendish letter and taken Hubbard into custody. It turned out that the fatal letter had been addressed to Richard Carter the coroner, who had been staying at the Hero of Waterloo public house not far away. The letter had arrived after the coroner had left, however, and Mr Okey the landlord had opened it himself to see if it contained anything important. The startled publican had immediately taken the letter to the local police station, where Superintendent Grimsall had only just had time to read and digest it when Inspector Field brought the news that Hubbard had left the murder house.

Mr Jeremy sternly asked Inspector Field whether he believed that the Cavendish letter constituted sufficient grounds to keep Hubbard in custody. The inspector stoutly answered in the affirmative, adding that if the letter was advertised in the newspapers, he felt that Mr Cavendish would certainly come forward. Mr Jeremy replied that he had no authority to publish this letter in the newspapers, and that it might not be such a good idea if this was done. Was it not still important to keep certain details of the murder investigation strictly secret, to make sure that hoaxers and anonymous letter writers would not interfere any further? The inspector fully agreed, and it was decided that although the fact that a highly incriminating letter signed 'Cavendish' had been received would be made public, its text would remain a secret. To argue the authenticity of the Cavendish letter further, Thomas Grimwood testified that a pair of lavender-coloured gloves had been found in the murder room, under the head of the bed, on the Monday after the murder.

Mr Jeremy decided that although he believed that charges should be supported by evidence and not by anonymous letters, he felt that it was his duty to remand Hubbard in custody for one week. The jailer was about to remove Hubbard when one of the police constables said that the prisoner wanted to speak. After being cautioned that anything he said could be used in evidence against him, Hubbard spoke up. He denied having made any attempt to escape from Wellington Terrace the previous evening. It had in fact been Thomas Grimwood who had persuaded him to leave the house, and given him 30s to do so! The reason he had travelled from house to house was that his mother had been ill, and that his brother Charles had been the only other relative willing to accommodate him. Thomas Grimwood wanted to contradict this statement, but the magistrate instructed him to be silent for now. As Hubbard was escorted out to the coach that was to take him to the Horsemonger Lane Prison, he was again recognised by the mob. There was a shout of 'There goes the murderer!' and a violent torrent of abuse from hundreds of angry voices. Had the police constables not protected the coach, the mob would have torn Hubbard to pieces.[8]

★ ★ ★

As we know, the police operation searching for the Foreigner had ceased on 9 June. But if the constables involved had hoped that their aching feet would be spared in the coming weeks, they received an unpleasant surprise on Tuesday 12 June. Inspector Field set the entire Grimwood task force, reinforced with several constables recruited from other police divisions, to work on a massive house-to-house search of the area around Goswell Road. Every householder was asked if they knew the elusive John Walter Cavendish, or indeed any person by that name. As the weary constables were trudging away, led by the faithful Sergeant Price, the inspector made use of his not inconsiderable talents for lateral thinking. If 'Cavendish' was a habitué of the Strand Theatre, perhaps he had a private box there? The theatre box-keepers answered in the negative. Had any of the toll-keepers or cabmen on Waterloo Bridge noticed a somewhat dishevelled-looking gentleman the night of the murder? They had not. Then there was the description of the ring with the bear's head crest. The inspector first went to see one of Eliza's former clients at Lincoln's Inn, but when this gentleman showed his crest, it contained no bear's head. He then went to the College of Heralds, where he was assured that no family named Cavendish had a crest with a bear's head.[9]

After a few days, the inspector must have felt like he was going mad. Since Sergeant Price and the constables had searched Goswell Road and its vicinities without finding the slightest clue, the search was widened to Clerkenwell, Islington and Highbury. After a £150 reward had been posted for the conviction of the murderer of Eliza Grimwood, there was a torrent of tips from all over London. One writer thought Cavendish was identical to an old schoolfellow of his, who had always been over-partial to the ladies; another letter-writer tried to implicate the local rector. A third writer thought Cavendish was a member of a distinguished noble family, who were going to hold a meeting to decide whether he was going to ruin his good name forever by coming forward. All over London, amateur detectives were on the lookout for any suspicious-looking person; the mysterious 'Cavendish' seemed to be sitting in every alehouse of the metropolis. After the news of the arrest of Hubbard had diffused into the provincial news-papers, there were tips from Reading, Brighton and Manchester.[10] On a coach from Bridgwater to Taunton, a well-dressed young man introduced himself to the other passengers as John Walter Cavendish, an engraver from London. He behaved strangely, more than once crying out, 'Murder!' At the Crown Inn in Taunton, he requested a room for the night under the name 'John Walters', but was fearful of entering it unless he was accompanied by the landlord. He searched the room minutely and looked under the bed. When this strange person saw the Cavendish letter advertised in the local newspaper, he abruptly left town by the Exeter coach. The *Taunton Courier* suggested that this must have been the timid Cavendish making his escape from London, since he was fearful of being murdered himself if he gave evidence against Hubbard."

When Mr Jeremy took his seat at Union Hall on 14 June, he complained that since the news of the Cavendish letter, and of the £150 reward, had been published in the newspapers, he had received an unprecedented number of anonymous letters. Some of these were threatening, some jocular, others just plain crazy. A few days after the reward had been posted, the situation for the police had also become almost intolerable. Every constable was employed investigating tip-offs from the public and dealing with amateur detectives eager for the reward. But Inspector Field thought of one final clue. Would it not be possible to find out where the Cavendish letter had been posted? After the stamp had been minutely examined with a strong lens, it was discerned that it came from the Highbury post office. This was a valuable clue and the inspector ordered his men to make inquiries at every receiving office for the twopenny post that sent its letters on to the Highbury post office. One of them was the shop of Mrs Humphries, fruiterer, at No. 4 Slayman's Row, Highbury. Although more than a week had gone by since the letter had been posted, the eagle-eyed sub-postmistress immediately recognised it, since she had been impressed that it was addressed to the coroner for Surrey. She could well remember that it had been delivered by young Mr M'Millan, the son of a stationer and newsman who had his business at No. 17 Wells Row, Highbury.

Sergeants Bays and Thomas, who had led the operation searching the Highbury postal service, immediately informed Inspector Field of this important breakthrough. Field went to Highbury to find out more about young Mr M'Millan. It turned out that this individual, who was 25 years old, had led a quiet and unassuming life as assistant to his father the stationer. After consulting the two sergeants, Inspector Field made a cunning plan. Sergeant Bays was to go into the M'Millan stationer's shop with a letter, purchase an envelope and request young M'Millan, who was behind the counter, to address it to Mr Carter, Coroner for Surrey. They would closely watch his reaction, and compare the writing with that on the Cavendish letter.

As planned, the sergeant stepped into the shop and ordered the letter to be addressed to the coroner. Young Mr M'Millan said, 'What, another letter to Mr Carter?' The sergeant replied, 'Yes; have you sent one?' M'Millan just said, 'No, but I know who has,' and wrote the address as requested. In triumph, the sergeant carried it out to Inspector Field, who felt satisfied it was the same handwriting as that on the Cavendish letter. All three policemen marched into the shop and confronted young M'Millan, gruffly accusing him of having written the Cavendish letter. The startled shopman denied everything: he had not visited Wellington Terrace the night of the murder, and he had certainly not written any letter to the coroner. Leaving young M'Millan with the two sergeants, Inspector Field went to confront his father, Mr Douglas M'Millan the stationer. This gentleman was very much surprised, since his son led a regular life; he had not been out the night of the murder, and although the handwriting on the Cavendish letter did resemble his, he thought there were also some notable differences. The inspector felt sure young M'Millan had written the letter, however. Since the penniless young shopman did not at all fit the description of the Foreigner, this would make him either a hoaxer or an accomplice. The way to find out would be to summon him to appear before the magistrates at Union Hall.[12]

★ ★ ★

As the police searched for the writer of the Cavendish letter, the brothers Grimwood made plans to milk the situation for all it was worth. Having disposed of the resentful Hubbard in the cunning manner described earlier, they did so with such alacrity that one must suspect that financial reasons rather than brotherly love had been the reason for their swift occupation of the murder house. Posters were pasted up all over London saying that the murdered Eliza Grimwood's belongings would be sold by auction. An auction catalogue headed 'By the Administrators of the late Eliza Grimwood' was printed and sold for threepence; no person would be admitted to the murder house unless they could produce one of these vouchers. Mr Wooler, the solicitor acting for Hubbard, threatened action since the Grimwoods were likely to make a pretty sum of money from admitting people into the house belonging to his client, but the brothers coolly replied that Hubbard had already received a fee of 30s to make himself scarce. Furthermore, the bricklayer was hardly in a strong position to sue, since he was himself in prison as the suspected murderer of their sister.

On the morning of Wednesday 13 June, a huge crowd assembled outside No. 12 Wellington Terrace, although the sale would not begin until one o'clock in the afternoon. A party of police from the 'L' division had to be stationed in and about the house, to protect the property. When the doors were opened, there was a tremendous rush for admission, including a number of well-dressed gentlemen and ladies. Although the sale was held in one of the first floor rooms, many people halted to admire the bloodstained floorboards in the murder room. The bidding was brisk for Eliza's chairs and sofa, and particularly for her fine mahogany chest of drawers. The deceased's bed was lot 41, described as a japanned French bedstead with chintz furniture and window-curtains to match, which attracted even fiercer bidding, since it was liberally marked with blood spatter. In total, the furniture sold for £64, a little more than the valuation, Eliza's watch and jewellery having already been sold for above £80. After the auction, it was impossible for the buyers to leave the house by way of Wellington Terrace, due to the dense crowd outside. At the advice of the auctioneer, they had to be let out through the back, before the angry mob outside, waving their auction catalogues and demanding entry, could be let in to see the murder room. Disappointed that no mementoes of the murdered woman remained, one of these rowdy fellows made a bid for the bloodstained carpet, which he swiftly rolled up and took outside, proposing to cut it up into smaller fragments to sell it to the mob outside. The covetous Thomas Grimwood must have been grinding his teeth that he had not thought of this stratagem himself.

Another 'gentleman' wanted to buy the bloodstained floorboards, but although Thomas Grimwood remained keen to do a deal, he had to turn him down at the advice of his solicitor: the floorboards, along with the rest of the house, remained the property of Hubbard and Best. Throughout the day, there were scenes of the utmost confusion outside the house, with frustrated ticket-holders demanding entry, and an angry mob being kept at bay by the police.[13] The crowd was such that traffic in Waterloo Road, and across the bridge, was seriously impeded. A *Times* journalist, who had seen these deplorable scenes first-hand, found this stratagem of turning the murder house into a freak-show to gratify idle curiosity and enhance the price of the articles sold most indecent. He wrote that 'It reflected alike disgrace upon those who promoted the sale, and those whose vicious and depraved taste drew them to the scene of the recent tragical affair.'[14]

★ ★ ★

As Hubbard was languishing in prison, and the brothers Grimwood were counting their money, young M'Millan faced the magistrates Jeremy and Traill at the Union Hall office on 16 June. After Inspector Field had explained how he and his men had tracked M'Millan down, the sub-postmistress Mrs Susan Humphries was the first witness examined. She made it her business to know the people in the neighbourhood, she said, and to identify their handwriting when they handed in letters. When the Cavendish letter was shown, she at once identified it as the one M'Millan had posted in her office. But from this promising beginning, things quickly went downhill. She had actually not seen M'Millan post the letter, but since she had also made it her business to recognise people's voices with unfailing accuracy, she could swear it was him, although she had been upstairs at the time. The prying postmistress remained convinced that the handwriting on the envelope was that of M'Millan, but she could not say the same about the handwriting on the actual letter. Had he posted it for someone else?

Young M'Millan did not deny visiting the post office the day in question. He was not sending any letter to the coroner for Surrey, however, but to a certain Mr Clark, of Warwick Lane. Since it had been an urgent letter, he was annoyed when being told that the post had gone. He had this letter with him to show the magistrates, but not unreasonably, they merely commented that if he had been so very anxious to get the letter sent off, then why keep it in his pocket for several days. Inspector Field had also found a certain Mr Talbot whom M'Millan had told, a few days previously, that the letter was for a gentleman in Highbury, whereas Mr Clark lived nowhere near those parts. After M'Millan had been sworn and sternly cautioned not to perjure himself, the Cavendish letter was put before him and he was asked if he had seen it before. The shopman denied this vehemently: he had never seen the letter before Inspector Field showed it to him the other morning. He had no idea who had sent it. He did not go out much, and was certain he had been at home the night of the murder, since he could well recall hearing about the Waterloo Road Horror the morning after.

The angry magistrates were not particularly impressed with young M'Millan, and they obviously shared Inspector Field's suspicion that he was really the writer of the Cavendish letter. They characterised the letter 'a foul fabrication, and as gross an attempt to warp justice as was ever attempted', adding that if the writer should be found, he 'could be indicted and found guilty of the highest misdemeanour committed against public justice'. In spite of these dire threats, M'Millan requested that the magistrates express an opinion that he was not the writer of the letter, but this they of course refused to do.[15]

The veracity of the Cavendish letter being severely undermined, the situation was now that very little hard evidence remained against Hubbard. Although the solicitor Pelham, who watched proceedings on behalf of the brothers Grimwood, pointed out that he did not discredit Owen's evidence, the magistrates did not agree. Surely this man was deranged in his intellect, and it was a travesty of justice to let him have several attempts to pick out the murderer. Instead, they suggested that all evidence against Hubbard should be reassessed in a few days, when he was re-examined once more. The solicitor Wooler, who acted for Hubbard, had no objection to this.

★ ★ ★

Knowing that Hubbard would be re-examined at Union Hall on Tuesday 19 June, Inspector Field was desperately clutching at straws to find new leads. All Sunday, he and Sergeant Price personally searched the murder house one more time. In the front attic room, they saw that a knot in one of the floorboards seemed to have been removed. They immediately raised the plank, finding a rusty old penknife underneath. For a moment their hopes were up, but the inspector saw that this knife was far too small to have caused Eliza's terrible injuries. On Monday morning, the inspector and Mr Pelham the solicitor collected evidence and took down statements of several witnesses. He then went to Highbury to make inquiries about a former lodger 'in the house of Mr McMillan the supposed writer of the letter signed Cavendish'.

At the end of another exhausting day, he received 'information that a woman who knew the deceased could give particulars about the person the deceased went home with, traced out her residence, stated to me that she saw the deceased the night of the murder in company with a person, saw them at the theatre before, gave a full description of him, found that the description answered to what the others had given'.[16]

Mr Keane, the governor of the Horsemonger Lane county jail where Hubbard was being kept, was becoming increasingly apprehensive when the date for the re-examination of his notorious prisoner was approaching. He went to warn the magistrates about the risk that Hubbard would be pulled out of the carriage and lynched by the mob before he even reached Union Hall. Having witnessed the uproar when Hubbard was first examined, Mr Jeremy and Mr Traill decided that the safest solution would be to let the bricklayer remain in prison. He would be represented by Charles Hubbard and the solicitor Wooler.[17]

Not knowing that Hubbard would be absent, a large and unruly mob gathered at Union Hall, baying for his blood. They were disappointed when proceedings began at one in the afternoon without the bricklayer being present. The magistrates examined Eliza's stays, Hubbard's trousers, the two razors found in the house, and the little penknife discovered by Inspector Field. The author of the Cavendish letter was formally called to come forward, but no person replied. Mary Fisher's evidence was looked into in some detail, without any new information being disclosed, except that the bloody napkin under the pillow probably emanated from the careless surgeon leaving it behind after wiping his hands on it. No mystery remained with regard to either the chamber pot in Eliza's room, or Hubbard's shirts and other garments. Mr Jeremy said that since Hubbard was only inculpated by the statements in the Cavendish letter, which had proved to be a stupid fabrication, he should be detained no longer. Mr Traill sagely added that, in his opinion, it was clear that the murder had either been committed by Hubbard, or by the Foreigner who had gone home with Eliza. Hubbard had been detained for eight days, but no new evidence had been added against him, and he should be discharged.

Charles Hubbard was called to stand forward, and it was formally proclaimed that in the interest of public safety, his brother would be discharged from the prison, since the mob might tear him to pieces if he was taken to Union Hall. Charles Hubbard objected that no person who knew his brother would entertain the thought that he was the guilty man, and that he was sure that his brother would prefer to be discharged in the proper manner rather than to skulk away from prison. Would it not convince people of his innocence if the magistrates formally discharged him from Union Hall? Mr Jeremy coolly retorted that the reason for all this prejudice against his brother was that Hubbard had led a life 'which was highly criminal on his part'. Charles Hubbard sadly shook his head and agreed that his brother's life had been disreputable.[18]

But the solicitor Wooler remained belligerent. He insisted that Hubbard should be formally discharged from the office and pointed out that since the crowd was now diminishing, it was becoming less likely that public safety would be endangered. Accordingly, Hubbard was brought up in a hackney coach late in the afternoon. But a considerable number of people were still lurking in the street outside; when they saw the hated Hubbard, he was at once 'assailed with groans and execrations'. The magistrates told him that since the letter incriminating him had been found to be a fabrication, he was now free to go. Until the real perpetrator of the murder was discovered, a certain amount of suspicion would still attach to him, and if he was an innocent man, he ought to do everything in his power to facilitate the detection of the offender. Hubbard declared his innocence, adding that he trusted that the murderer would be discovered.

Due to the size of the angry mob waiting outside in the street, it was not possible to let Hubbard out that way, since they would certainly have attacked him. The magistrates tried the old tactic of having the coach in which he would have taken his departure driven away, but the mob was wise to this trick. In the end, Hubbard had to be let out through the back of the office, where he climbed some palings and other impediments, before safely mixing with the crowd of pedestrians in the Borough.[19]

★ ★ ★

One of the most notorious personages in London in the late 1830s was Charles, Duke of Brunswick. Born in 1804, he had been the absolute ruler of Brunswick for some years, before his extravagance, eccentric manner and petty tyranny stirred full-scale revolution in 1830. The ducal castle was burnt down and the duke dethroned and evicted. He was declared insane by his brother Duke Wilhelm and by his cousin, King William IV, in 1833. The Duke of Cambridge was appointed his guardian and took control of his fortune in England. In 1836, the Duke of Brunswick came to London to try to reclaim his money. He also wanted the Royal Navy to mount a naval expedition to recover his landlocked territory, something that gained him a good deal of ridicule, although the duke pointed out that they could land at Bremen and cross through Hanoverian territory to reach Brunswick.[20]

King William IV and the government considered the Duke of Brunswick a madman and ignored his various appeals. Among Londoners, the extravagant duke soon became quite notorious. Nothing like his elegant carriages, over-large wigs and whiskers, diamond-studded waistcoats, and powdered and rouged face had ever been seen in the metropolis. He spent money lavishly to gain allies against the government, and enlisted various shady radicals for his cause. He partied and revelled to excess and was an inveterate customer of prostitutes. Bow Street Runner Henry Goddard, who was employed as a secret agent to spy on the duke in 1836 and 1837, marvelled at his nightly visits to Drury Lane, Covent Garden and other theatres, and the low company he kept.[21]

The Duke of Brunswick took great interest in the murder of Eliza Grimwood. When he visited the inquest in person, the other spectators marvelled at his outrageous dress. When Hubbard was at Union Hall, the duke followed the proceedings with much interest. When Hubbard

LE DUC DE BRUNSWICK
OCTOBRE 1822

Charles, Duke of Brunswick as a young man, from the anonymous book *Le Duc de Brunswick* (Paris 1875).

had been discharged, the duke suggested, in his imperfect English, that he ought to cut off his bushy whiskers to disguise himself and facilitate his escape from the office. Hubbard, having no appreciation of the rank of the person who had just addressed him, replied in his usual surly manner, referring to the duke's moustache: 'And if I were you, I would cut off those two black patches you wear upon your upper lip; I think it would improve your beauty!'

When the startled duke replied, 'But it is my fashion', Hubbard just said, 'Well, if it is your fashion to wear so much hair over your mouth, it is my fashion to wear the pair of whiskers you now see, and I shall not cut them off, for I have done nothing of a criminal nature that should make me attempt to disguise myself!'[22]

Since it was well known among Londoners that the Duke of Brunswick was very partial to female company, rumours soon began to circulate that it was in fact he who was the Foreigner who had accompanied Eliza Grimwood home, only to brutally murder her. People booed the duke in the streets and called him 'Don Whiskerando', the name they had given the bewhiskered 'Foreigner' who had taken Eliza Grimwood home. But in real life, there is nothing whatsoever to connect the foppish duke with the murder: he was a weak, vacillating character, with no liking for violence or bloodshed. Although he was very partial to the ladies, and quite possibly an established customer to the better class of London prostitute, there is nothing to suggest that he ever had anything to do with the murder of Eliza Grimwood.

THE CLUE OF THE LAVENDER-COLOURED GLOVES

After Hubbard had been discharged, the murder investigation was back at square one. Inspector Field tried his best to keep open three parallel lines of inquiry: firstly, to keep an eye on Hubbard's movements; secondly, to keep looking for the elusive Foreigner; thirdly, to find the owner of the lavender-coloured gloves. Far from showing any signs of wanting to flee London, Hubbard provided the inspector with his address and said he would be pleased to help with any inquiries. The dismal M'Millan was less bonhomous. He applied to the Commissioners of Police, claiming that the inspector had misconstrued his evidence, and demanding to be formally freed of suspicion of having written the Cavendish letter. To get rid of him, Mr Traill the magistrate expressed his opinion that M'Millan was not the author of the letter, and the stationer was satisfied.[1]

The magistrates still received large amounts of anonymous letters. Many of them came from people who confessed they had committed the murder. One of these individuals, who called himself 'Captain P.L. Roberts, Kennington', said that he would have come forward if Hubbard had been remanded for trial, but now he would remain quiet, although he was an unhappy man after committing the murder. Captain Roberts did not exist, however, so the letter was the product of some joker who wanted to waste police time. Two more letters, from a man who called himself 'Philip Jardine' and claimed to be on his way to Van Diemen's Land to escape the police, were more detailed. After cutting Eliza's throat, 'Jardine' had wiped his bloody hands on a towel, which he had thrown into the Thames from the middle arch of Waterloo Bridge, together with the murder weapon. The letters were sufficiently compelling for Mr Jeremy to send Inspector Field on another wild goose chase to try to track down 'Jardine' in Hornsey.[2] Another letter came from a psychic named James Holman, who had dreamt that he was present when Eliza Grimwood was murdered, and that the killer had hidden the murder weapon by thrusting it down her throat. Another busybody claimed that it was possible to cut someone's throat without becoming stained with blood, if the victim was grasped hard from behind. The surgeons who had committed the autopsy pooh-poohed both these notions.[3] Another anonymous letter writer asked himself why Eliza's dog had not attacked the murderer: had the faithful animal been remiss in its duty, or did the dog in fact know the murderer?[4] Inspector Field knew that the dog was just a small spaniel, however. Even if the dog had been of a larger and more ferocious breed, the parlour door would have impeded it, since it had its sleeping quarters in the kitchen. The absence of prolonged and angry barking from the animal still puzzled him, however.

In late June, Inspector Field was kept busy trying to find the owner of the lavender-coloured gloves. Today, it would have been like looking for a needle in a haystack to find the owner of a pair of gloves found somewhere in London. It cannot have been much easier back in 1838, although the canny inspector did have one vital clue. The gloves were marked 'S.K.R.'.

It was not known whether this referred to the owner or the manufacturer, but it at least offered some help for the detective. Not unreasonably, he deduced that if there was such a thing as an expert on the marking of gloves, it would be a professional glove-cleaner. On 20 June, the inspector went to see one of these individuals, but all the glove-cleaner said was that he had a very good idea who had not cleaned them, namely himself. There were not more than eight or nine regular glove-cleaners in London, however, and he gave Field their addresses. For three days, the inspector went from glove-cleaner to glove-cleaner, but without success. As he later told his friend Charles Dickens:

On the evening of the third day, coming over Waterloo Bridge from the Surrey side of the river, quite beat, and very much vexed and disappointed, I thought I'd have a shilling's worth of entertainment at the Lyceum Theatre to freshen myself up.

Having gone into the pit, for half-price, the inspector sat down next to a young man who thought he was a stranger to London and explained who the actors were. The two became good friends and went together to a pub nearby, bought some beer and lit their pipes. After they had spoken for a while, the young man said that he must soon go home, since he had to work all night. When Field asked if he was a baker, he replied that he was in fact a glove-cleaner![5]

Having recovered from his astonishment after this great coincidence, the inspector pulled out the lavender-coloured gloves and asked if he could tell who had cleaned them. The crafty detective had not introduced himself to his new acquaintance. Presuming that the hope of financial reward would act as a stronger stimulant than the risk of becoming involved in a criminal investigation, he invented a story about a pair of gloves left behind at a party and a bet that he would be unable to find their owner. The glove-cleaner had a good look at the lavender-coloured gloves, before exclaiming that he had seen dozens of pairs just like them at his father's shop. Field lost no time before accompanying his young glove-cleaner friend back to the father's shop nearby, where they found an old man in a white apron and his two daughters rubbing and cleaning away at a lot of gloves in the front parlour. The old glove-cleaner immediately identified the lavender-coloured gloves: they belonged to Mr Skinner, the great upholsterer in Cheapside. This magnate did not handle his dirty laundry himself, but always sent it through a certain Mr Phibbs, a haberdasher opposite his shop.

The day after, Inspector Field went to see Mr Phibbs, with high hopes of a vital breakthrough. The haberdasher also recognised the gloves: indeed, he had sent them to be cleaned, but they did not belong to Mr Skinner the upholsterer, but to his son, young Mr Skinner the tobacconist. Having spent some time pondering how to proceed, the inspector decided not to confront young Skinner directly, but instead to make some inquiries about his habits and situation in life. It turned out that just like his father, young Skinner was a wealthy and successful tradesman; a newspaper article refers to him as 'the extensive tobacconist near Temple-bar'. He was in the habit of seeing loose women, however, and 'partly kept a woman in East-street, Red Lion Square'.[6]

★ ★ ★

On 24 June, Inspector Field went to confront young Mr Skinner, carrying with him the lavender-coloured gloves. The startled tobacconist had to admit that they were his, although he had not seen them for several months. He thought he might have left them in the house of his mistress in Red Lion Square, but he was not sure. He vehemently denied ever having seen Eliza Grimwood, or having anything whatever to do with the murder. After having made sure that Skinner was secretly watched by a police constable, Field went to Red Lion Square to find the 'gay woman' the promiscuous tobacconist was in the habit of visiting. Although having already had his fill of strange coincidences since the start of the Grimwood murder investigation, it must have given him quite a turn when he discovered that this woman was none less than Harriet Caroline Chaplin, the niece of Eliza Grimwood, who had given such dubious evidence at the inquest.

Harriet Chaplin could well remember the incident with the gloves. Mr Skinner had left them behind and she had not seen fit to return them, instead using them to clean her teapot. She had then given them to her friend Rebecca Ryan, who had shared her lodgings at the time. Inspector Field remained suspicious, however. Had the promiscuous Mr Skinner murdered Eliza Grimwood, left the gloves behind, and then persuaded or bribed his mistress to concur with his story? Or could it be that Harriet Chaplin had nourished some secret grudge against her aunt? The inspector managed to track down Rebecca Ryan to a house of ill repute at No. 2 Ann Street near Waterloo Road. She could not recognise the gloves, although she might well have seen a similar pair in Harriet Chaplin's possession. She had herself had nothing to do with them, and had certainly never taken them anywhere near the murder house. Thus the stories of the two 'loose women' contradicted each other, which was bad news for Mr Skinner. Although he did not resemble the description the Strand Theatre witnesses had given of the Foreigner, the inspector began to regard the tobacconist as a serious suspect.[7]

There were three ways for Inspector Field to tighten the net around this latest suspect. Firstly, he made further inquiries into the habits of Mr Skinner. It soon became apparent that for several years, the tobacconist had been in the habit of spending money on prostitutes all over London. Secondly, the inspector kept visiting the two women to keep up pressure on them. It turned out that Rebecca Ryan had actually been the servant of Harriet Chaplin, although they had parted on good terms. Poor Rebecca had since sunk low to become a miserable whore in a brothel, whereas Harriet remained a better class of prostitute, entertaining fun-loving gentlemen like Mr Skinner in her rooms at Red Lion Square. Thirdly, the inspector leaked the news about the gloves to the press, making sure that it became known that the new suspect, who was not named, was the owner of the lavender-coloured kid gloves marked 'S.K.R.' that had been found in the murder house. There were no tips from the public regarding the gloves, although a prostitute told him that in a house of ill repute not far from Red Lion Square, a gentleman had left behind a white pocket handkerchief marked 'Eliza'. When she had read the story of the gloves, she thought the search should be widened to include other suspicious garments. But as Inspector Field expressed it, he 'traced out this gentleman who gave a satisfactory account of the same that it belonged to his cousin which upon inquiry turned out to be correct'.[8]

On 2 July, Inspector Field called at Skinner's house, inviting the tobacconist to join him for a series of witness confrontations. Happy to clear himself of any suspicion, Mr Skinner willingly joined him. The result was that neither witness thought him at all like the 'Foreigner' they had seen with Eliza Grimwood the night of the murder.

★ ★ ★

On 7 July, Mr Skinner was taken to Union Hall, where he was questioned by Mr Jeremy and Mr Traill in their private room. He said that in January 1838, he had been in the habit of visiting the woman Harriet Caroline Chaplin at her lodgings at No. 39 East Street, Red Lion Street, Holborn. He was not certain he had left the gloves there, but thought he might have. In February, Mr Skinner had suffered from an illness that prevented him from visiting young ladies. He had not seen Harriet Chaplin again until after the murder.

When this excitable young lady fell down on her knees and cried violently, he enquired the cause and she told him that the murdered Eliza Grimwood had in fact been her aunt. The glover Mr Cording deposed that he had sold the gloves to Mr Skinner, and that he had cleaned them twice since that time. The marking 'S.K.R.' had been done by him.

Harriet Chaplin testified that she could recollect having the gloves in her possession, although at the time, she did not know where they had come from. They were too large for her to use herself so she had cleaned a teapot with them instead. She could now recollect that, in February, Eliza Grimwood had come to see her, which was the only time she had visited her niece's lodgings in the last three years. Whether Eliza had taken the gloves with her to Wellington Terrace she could not say with certainty. Just like at the inquest, she then made the most of her few seconds of fame by adding some quite sensational new material. The Sunday after the murder, she had visited Hubbard and his mother at Wellington Terrace. William Best and Mary Glover were also there. When Hubbard saw her enter, he threw himself to his knees, seized her by the hand and exclaimed, 'Oh! Oh! Oh!' He told her that he presumed that Eliza had brought home some foreigner, who had wanted to ravish her against her will, and that her refusal had led her to be murdered. Hubbard had also said that he had heard the little dog bark at night, and that it made him feel so strange that he could not sleep. At four o'clock he had come downstairs and seen that Eliza had been murdered. She had put her hands to her breast and her eyes had moved. When Best interposed, saying that Hubbard must be mistaken, the bricklayer angrily exclaimed, 'I tell you that her eyes were open; she looked at me, and I never shall forget the look she gave me!'

According to a newspaper reporter, this new and startling evidence made an evident impression on the magistrates, who made a pause to discuss it. The misogynist Inspector Field, who knew Harriet Chaplin's histrionic tendencies, probably took the opportunity to inform them that, at the inquest, she had in fact given some equally dubious evidence *incriminating* Hubbard as the murderer. The magistrates went on to question Rebecca Ryan, who assured them that although she had seen the gloves in Harriet Chaplin's possession, she had no idea how they had come to Wellington Terrace.[9]

As the meeting ended at this unsatisfactory note, Mr Skinner was free to go. The magistrates sagely commented that it was now placed beyond doubt that the Cavendish letter was a wicked fabrication. The fact that a pair of gloves had been found in the murder room had given it some spurious authenticity, although these gloves had not been black, but lavender-coloured. The finding of the gloves was probably just another coincidence and Mr Skinner had steadfastly denied any involvement in the murder. Inspector Field had to agree with these deductions, although his diary hints that he still had some doubts about the tobacconist. As late as 14 July, he 'saw Mr Skinner in the afternoon the owner of the Gloves wished him to try all in his power to ascertain how the Gloves got to the deceased house'.[10] But the inspector later told Charles Dickens that although the finding of the lavender-coloured gloves had been 'a singler story', it had not brought him any closer to solving the mystery.[11] The most likely explanation was that Skinner had left the gloves behind with Harriet Chaplin and that Eliza Grimwood had taken them away to give them to her servant for use in cleaning the stoves.

★ ★ ★

While Inspector Field had been investigating the lavender-coloured gloves and their owner, Hubbard's miseries had continued. Although he had been set at liberty by the magistrates at Union Hall, he remained a marked man among the Londoners. To avoid someone calling out, 'There he is – the murderer!' he stayed in his mother's house and always kept indoors. When Inspector Field went to see him at his lodgings, he was always keen to hear of the new developments in the hunt for the murderer, but since the inspector still disliked and distrusted him, he told him very little.

When Hubbard was told the shameful news of the brothers Grimwood selling the entire contents of his house at auction, he became almost apoplectic with rage. His bed, his chest of drawers, and even his clothes had been disposed of. His solicitor applied to the Union Hall magistrates, but although he managed to recover Hubbard's writing-desk, which had been confiscated by the police along with its contents, there was no way of dealing with the covetous Thomas Grimwood, who was openly crowing at his cleverness in outfoxing the dismal Hubbard. But Grimwood would not have long to exult at his success. Just a few days later, he was run over by a carriage in the street and carried to the London Hospital with several broken ribs. One day, Hubbard and his two brothers came bursting into the ward. They cursed and abused the injured builder in a shameful manner and swore that they would be damned if they did not recover the property he had stolen from Hubbard. They left behind a highly threatening letter signed by the solicitor Wooler, saying that if the Grimwoods did not pay Hubbard full compensation for the effects sold at auction, they would be sued for their last penny. Most imprudently, this letter also threatened Inspector Field, saying that for his role in these shameful proceedings, he would also face a lawsuit. It was thanks to the inspector's prejudice and lack of judgement that William Hubbard's character had been injured and his personal safety put at risk.

The ailing Thomas Grimwood consulted the solicitor Pelham, who applied to the Lambeth Street magistrates to protect his client against the violent and threatening Hubbards. The magistrate objected that it was surely the task of the house surgeon and porters of the hospital to protect the patients against unprovoked assaults and blackguarding. The solicitor retorted that Thomas Grimwood was 47 years of age and that the surgeon had put him on a very low diet; the excitement of being blasted and damned by the Hubbards while lying in his hospital bed could have had potentially dangerous consequences. When the ill-advised threatening letter written by the solicitor Wooler was read aloud, it further strengthened the anti-Hubbard bias. In particular, the unfounded accusations against Inspector Field angered the magistrate, who commented that he did not think the inspector had much to fear from this threat. He ordered Inspector Field to liaise with the hospital staff to make sure that Thomas Grimwood received proper protection against the Hubbards.[12] But the solicitor Pelham was still not done. He handed over two anonymous letters addressed to himself, signed 'Philippe de Sasseau'. The first one, written in French, was translated thus:

Mr Lawyer – Indeed you are a fine subject for the worms. Take care of your precious throat! The stiletto is yet further capable, and your person pretty well known.

The second letter seemed to imply that the writer, whose crime was very dark and for whom there was no peace on this side of the grave, wanted to give himself up for murdering Eliza but could not find the courage to do so.[13] The magistrate and Inspector Field had had enough of anonymous letters for the time being, however, and treated them with scorn.

★ ★ ★

In spite of the rebuff at Lambeth Street, Hubbard continued his struggle against the Grimwood brothers, who had deprived him of all the furniture in his house, even his own bed. He had found out, through large advertisements pasted up throughout London, that Eliza Grimwood's dog was to be seen at the Gun public house in Shoreditch. This was a cunning ploy by the landlord Mr Chamberlayne, since the beer barrels were speedily emptied by the crowd of curious Londoners who came to admire the pretty little spaniel dog, the purported murder witness, whose lack of barking the night of the murder remained a mystery. Hubbard went to the pub and accused the landlord of being a damned scoundrel: not only was it indecent to exhibit Eliza's dog in this manner, but the animal was his own property and had been stolen from him by the brothers Grimwood. Since the publican refused to give up the dog, Hubbard summoned him before the Worship Street magistrates.

On 4 July, the magistrates asked the publican to explain himself. As cool as a cucumber, Mr Chamberlayne said that, although he had exhibited the dog in his public house with a mind to improving the trade, he was not the owner of the animal. It had been lent to him by the shoemaker Mr Sparrow, who was also present in court. The shoemaker said that he was a friend of the brothers Grimwood, and that he had greatly desired to buy some of Eliza's jewellery as a curiosity, but he had been outbid at the auction. Instead, Thomas Grimwood had given him the dog. The angry Hubbard objected that Grimwood had had no right to dispose of the animal in the first place, but the magistrates adjourned the case until next week, when the ailing Thomas Grimwood would have been discharged from London Hospital.

When the parties again met before the Worship Street magistrates on 11 July, quite a crowd of onlookers had assembled to see Hubbard.

Thomas Grimwood was also present, along with the solicitor Pelham. The latter individual effectively demolished Hubbard's claims, stating that Thomas Grimwood had acquired his right to the dog by virtue of letters of administration. Just like the remainder of his late sister's effects, the animal was his to dispose of. Mr Pelham produced a witness who had heard Hubbard admit that he had purchased the dog, as a puppy, and given it to Eliza as a present. This settled the case in the minds of the magistrates, who took no further action except to censure the publican Chamberlayne for pandering to the depraved curiosity of the public by making a show of Eliza's little dog. Aided by the solicitor Wooler, both Hubbard and his brother objected. Charles Hubbard declared that Thomas Grimwood had lured his brother away from the murder house with a shabby trick, before availing himself of William Hubbard's imprisonment to take possession of all his effects, including the dog. Thomas Grimwood 'denied this assertion with some warmth, upon which a loud and wrathful altercation ensued between them, in the course of which sundry scurrilous epithets were applied on either side'. The magistrates had to dispatch an officer to prevent a fight breaking out, before the Hubbards and Grimwoods went wrangling out of the office.[14]

RED HERRINGS

After Mr Skinner had been cleared at Union Hall, Inspector Field and Constable Goff were the only remaining members of the Grimwood task force. They kept an eye on Hubbard, who was again working as a bricklayer, and more than once followed him clandestinely back to his mother's house in Mile End, which served as the wretched man's only refuge. A busybody named Mr Golding wrote to the police that he was sure that some of Hubbard's relatives lived next door to him, and suspected that the murder weapon had been thrown down the privy of these premises. But the inspector found that Hubbard the neighbour, a respectable customs officer, was not related to Hubbard the bricklayer. Another letter-writer pointed the finger at a former 'customer' of Eliza Grimwood, but the inspector 'found that he was a reputable gentleman and had only seen her three times'.

On 12 July there was some drama after a foreign criminal had been taken in Clerkenwell. Since the local police thought he resembled the Foreigner, Inspector Field was ordered by Mr Jeremy the magistrate to bring the cabman Spicknell and the waitress Parker, the two people who had had the best look at Eliza Grimwood's sinister companion the evening of the murder, to the Clerkenwell police station. The prisoner was a foreign Jew and a noted gambler, who had been in prison from March until early May 1838 under another charge. But neither cabman nor waitress could identify him as the Foreigner and so he was released.[1]

Inspector Field's police diary about the Grimwood murder investigation ends on 14 July 1838, just seven weeks after the murder was committed.

After that date, he was probably assigned to other duties, although he never entirely lost touch with the most mysterious murder case of his career and from time to time was called upon to continue his investigation. On 14 August 1838, a tobacconist named Goodlad, who kept a small shop in the Mile End Road, applied to the Lambeth magistrates to have a ditch in his neighbourhood searched for the murder weapon and other articles that might give a clue to the identity of the murderer of Eliza Grimwood. He carried with him a large bundle of correspondence, having already written to the Secretary of State as well as to the Union Hall magistrates. But since Inspector Field had already considered his proposal and turned it down, the magistrate would have nothing to do with this matter. Mr Goodlad, who was said to be 'exceedingly fond of interfering with matters that do not at all concern him', left the justice room very dissatisfied with their lack of interest.[2]

In March 1839 there was some further buffoonery. A man named James Howard, respectably dressed but in a very excited state of mind, had gathered a large mob in George Street, Grosvenor Square. When a police constable came to the scene, Howard told him that he was annoyed because he had been waiting for more than two hours opposite the residence of Lord Melbourne, the Prime Minister, in order to 'crack his Lordship's head', for which purpose he had armed himself with some large stones. When brought to the Marlborough Street police office, Howard introduced himself as the son of King George IV and Queen Caroline and went on to say he had undeniable evidence that Lord Melbourne had murdered Eliza Grimwood, in the Waterloo Road. Aware that his dark secret was known, the wicked nobleman was tormenting Howard by means of electricity, administered through a vast network of agents. When searched, his pockets contained several stones, a sharp dirk, and a letter to the Queen outlining how Lord Melbourne had committed the Grimwood murder. The magistrate said that after such threatening conduct, Howard could not be permitted to be at large. He was committed to prison, and the police were ordered to search out his friends, since the poor fellow was obviously quite insane.[3]

Just a few weeks later, there was further sensational news. The Union Hall police office received a letter that began with these highly charged words:

Gentlemen, – Before you receive this hurried note the body of the murderer of Eliza Grimwood will be in the Thames. Yes, I, and I alone, am the guilty villain who perpetrated this hellish deed and in a few hours will receive my desserts. Stricken in conscience, and shunning all mankind, I add to my character the name of a suicide rather than meet with an ignominious death on the scaffold …

Having already had enough of anonymous letters, the magistrates first decided to ignore this animated missive, but when Inspector Field attended at Union Hall on some other business, they showed it to him. The inspector immediately became interested, since he knew that a man's body had been found in the Thames the morning after the letter had been sent, namely that of George Green, a former captain's steward on board the East India trader *Victory*, who had for some time been in bad health from a liver complaint. When his body was fished out of the Thames, his pockets had contained a fine silver hunting watch, nine shillings and a halfpenny, and a half-pint bottle of sherry. Green had been drinking hard for many years, although the waiter at the Bengal Arms in Birchin Lane had observed that the evening of his suicide, Green had for once been reasonably sober. At his lodgings was found a large amount of Indian copper money and 'a singularly extensive wardrobe of linen and general clothing', but no letter or other document that allowed comparison with the handwriting on the letter the magistrates had received.

At a second inquest on Green, in early April, it was concluded that apart from the timing of his suicide, there was nothing to connect the sottish ex-steward with either the letter or the murder of Eliza Grimwood. Some letters of his had been discovered and there was no resemblance between his handwriting and that on the letter to the magistrates. It also appeared as if he had been confined to some kind of hospital or asylum at the time of the murder. The jury returned a verdict of 'Found drowned'. Hubbard was present at the inquest and paid great interest to the proceedings.[4]

★ ★ ★

In August 1839, the anonymous letter writers were up to their old tricks again. The Union Hall magistrates received a letter signed 'M. Duke, 99,

Chancery-lane, Fleet-street', claiming knowledge that would unravel the Grimwood mystery and disclose the identity of the Foreigner, who was in fact a distant relation of the writer. It ended with the words, 'I shall not be easy until I have betrayed the villain!' It was discovered that there was a law stationer named Mr Duke at the address stated, but he turned out to be a respectable man. The letter did not at all match his handwriting, and must have been written by some mischievous fool, like so many others in the Grimwood drama.[5]

In December 1840, a man named Edward Hughes wrote to the Under Secretary of State, the Rt. Hon. Fox Maule, that he knew who had murdered Eliza Grimwood. In a further letter, he dropped the bombshell that the perpetrator was a woman, Mary Leary, 'now residing at Hull – and to be easily found'. This jealous virago had suspected that the man cohabiting with her was in the habit of visiting Eliza Grimwood, and set in motion a diabolical plan to make sure their liaison was ended. Wearing an elaborate disguise, she had sneaked after her boyfriend to the Strand Theatre, where sure enough, he met up with Eliza. She had then followed them all the way to Wellington Terrace, where she lurked outside waiting for her boyfriend to exit the house. She then dashed into the house, seized a large knife lying on a table, killed Eliza and rushed out again, throwing the knife into the Thames from Waterloo Bridge on her way home.

This story had been told to Hughes' sons by a man named Roberts. It does not seem to have evoked any police response, probably due to its innate implausibility. Firstly, a woman could hardly have cut Eliza's throat with such force. Secondly, would the other inhabitants of the house not have heard this madwoman barging into the premises? Thirdly, the toll-keepers on Waterloo Bridge had not observed any bloodstained woman, or indeed any likely suspect, crossing the bridge shortly after the murder. Nor did it inspire confidence that Hughes wanted to involve the government in a quarrel he had with a magistrate in Hull, who had imprisoned his sons on a charge of obtaining money by false pretences.[6]

★ ★ ★

In late August 1845, more than seven years after the murder of Eliza Grimwood, there was some sensational news that actually seemed to solve the mystery. A private soldier in the 67th Regiment stationed at Portobello Barracks in Dublin, 30-year-old George Hill, had been arrested for being absent without leave. When the drunken private was taken into the College Street police office, he seemed quite jolly, saying that he knew something that would surprise everybody. He was the son of a London silversmith, and seven years earlier, he had murdered Eliza Grimwood, whose death had caused such a sensation in London back in 1838. Hill was given pen and paper and wrote down his confession in a very shaky hand, getting it almost right in his second attempt.

The news of the arrest of George Hill was speedily transmitted to London, where it caused considerable stir. Would the murder of Eliza Grimwood be solved after all? Without delay, Inspector Field and Sergeant Goff set out for Dublin to question the prisoner. It turned out that Hill had joined the regiment in 1843 and that his conduct had been extremely bad. He was a heavy drinker who had deserted several times, once being absent for more than a month. During one of these drunken expeditions, he had stolen a watch in Dublin and been sentenced to six months in prison. Inspector Field listened with interest when Hill's commanding officer told him that the drunken private came from a respectable family in London, his father Mr E. Hill being a jeweller and watch-maker by trade, and that he had enjoyed a good education, learning to speak both French and Italian. George Hill had quarrelled with his father, however, and after being turned out of doors by his irate parent, he became a street hawker of sandwiches, newspapers and books, residing in the City of London. He then became a collector of fares in a steamboat company, but was discharged after embezzling £5. He then fell low for a while, living in the streets as a seller of sandwiches, before marrying, fathering a child, and moving to lodgings in Bishopsgate. Hill had joined the army in 1842, and due to his superior education, it had originally been proposed that he should be promoted to corporal, but his perpetual drunkenness and misconduct had upset this plan. When Inspector Field confronted Hill with his confession that he was the murderer of Eliza Grimwood, the private said that since he had been very drunk at the time, he had not known what he was doing. He greatly

Confesssion of the Murderer of
ELIZA GRIMWOOD.
And the Murders at Greenwich, & near Hertford.

We are happy in laying before our readers the full particulars of the Examination and Confession, of the actual murderer of Eliza Grimwood, the unfortunate female that was cruelly murdered at No. 12, Wellington Terrace, Waterloo-road, on the last Saturday morning in the month of May, in 1838, which is above 7 years ago.

It will be reccolected a man named Hubbard had been examined on several ocassions for the murder. And when he was on his death bed, he sent for the Minister, and on his arrival; made a dying statement that he did not know anything concerning the murder. Which it know appears to turn out to be correct.

A private soldier of the 67th regiment, now lying at Portobelo Barracks, was charged at College-street police-office, Dublin, on Wednesday evening, with being absent from quarters without leave. On being given into custody, he asked for pen and paper, remarking to the inspector that he would surprise him. His request being complied with, he stated that his name was George Hill, a native of London, & son of a silversmith residing near Temple-bar, in that city; that he was the murderer of Eliza Grimwood, whose death caused so much sensation in London some years ago, The prisoner was brought before the magistrate on Thursday. After proper caution being given, he was asked by Alderman Tyndal if he had any communication relative to his disclosures of last evening, to make. He replied, after some minutes' hesitation, that he had nothing further to state at present; but he begged to be understood that he retracted nothing he had stated remanded. The prisoner will now be brought to London.

day night last Warman's temper was uunsually ruffled. The unfortunate deceased in consequence, concealed herself in the garden, but Warman went out, and discovering her retreat, beat her in such a manner about the head, that she was shortley afterwards found by her daughter lying on the ground quite dead. An inqnect has been held and a verdict of "Wilful murder" returned against Levi Warman, wno is committed to the County gaol, to take his trial.

Murder near Greenwich.

Within this last day or two Greenwich & Wapping have been the scene of great sensation, in cousepuence of a report gaining circulation that a woman named Ellen Tyrell, about 40 yrs of age, had been murdered by a man named John White, of Gravel Lane, Wapping. The body of the deceased was found in the Surrey Canal, the head was very much swollen. The prisoner underwent a long examination yesterday at Greenwich, and it appears from the evidence adduoed, that the prisoner

A handbill announcing Private Hill's confession. The main image, wrongly showing Hill shooting Eliza Grimwood, had probably been 'lifted' from some other broadsheet.

abhorred military life, and would prefer being executed as a murderer to remaining with this miserable regiment.

Supplied with certificates from the Colonel of the 67th Regiment concerning Hill's disastrous military career, and from the Dublin police about his confession as the murderer of Eliza Grimwood, Inspector Field and Sergeant Goff set out for North Quay with their prisoner, planning to travel to Liverpool on a steamship. On their way, the axle of the 'jaunting car' they travelled in broke and all three were thrown into the ditch. Hill tried to escape, but the athletic Inspector Field pursued and recaptured him. During the journey to Liverpool, and then by coach to London, the truculent prisoner hardly spoke a word. Inspector Field knew that habitual deserters sometimes made spurious confessions to notorious crimes, in order to escape from the military. Still, even the most drunken deserter must surely realise that this was a very dangerous practice indeed, particularly when the confession had been put down in writing before several police witnesses. It was also considered damning that Hill had said he had killed Eliza Grimwood by cutting her throat. Just like the Foreigner, Hill was nearly 5ft 8in tall and had dark hair and whiskers. He did not look particularly foreign, however, being a rather thin, pale, timorous-looking fellow, already marked by his addiction to the bottle. Inspector Field rather doubted that such a miserable specimen of humanity could carry out an accomplished murder and then escape without a trace. And what could have been the motive? The London newspapers were openly jubilant that the murderer of Eliza Grimwood had finally been brought to justice, however. There was even a 'murder broadside' about the 'Confession of the Murderer of Eliza Grimwood', wrongly depicting Hill as shooting Eliza with a pistol.

On 8 September, George Hill was brought before Mr Traill, the Southwark magistrate. Inspector Field detailed the evidence against him: his bad character and conviction for stealing a watch, his escape attempt when they had left Dublin, his resemblance to the murderer with regard to age and height, and most important of all his written confession. Hill's father told Inspector Field how he had 'discarded' his worthless son, as he described it, and how he had thrown away all his begging letters. George Hill had once written to his mother asking for money to purchase his discharge from the army, but she had ignored him. But when asked to explain himself, Hill made a much better impression than before, probably because the alcoholic fumes had cleared from his brain. He admitted that everything the inspector had said was correct, but he had made the confession only because of the tyranny and oppression he had suffered in the regiment. In his desperation, he had thought transportation or even execution preferable to staying in the army. Since he had lived in London in 1838, he could well remember the notorious unsolved murder of that year, and in his drunken state, he had decided to falsely confess to it. The magistrate remarked that although Hill's wife and parents knew that he had been arrested for murder, none of them were present in court. Although he could understand how a desperate man might be driven to making a false confession, there was a need for Inspector Field to investigate what the prisoner had been doing back in 1838, and to confront him with the witnesses who had seen the Foreigner with Eliza Grimwood on the night of the murder.

When George Hill was back before the magistrate on 15 September, his wife, described as a genteel-looking woman, and her daughter, were present. Mr Thomas, the superintendent of the London & Westminster Steam Packet Company, testified that in May 1838, Hill had been in his employ as a ticket collector. He produced an account book showing that Hill had not absented himself from work at the time. Nor had he 'exhibited any conduct to induce a belief that he had committed a murder'. A friend of Hill's testified that they had often met in May 1838 and that Hill had behaved perfectly rationally and 'manifested the same degree of sympathy' when reading the newspaper reports of the murder of Eliza Grimwood. The cabman Spicknell, who had seen the face of the Foreigner, was certain that Hill looked nothing like him. Inspector Field concluded that in his mind, Hill was certainly innocent. The magistrate discharged him, but he was advised to report to the Horse Guards barracks at once, or he would be charged with desertion. Poor George Hill, who had not uttered a word during these proceedings, left the court by one door, his wife and child by another.[7]

★ ★ ★

The next drama in the Grimwood mystery was provided by the Duke of Brunswick. In 1843, the duke took legal action against Barnard Gregory, editor of the *Satirist* weekly paper, for calling him, among other things, the murderer of Eliza Grimwood. There was prolonged legal wrangling and the case went on for almost a decade; one of the points argued was how it could be known that the libel was directed against the exiled Duke of Brunswick and not his brother, the reigning duke.[8] In 1845, Mr Carter and Inspector Field testified that the only person who had been charged with the crime was William Hubbard. In the end, the duke won and Gregory was sentenced to eight months in prison. The scribbler knew every legal loophole, however, and appealed the verdict claiming to have new evidence. But the crazy duke had prepared some unpleasant surprises for him. Gregory was an amateur actor and when he played Hamlet at the Covent Garden Theatre, the duke led a mob pelting him with rotten fruit. When Gregory brought a lawsuit against him for this outrage, the duke argued that the journalist's libels against himself and others made him a person unfit to appear on the stage, and won his case. In 1846, Gregory again appeared as Hamlet, with the same disagreeable consequences.

After this second pelting, Gregory decided to fight back. When acting the part of Shylock at the Strand Theatre, he uttered a lengthy monologue that was not in the play, reminding the audience that it was at this very theatre that Eliza Grimwood had met the Foreigner – and had there not been plentiful rumours at the time that the murderer was none other than the Duke of Brunswick? Further court action ensued, in which Gregory was strictly forbidden to repeat the offending statement in public. In 1848, the duke brought a second lawsuit against the *Satirist*, complaining that being libelled as the murderer of Eliza Grimwood had made him a marked man in society. He was awarded £1,500 in damages and the next year, the *Satirist* went out of business; Gregory was later sentenced to six months in prison.

But still it would be Gregory who had the last laugh. The duke, whose passion for litigation had got the better of him, proceeded to sue the *Weekly Dispatch* for calling him a lunatic. There was a debate whether a wealthy foreigner should really be able to sue for libel in British courts, but it was allowed, thus creating a legal precedent that has worried some of the Internet calumniators of the present day. The Duke of Brunswick won £500 damages this time, but after it had turned out that he had actually bribed two men to perjure themselves in court, the verdict was overturned. When the duke was charged with perjury, he escaped to France in a balloon and never set foot in England again.[9]

★ ★ ★

As late as September 1853 came some last-minute drama. A Dane named Peter Lunischall was arrested as the murderer of Eliza Grimwood after being accused by the prostitute Ann Jennings. When the Dane first appeared before the Southwark magistrates, he said that he had been very intoxicated at the time. A police constable testified that the woman Jennings had been sober when she accused the Dane. With some trepidation, Ann Jennings testified that the prisoner had threatened 'to serve her the same as he had served Eliza Grimwood'. Sergeant Goff next took the stand, to give the court a short summary of the Grimwood case, as he remembered it. Indeed, the murder had been a most mysterious one, and a man named Hubbard, who was since dead, had been the only man charged with the crime. The most likely culprit had been the man who had accompanied the murdered woman home that night. When asked whether the prisoner resembled that man, Goff responded in the negative, since the Foreigner had been a good deal taller. But when asked whether he could definitely exclude the prisoner as the murderer, the cautious Goff again said no, and the Dane was remanded for further questioning. An anonymous letter to *The Times*, signed 'a Magistrate', exulted that the Dane had been charged with the murder of Eliza Grimwood and that his accuser was a woman who supported him with the wages of prostitution, just like Eliza Grimwood did to the *English* wretch.

A few days later, Lunischall was again examined. By this time, Goff had examined the documents on the case held by the Commissioners of Police at Scotland Yard, and found the original descriptions of the Foreigner as a man much taller than the hapless Dane. Goff now declared himself certain that the drunken sailor was wholly innocent. The cabman Spicknell, the witness who had had the best look at the Foreigner at the time, had been transported seven years ago for stealing a watch and was now coachman to a judge at Hobart-town! When gruffly asked whether she still persisted in her story, Ann Jennings meekly answered 'I do, your worship. He not only threatened to serve me as he had Eliza Grimwood, but said he would cut me up, put me in a pickle tub, and send me to Holland!'

Commenting that this was a ridiculous affair altogether, the magistrate said that these words were the idle threat of a lazy vagabond towards a prostitute. The words uttered by such a man were without meaning and there was not the slightest pretext for the charge.[10]

★ ★ ★

Throughout the Victorian era, the murder of Eliza Grimwood was vividly remembered in London folklore. Indeed, it became a byword for any unsolved murder mystery, as well as for the wild accusations that had been going round at the time. In 1848, a ludicrous list of accusations against Lord Palmerston in the satirical monthly *The Man in the Moon* included that of murdering Eliza Grimwood. The next year, the same periodical lampooned Charles Dickens for his short story 'The Haunted Man', the reviewer saying that he had not the slightest idea 'what the crime committed by the Chemist might have been. For all that appears it may have been murdering Eliza Grimwood. Should not wonder if it was.' George Augustus Sala wrote in a similar vein about people 'who accuse you of having set the Thames on fire, and murdered Eliza Grimwood, if you do not accept their interminable romances ...' and the Radicals being accused of having 'invented the Income Tax, caused the Irish potato famine, set the Thames on fire, and murdered Eliza Grimwood'. When the actor William Charles Macready played a character named Gabriel Grimwood in a boring religious melodrama, a voice from the audience interrupted his harangues with the question, 'Look here, old bloke, who cut Eliza's throat?'[11]

For many years to come, the ghost of Eliza Grimwood would be conjured up when London was shaken by some gruesome unsolved murder. It was something like the epitome of a murder mystery: the beautiful but flawed victim, the base and unworthy Hubbard, and the multitude of other suspects. In late 1857, when a large knapsack containing human remains was found on the abutment to Waterloo Bridge, there was debate whether this was a hoax by some medical students, or a murder with dismemberment by some student of James Greenacre, the Edgware Road murderer of 1836. For topographical reasons, a journalist thought the hideous relics on Waterloo Bridge more reminiscent of the great murder sensation back in 1838: 'In some respects, it seems more to resemble the case of Eliza Grimwood, that castaway whose murder has probably haunted the memory of some brutal "gentleman" …' Another writer on the Waterloo Bridge Mystery of 1857, which would never be satisfactorily solved, commented on this most recent addition to London's unsolved murders: 'will the assassins ever be discovered, or will this horrid tragedy remain for ever, like the murder of Eliza Grimwood, years ago, a mystery, utterly beyond solution …'[12]

When, in January 1860, a young prostitute named Marie Tourtoulou was found murdered at No. 39 rue Sainte Anne, a newspaper headline exclaimed, 'An "Eliza Grimwood" case in Paris!'[13] In 1863, the young prostitute Emma Jackson was found murdered with her throat cut from ear to ear, inside a seedy brothel at No. 4 George Street, St Giles. Although twenty-five years had passed since the Waterloo Road Horror, there was immediate comparison with the case of Eliza Grimwood, and prediction that the murder would remain unsolved. 'While England has a memory, it will ponder upon the ghastly mystery of Eliza Grimwood's fate. … When will the murders of Eliza Grimwood, the child at Road Hill House, and the girl in George Street, St Giles, be "out"?' exclaimed the *London Reader*.[14] Later in 1863, the bricklayer Samuel Wright murdered his girlfriend Maria Green at No. 11 Waterloo Road, 'adjacent to the spot where the unfortunate Eliza Grimwood was murdered upwards of 20 years ago'. An eloquent *Morning Post* journalist wrote:

> It would almost seem that some localities in London are doomed to bear a fatal reputation, either from having been the scenes of crimes or accidents, or from possessing evil reputations gained in other ways. Waterloo-road is, unfortunately, particularly distinguished on account of the doubtful reputation attached to it in times not far gone by … The tragedy of which Eliza Grimwood was the victim, from the mystery attending the circumstances, and from the fact that the perpetrator has never been brought to justice, was enough to impress the name of the locality on the public mind for a long time, even had the road not borne a name which history will not let die.[15]

The ghost of Eliza Grimwood was again called to rise up after the mysterious murder of the young prostitute Harriet Buswell on Christmas Eve 1872, and after a woman's dismembered remains had been found in the Thames near Battersea:

> It is greatly feared that we are now in possession of all we shall ever know concerning the unfortunate woman, murdered and mutilated, whose remains have been found in the Thames. The reward of £200 has failed to bring to light any fresh particulars of the affair, which bids fair to be consigned to Lethe along with that of Eliza Grimwood and Harriet, of Coram-street ...[16]

An indignant writer on the Buswell case was scathing about the skill possessed by the Scotland Yard detectives:

> They possess none, and it is notorious that they make a mull of nearly every intricate case taken in hand. What about the Eltham murder, the Hoxton murder, or the murder of Eliza Grimwood (which in its features was counterpart with the present Coram-street Tragedy). Moreover, the circumstances connected with the George-street murder are somewhat identical with those of the present, and the criminal is at liberty.[17]

Due to the passage of time, the accounts of the Grimwood case became increasingly confounded. One journalist wrote that 'in the famous case of Eliza Grimwood at least a dozen persons claimed the credit of being her assassin. They were all, of course, lunatics, or in delirium.' A writer on Waterloo Bridge, which had become toll-free after being purchased by the Crown, said that in Waterloo Road, 'Eliza Grimwood was murdered by some miscreant, of whom the only trace was a glove, bearing a ducal coronet'![18] In 1876, the murder of Eliza Grimwood was featured in the *New Zealand Evening Star*; in 1881, in the *Memphis Daily Appeal*; and, as late as 1929, in the *New Zealand Herald*.[19]

In a magazine article about unsolved murders, there was another long but dangerously inaccurate passage about the Grimwood case, showing how facts get distorted in the popular imagination:

The murder of Eliza Grimwood excited a most painful interest in the public mind. She was singularly beautiful, of the class termed 'unfortunate', but loathing her way of life, which she was in a manner coerced into following by her cousin, originally a working carpenter, but at the time of the murder occupying a house in the Waterloo road, twelve doors from the bridge, where he offered a mercenary shelter to vice. Eliza Grimwood occupied and received her friends in the first floor of that house. One of the most frequent of her visitors was a foreign gentleman, called by the neighbours whose notice he came under, Don Whiskerandoes, from the luxuriance of his whiskers and beard. This person, it was observed, invariably wore lavender-coloured gloves. The same peculiarities – a hairy face and lavender gloves – distinguished a dethroned potentate then residing in exile in England, for which and no other tangible reason his Serene Highness fell under the ban of suspicion. A few days previous to the catastrophe Eliza Grimwood had a clear prospect of escaping from the loathed life to which circumstances had condemned her. A commercial traveller had fallen deeply in love with the beautiful unfortunate, to whom he proposed marriage. His offer was accepted, greatly, it was said, to the cousin's chagrin, rage, indeed, as also, there was reason to believe, in opposition to the jealous will of Don Whiskerandoes. A day was fixed for the ceremony, late in the evening previous to which Whiskerandoes was seen to enter the house. He was admitted by the cousin. A room on the second floor, directly over Eliza Grimwood's sleeping apartment was occupied by another courtesan who, as well as her companion, heard at about the dead waste and middle of the night, a noise as of quarrelling below. The chamber door was presently opened, shut again, and the listeners heard the creaking of a man's step as he descended the stairs and passed out at the street door. So common an incident in that house could excite no surprise. It was afterward remembered that Eliza Grimwood's little dog, though a fierce animal, except in the presence of any one he knew well, did not bark! In the morning, Eliza Grimwood was found, fully dressed, lying on the floor (the bed had not been occupied) quite dead. A sharp instrument, a thin poniard it is believed, was driven into her heart, and life must have been instantly extinct. Instead of the escape, poor girl, so near as it seemed at hand, from pestilential, moral death to hearty, hopeful life, she had been hurled (because, there can be little doubt, of the seeming certainty of that near escape, and her fixed resolve to avail herself of the blessed chance) – hurled ruthlessly into a terrible eternity, with all her sins broad-blown, as flush as May – unhouseled, unanointed, unannealed. By the black-bearded foreigner nicknamed Whiskerandoes? Few doubted that he was the murderer. But where was Whiskerandoes, so-called? Where was he to be found? None knew.[20]

The final appearance of the ghost of Eliza Grimwood was in 1888, when it was conjured up by Jack the Ripper's sanguineous handiwork in Whitechapel. A writer in the *Daily Telegraph* commented:

> Those with retentive memories may be comparing notes regarding the strange similarity existing between the Whitechapel case and that of Eliza Grimwood, who about half a century ago was found in a house in the Waterloo-road under circumstances of closely analogous horror, her murderer never having been discovered.

The journalist speculated:

> Foul deed has been wrought by a lunatic suffering from a recognised and hideous form of homicidal monomania – possible in the case of Eliza Grimwood, and incontrovertibly established in that of the 'Monster' Renwick Williams, whose intended victims, however, escaped with life – or whether the poor waif and stray of a woman in Whitechapel was done to death by a gang of fiendishly ferocious roughs.[21]

A letter writer to the *Irish Times* wished to point out that:

> Undetected crime in London has assumed a very formidable and disappointing shape. Note the Great Coram Street murder, the Waterloo Road murder, the Euston Square murder, the Burton Crescent murder, the Stoke Newington murder, and various minor atrocities … Again is London startled with most appalling murders, committed with impunity in its most crowded thoroughfares.[22]

★ ★ ★

After Eliza Grimwood's effects had been sold at auction by her covetous brothers, it must have been very difficult for Hubbard to find a tenant for the house in Wellington Terrace, since every Londoner knew that a particularly gruesome murder had been committed there. Rumours soon spread that the empty house was haunted by Eliza Grimwood's restless spirit. Hubbard stayed at his mother's house, and did not dare to move back to Wellington Terrace, although he still had the let for the house. In September 1838, a newspaper wrote:

> Notwithstanding the length of time which has elapsed since the murder of Eliza Grimwood, the house which she occupied in the Waterloo-road has remained untenanted ever since Hubbard quitted it. In order to facilitate the letting of it, the landlord has reduced the rent considerably, but all to no purpose. Numerous have been the applications from individuals of both sexes to look over the house, upon the pretence of taking it, should it suit their convenience, but it has afterwards been apparent, with no other object than that of gratifying an idle curiosity. From present appearances no one is likely very soon to become the inmate of this dwelling, so notorious is it in the annals of crime, while the landlord has the mortification of knowing that he is not only pestered by inquisitive observers, but is sure to be a very great pecuniary sufferer by its inoccupancy.[23]

The gloomy prediction of this newspaper journalist would prove to be nothing but the truth.

The haunted murder house at No. 12 Wellington Terrace stood empty throughout 1839, 1840, 1841 and 1842, but the Post Office directory for 1843 shows that it had finally got a tenant, the German wine merchant Adolphus Feistel, who may well have been a foreign immigrant who could not understand what all the fuss was about this notorious murder house. In 1844, the various 'Terraces' in Waterloo Road were incorporated in the main road, and the houses renumbered: Mr Clayton's shop at No. 11 Wellington Terrace became No. 191 Waterloo Road, the murder house at No. 12 Wellington Terrace No. 192, and the Feathers tavern at No. 25 Wellington Terrace No. 205 Waterloo Road. The old numbering also remained, however, and the phrase 'Wellington Terrace, Waterloo Road' remained in use well into the 1860s.

Adolphus Feistel lived in the murder house until 1851, along with his wife who was a foreign toy dealer; the next tenant was the violin maker William Ebsworth Hill, who would remain in the house until 1868. In 1864, a journalist wrote, in an article on cheap dinners and where to find them, 'If the gastronomic student will cross Waterloo-bridge, will walk down that combination of dubious tenancy and faded respectability known as the Waterloo-road, will pass the half-forgotten site of Eliza Grimwood's murder, will proceed under the railway bridge, and continue his pilgrimage almost due south …'[24]

In 1865, the houses in Waterloo Road were again renumbered, from the centre of London towards the periphery, those on the eastern side of the road receiving uneven numbers: the Feathers tavern became No. 1 Waterloo Road, and the murder house No. 27 Waterloo Road.

In the years to come, a number of respectable tradesmen would live in the rehabilitated murder house at what had become No. 27 Waterloo Road: the portmanteau-maker Wollrath Zwanziger, the cork manufacturer Henry Clemence, and the watchmaker Abraham Kaufmann. When that intrepid ghost-hunter, Mr Elliott O'Donnell, made some enquiries about local ghosts in the 1890s, he found a street hawker named Jonathan who had been a boy at the time when Eliza Grimwood was murdered. Jonathan's mother, who had known both Hubbard and Eliza, used to say that the latter was 'as tidy a looking girl as was to be found in the 'ole neighbourhood'. A Mrs Glover, who used to visit someone lodging in Hubbard's house (her daughter Mary Glover?), had twice seen Eliza Grimwood's ghost, dressed just as she had been in her lifetime, making the bed in the murder room. People in what had used to be Wellington Terrace saw the ghost looking out through the ground-floor window so often that they got used to it, and were not alarmed by its presence.[25]

In contemporary articles on 'murder houses', the sinister dwelling in what had used to be Wellington Terrace was compared with the Curse on Mitre Square, the site of one of the 'Ripper' crimes, and with the house and shop at No. 22 Wyndham Road, Camberwell, where an entire family had been exterminated. Similar in notoriety was the strange 'murder neighbourhood' that had been the site of the unsolved Euston Square, Burton Crescent and Great Coram Street mysteries. In the early 1900s, the

A house in Wellington Terrace, showing the deep chasm below, from the *Penny Illustrated Paper* of 27 February 1872.

murder house was still standing. The area remained a seedy and rundown part of London, although traffic across the bridge gathered apace. In 1905, the journalist Guy Logan wrote:

> No. 12, Wellington Terrace, is daily passed by thousands who have no idea that it was once the scene of a most mysterious murder. There Eliza Grimwood, fair and frail, was cruelly done to death by a male 'fiend' whom she had permitted to accompany her home from the Strand Theatre ...[26]

Old Waterloo Bridge was closed to traffic in 1924 after becoming increasingly unstable. After a heated debate over whether it should be repaired or destroyed, it was demolished in 1936, and a new bridge constructed next to it.

The murder house at what had become No. 27 Waterloo Road still stood in 1937, but its days were numbered: in 1938, it was recorded to have been empty, and in 1939, it was no longer listed in the Post Office directory. In 1940, only the Feathers tavern at No. 1 Waterloo Road, and a shortened terrace consisting of the remaining Wellington Terrace houses at Nos 3–11 Waterloo Road, remained standing.

New Waterloo Bridge.

The site of Wellington Terrace today. On the left is the Waterloo Campus, King's College London; on the right, Conway Hall, University of Notre Dame.

St John's Waterloo, where Eliza Grimwood was buried, as it stands today.

Some remaining older houses in Waterloo Road, at the corner with Exton Street.

The Cornwall House annexe of the HM Customs and Excise had been constructed where the remainder of the terrace had once been, with the Royal Waterloo Hospital for Women and Children occupying the corner with Stamford Street. In 1951, only No. 11 Waterloo Road still stood, but this *ultimus* of old Wellington Terrace was pulled down the following year. Although some older houses in Waterloo Road remain at the corner with Exton Street, nothing whatsoever remains of Wellington Terrace; the Cornwall House annexe is today the Waterloo Campus of King's College London, and the Royal Waterloo Hospital has become the Conway Hall of the University of Notre Dame.

If the ghost of Eliza Grimwood has not been exorcised by constant noise from motor vehicles in busy Waterloo Road, the clatter from the trains on their way to Waterloo station and the revel of the jolly young students, then it will gaze in horror at the Southbank Centre and the National Film Theatre, and that curious contraption, the London Eye.

WHO MURDERED ELIZA GRIMWOOD?

So what are we to make of Inspector Field's handling of the Grimwood murder inquiry? Quite a few of his decisions do not agree with the modern concept of how a police detective ought to conduct his business. It is surprising that more than once he ruled out potential suspects for the reason that they were, or perhaps rather seemed to be, respectable people of fixed address. Murderers come from all walks of life and the witnesses had, after all, testified that the Foreigner was smartly dressed. The inspector's notes also make it clear that he was a misogynist even by the standards of the time: women, to him, were an inferior breed, and their reliability as witnesses accordingly diminished. It is ironic that the antics of some of the female witnesses from the Strand Theatre actually seemed to support this notion.

Inspector Field deserves praise, however, for his ability to keep a cool head in what must have been a most trying situation. He was under pressure from the magistrates and coroner, from the newspaper journalists, and from the Londoners themselves, who demanded a speedy solution to the murder mystery. Another admirable quality was his considerable talents of organisation. It has been claimed by some historians that it was a major weakness of the New Police that its divisions had no tradition of co-operating, and that even major cases were handled by just a few officers. But the data on hand from the Grimwood investigation does not agree. Inspector Field was capable of raising considerable manpower when facing tasks that exceeded the capacity of his small core team of three, like the search of the vicinity of Waterloo Bridge, the hunt for the Foreigner, and the tracking down of the writer of the Cavendish letter. In the latter two operations, he successfully liaised with policemen from other divisions.

Inspector Field's notes also testify to how much influence the coroner had on the proceedings during the inquest, and to what degree the magistrates directed the subsequent murder inquiry. Out of the window goes the idea of the omniscient Victorian policeman running his own inquiry, like Inspector Bucket in *Bleak House* or Sergeant Cuff in *The Moonstone*. In the Grimwood murder inquiry, the majority of the important decisions were made by the coroner and magistrates, sometimes without Inspector Field even being consulted. But although these magistrates may have been competent in administering summary judgement in the various petty offences that were brought before their bench, they lacked experience when it came to investigating a serious crime. In particular, Inspector Field rightly objected to their enthusiasm for easy 'solutions': the sensation witness John Owen, the unreliable Catherine Edwin, and the ubiquitous anonymous letters naming some novel suspects.

Charles Frederick Field continued his police career with considerable distinction. Far from receiving any criticism from his superiors for his running of the Grimwood investigation, he seems to have improved his position within the police hierarchy. In 1842, when the New Police finally formed its Detective Division, he became one of its inspectors. In 1846, he was promoted to Chief of Detectives, serving with considerable distinction until his early retirement in 1852, at the age of just 47. He then became a private inquiry agent in London. The Waterloo Road Horror remained the greatest unsolved murder mystery of Inspector Field's career and he never ceased pondering it. In 1850, Field and six other detectives were invited by Charles Dickens to the office of his new magazine *Household Words*. Described as a portly, middle-aged man 'with a large, moist, knowing eye, a husky voice, and a habit of emphasising his conversation with the aid of a corpulent finger, which is constantly in juxtaposition with his eyes or nose', the inspector told the story of the murder of the beautiful Eliza Grimwood, and his own pursuit of the owner of the lavender-coloured gloves. Dickens published Field's account as the second of his Three Detective Anecdotes in his magazine.[1] The

1871 census lists Charles Frederick Field as a retired Inspector of Police, living at No. 5 Stanley Villas, Chelsea, with his wife Jane and their two servants; he died in 1874, aged 69.

* * *

Criminologists recognise that murder can either be spontaneous or planned. The former variety is by far the most common, in the 1830s as well as today. Alcohol plays a major part in fuelling mindless violence, being cheap and readily available; it was even cheaper back in 1838, and frequently enjoyed to excess. Drunken sailors bashed each other's heads in with heavy instruments, drunken husbands cut their wives' throats with their razors, and drunken wives returned the compliment with their kitchen knives. These spontaneous, chaotic murders were usually easily solved by the Victorian police. They were often committed in front of witnesses, the victim was quickly missed and the body found, and the befuddled killer usually screamed out ,'Yes, I did it!' as soon as he or she was confronted by the authorities. In contrast, the early London detectives often struggled in cases of planned murder. The mysterious murders of Mrs Donatty in 1822 and Elizabeth Jeffs in 1827 both remain unsolved to this day. The arrest and conviction of James Greenacre for the murder and dismemberment of Hannah Brown in 1837 owed more to luck than to the detective work of the officers involved.

In a logical analysis of the murder of Eliza Grimwood, Inspector Field's original three alternatives are a useful way to start: either the Foreigner did it, Hubbard did it, or Someone Else did it. The third of these alternatives is of course the least likely, and seems to have been excluded by the police at an early stage. It would either concern an intruder entering the house after the departure of the Foreigner, or that one of the other three people living in the house (the commercial traveller William Best, the prostitute Mary Glover, or the servant Mary Fisher) committed the murder. To begin with the intruder scenario, this would imply that this individual was in possession of a key to the house, since there were no sign of either the front or rear doors being tampered with. Hubbard and Best had keys to the house, whereas its two female inhabitants had to rely on the servant Mary Fisher, who was in charge of a third set of keys, to let them in. It is highly unlikely

THE MURDER OF ELIZA GRIMWOOD.

The murder of Eliza Grimwood, from the novel *Eliza Grimwood, A Domestic Legend of the Waterloo Road*.

that any of these people would have surrendered their keys to any person with violent or burglarious intent. Nor is there any record of Eliza herself giving keys to any of her admirers, even her favourite, the Birmingham sword cutler. As we know, there was some gossip at the time that a jilted admirer, an envious fellow prostitute, or even Hubbard's estranged wife, would have committed the murder. Neither of these individuals would have been able to enter the house without inside assistance, however, nor would they have been in a position to commit the murder without an uproar or a struggle. Alternatively, the scenario in which the murder was committed by one of the other residents would really amount to a murder conspiracy in which Mary Glover and Mary Fisher aided and abetted William Best. But neither of them held any grudge against Eliza Grimwood; in fact, Mary Glover was an old friend of hers, and the young servant Mary Fisher very fond of her mistress. And if the murder was done for profit, why leave eight prominently displayed large silver coins, as well as Eliza's gold watch and jewellery, when they knew where she kept her valuables? Inspector Field got the impression that Best was an honest man and that Mary Fisher was a timid young girl. It seems extremely unlikely that either of these people had anything to do with the murder.

★ ★ ★

It is clear from Inspector Field's notes that immediately after the murder he viewed William Hubbard with the greatest suspicion. The bricklayer was a rough diamond who led a dissolute life. His motive would be either jealousy (of Eliza's customers, particularly the sword cutler who was going to take her to Epsom) or gain (the missing purse full of gold sovereigns). Since Eliza knew and trusted him, he would have had the option of entering her bedroom after the Foreigner had departed, ready to noiselessly cut her throat with a formidable knife or bayonet he had purposely procured beforehand.

DISCOVERY OF THE MURDER.

The murder is discovered, from the novel *Eliza Grimwood, A Domestic Legend of the Waterloo Road*.

Hubbard was strong enough to have committed the murder and mutilation of the corpse in the manner described. As we know, it had attracted some curiosity that although Eliza's little dog had yapped briefly during the night, it had not barked loudly nor lengthily; was this because the murderer was someone it knew well? Inspector Field also found it strange that Mary Fisher, who had actually been sleeping only one thin wall away from the murder room, had not woken up, and he suspected that she might be in league with Hubbard. But although he questioned her several times, she was not caught in any prevarication or contradiction, and he formed the impression she was an honest girl who had been genuinely attached to her mistress. A combination of youth and hard toil may well have rendered her semi-comatose and entirely oblivious to the murderer's swift and silent strike.

As the murder investigation went on, the case against Hubbard weakened day by day. If he had been the murderer, his acting talents would have been considerable, since he seemed entirely distraught, drank and smoked excessively, and gave way to violent outbursts. Several witnesses attested that although their relationship had sometimes been tempestuous, Hubbard and Eliza had been genuinely fond of each other. With the exception of the unreliable prostitute Harriet Chaplin, no person testified upon oath that Hubbard was in the habit of beating or ill-treating Eliza. The three people who knew them best, namely Mary Glover, William Best and the servant Mary Fisher, all said that Hubbard and Eliza did get along quite well, and that they seldom quarrelled. Nor did any person, apart from Harriet Chaplin, testify that Hubbard had disapproved of Eliza's friendship with some of her clients, or that he had ever threatened her. As for the veracity of the witness Chaplin, it must be remembered that at the inquest and at the proceedings against Mr Skinner, she told two wholly contradictory stories sprinkled with several demonstrable untruths.

Another singular circumstance is that two deliberate attempts were made to incriminate Hubbard for the murder. The first of them seems to have been initiated by that miserable creature John Owen, with the aim of gaining pity and recognition for himself.[2] It was very fortunate for Hubbard, considering the amount of prejudice that existed against him, that Owen picked out another man at the inquest! The second attempt, that of the Cavendish letter, was more stealthy and its instigator a more obscure figure.

It may be that young M'Millan wrote the letter, but then it may not. Since there is no doubt that the brothers Grimwood bribed Hubbard to leave the murder house, and at the same time tried to make Inspector Field arrest him for attempting to escape from London, the timely appearance of the letter seems a little too convenient. Could it be that the Cavendish letter was written by or on behalf of the Grimwood brothers, to put Hubbard securely behind bars while they disposed of Eliza's property? As judged by their various altercations in court, the brothers Grimwood hated Hubbard intensely and blamed him for their sister's murder. If the letter had succeeded in its purpose, and led to Hubbard being convicted for the murder, the Grimwoods are unlikely to have shed any tears for the man they blamed for Eliza's downfall.

Hubbard and Eliza had a very strange relationship. Being first cousins, they must have known each other since an early age and there may well be some truth in the story that they had been childhood sweethearts. According to Hubbard, they had been living together in London for as long as ten years. During most, if not all this time, Eliza worked as a part-time prostitute. She had considerable success, as judged by her savings of at least £200, elegant clothes and expensive gold watch and jewellery. Although Hubbard worked as a jobbing bricklayer, his earnings were inconsequential compared to hers, and there is no question that she supported him financially. There was much sympathy for prostitutes among the Londoners at this time: they were considered as 'unfortunates' that had to be 'saved' from the evil men who preyed on them. As Hubbard found out the hard way, a prostitute's bully was generally detested among honest people. It is ironic that the truth was that Eliza had in many ways been the one 'wearing the trousers' in the household: she possessed money and independence, choosing to prostitute herself with clients she usually knew well, if and when she liked it. Hubbard was a hard-working and badly paid manual labourer, who spent most of his earnings on strong drink, and had no ability to save money or improve his situation in life.

There is strong technical evidence in favour of Hubbard's innocence. Firstly, it is obvious from the nature of the wounds, and the extent of blood spatter in the murder room, that the garments worn by the murderer would be extensively stained with blood. Hubbard was the owner of seven shirts, all of which were found to be free of blood, including the collar and cuffs. Nor were there any bloodstains on his other clothes, except what could be expected from a person stepping into a large pool of blood. According to the washerwoman and other people who knew about Hubbard's rather limited wardrobe, all his garments were present and correct. One could of course suggest that he committed the murder naked or dressed only in his underpants, but there was no way for him to have a bath afterwards unless he dived into the Thames from Waterloo Bridge. It would of course also have been possible for him to have clandestinely purchased another complete suit of clothes in which to commit the murder, but this would have demanded a degree of cunning that is not consistent with the other observations of Hubbard. And then there is the point of how to dispose of these extra clothes, and for that matter also the murder weapon. No person saw Hubbard sneak out of the house, through the front or rear entrances, and making such an attempt would have been hazardous indeed, since there were still people in the streets this warm and balmy late May evening, and since he was quite well known locally. The environs of the house were thoroughly searched by the police, but neither bloodstained clothes nor murder weapon were found. Hubbard's own account of how he found Eliza's body makes good sense and contains no contradictions or inconsistencies. The conclusion must be that not only were the magistrates quite right when they acquitted Hubbard, he was almost certainly innocent of committing the murder.

Although acquitted for the murder, Hubbard remained a marked man among Londoners. Since many people knew him by sight, he was frequently booed and jeered, particularly attempting to return to his old haunts in the vicinity of Waterloo Road. He was desperately poor, and it must have been hard for him to obtain employment. In November 1838, there was a newspaper story that Hubbard had absconded to New York and that the police officer Keys had been dispatched to bring him back to London, since new evidence had been discovered linking him to the murder of Eliza Grimwood. But Hubbard himself wrote a letter to the *Morning Advertiser*, saying that he had never been out of England since liberated from Union Hall.[3] As we know from the George Green story, he was still in London in April 1839.

There are several versions of what finally happened to poor Hubbard. *New Newgate Calendar* states that he did indeed go to America, but returned a few years after. He finally 'died a miserable death of starvation, uncared for, unpitied, and believed by all to be the murderer of the unfortunate girl, Eliza Grimwood, who had been so cruelly assassinated years before'.[4] According to the proceedings when George Hill was arrested in 1845, Hubbard had died in Hampton in 1843.[5] The curious 'murder broadside' issued to announce the Hill confession adds that, on his deathbed, Hubbard sent for the minister and swore that he had had nothing to do with the murder of Eliza Grimwood.

The truth would seem to be that, although Hubbard had announced his intention to stay in London until the murderer of Eliza Grimwood had been caught and convicted, he was soon driven out of the neighbourhood around Waterloo Road by the universal hostility he encountered. According to a newspaper article, he was living with his brother in Castle Street in March 1841. He often spoke of the murder, claiming that he had nothing to hide, although he knew that the police had been tracking his movements ever since. One day he collapsed and the doctor diagnosed inflammation of the lungs. Since his condition gradually deteriorated, 'He was aware that his end was approaching, and shortly before he expired he exclaimed "Eliza, I see you. You have been waiting for me a long while. Wait a minute. I am coming." He then placed his right hand upon his heart, and, in a few minutes after ejaculated, "Release me now." He was supported by his sister, and soon after died in her arms, without alluding further to the dreadful deed!'[6] This perhaps rather fanciful story was criticised by *The Examiner*, which suspected that it had been 'manufactured for the express gratification of a certain class of newspaper readers', but the fact remains that William Hubbard, aged 33 years and a bricklayer, expired from 'inflammation of the lungs' at No. 24 Castle Street on 22 February 1841, as proven by his death certificate.[7]

★ ★ ★

If the reader agrees with my deductions thus far, this will leave us with the same conclusion as Inspector Field – namely, that the Foreigner murdered Eliza Grimwood. But who the Foreigner was, the inspector had no idea. For some time, he entertained suspicions against Mr Skinner the tobacconist, and later briefly against the drunken private George Hill, but the cabman Spicknell resolutely ruled both of them out. The official verdict on the

Grimwood murder seems to have been that the culprit was a foreign sailor, who left London very soon after the murder, thus avoiding being caught by the police operation searching all foreign hotels and lodging-houses.

It can of course not be ruled out that the police were right and that the murder of Eliza Grimwood was just a random act of violence, committed by some nondescript ruffian who had the luck to be able to leave London on one of the ships lying on the Thames the very next day. But still, the 'foreign sailor' hypothesis has several serious drawbacks. Firstly, we know from the testimony of Mary Glover and some of the Strand Theatre witnesses that Eliza was quite cautious when selecting her customers. Most of her clients were 'regulars' with whom she had been acquainted for months, or even years. When some fun-loving gentleman wanted to make her acquaintance, he was introduced to her by some friend who could vouch that he was a respectable man and that he could pay for himself. It seems unlikely that a foreign sailor would have access to such a resource. Secondly, we know that Eliza charged at least half a sovereign for any customer who wanted to accompany her home to Wellington Terrace. This would be an excessive amount for a sailor to pay for one single night of pleasure, since such a considerable sum could have kept him going at the cheap brothels for the entire period of his leave. Thirdly, the Foreigner is multiply recorded to have had elegant dress and suave manners. All the witnesses who saw him thought he looked rather like a gentleman, and not a single one of them even entertained the notion that he might have been some rough seafaring man. Although he spoke French (and possibly also Italian), he could also speak good English. Several witnesses observed that he addressed Eliza Grimwood as 'Lizzy' and that they seemed to be on familiar terms, as if they had met under similar circumstances in the past. Bearing in mind what we know about Eliza's habits, it is likely that they had made an appointment to meet at the theatre. This is supported also by the reporter Sharpe, who heard Eliza say 'there he is', as if she had been waiting for someone she knew, followed by some indistinct words that sounded like 'he is here'.

There are also some important observations indicating that, far from being the random act of a violent sailor, the murder had been carefully planned. Firstly, several witnesses agree that the Foreigner wore a broad-brimmed hat. Did he use this as a disguise, since he was worried about possible witnesses? Importantly, the servant Mary Fisher added that when entering the murder house, he hid his face from her by pulling his hat down and walked quickly into Eliza's room. This would indicate that already when entering No. 12 Wellington Terrace, he had some fell purpose in mind. And why did he carry a long mackintosh across his arm? After all, it was late May and the weather was warm and fine. This garment would become very useful to protect his other clothing from the blood spatter when he committed the murder. If he was also carrying a cloth bag, into which to put his blood-stained mackintosh, gloves, hat and gaiters, he would present a perfectly normal appearance when leaving the house.

At the time, there was some speculation that some old enemy might have killed Eliza, possibly a jilted lover or some person with an old grudge against her. But several witnesses agree that the Foreigner and Eliza seemed to be on perfectly good terms during the evening, and that they seemed to know each other. Eliza's comment to the cabman Spicknell, 'You have a nice horse', and her perfectly normal behaviour towards the servant Mary Fisher when she came home, also seems to indicate that she was at ease with the Foreigner, and that the murder came as a complete surprise to her.

So, what do we know for certain about the Foreigner? The descriptions given by several reliable witnesses agree that he was between 20 and 30 years old, 5ft 7 or 8in tall, with dark hair and whiskers. He was well groomed and dressed, and certainly not a rough labourer or sailor. The witnesses agree that he looked like a foreigner, probably a native of some French-speaking country. He could speak French and possibly also Italian, but was also quite fluent in English, with some degree of a foreign accent. This is an important point, since the French are notorious for their reluctance to learn foreign languages. How many young Frenchmen in London fulfilled the criteria listed above, and could also speak fluent English? Certainly not very many. The singer Ernest Tondeur, picked up as a suspect by Inspector Shamling's men, appears to have been one, the unnamed foreign gambler apprehended in Clerkenwell another, but both these men were found to be innocent. When Inspector Field and his men made their extensive search of various foreign hotels and taverns in London, they found not a single suspect worthy of bringing before the magistrates.

Since the Foreigner knew Eliza Grimwood, and since he seemed to know his way about the Strand Theatre, it seems likely that he was a resident of London or its immediate vicinity. As to his trade and situation in life we can deduce even less. One witness thought his coat not unlike those worn by some master mariners and customs officials; another speculated that he looked more like a respectable gentleman's servant. Another unsolved mystery is where the murderer went after leaving Wellington Terrace. There was not a single observation of a man behaving suspiciously in the vicinity of Waterloo Bridge the morning after the murder, although quite a few people were still out and about in the early hours. Did the Foreigner trust his calmness and cunning, and hope that the drunken London revellers would hardly remember his countenance, or had he access to some vehicle nearby? The latter alternative would also explain why the toll-keepers at Waterloo Bridge did not take any note of his escape across the river.

★ ★ ★

When the debate about the Cavendish letter was raging in the London newspapers, a novel suggestion was made by a correspondent to *The Observer* newspaper. Pooh-poohing the idea that the miserable Hubbard had killed the goose that laid the golden eggs, and blasting the Cavendish letter as an elaborate hoax, he brought forward a novel theory of his own. Clearly, the Foreigner must be the guilty man, but what about the extreme brutality of the murder and mutilation of the body, and the absence of a credible motive? The writer knew about the London Monster of 1790, who took such an insane delight in stabbing ladies' bottoms, and also various other 'monsters' of similar proclivities that London and Paris had produced. Might not the murder of Eliza Grimwood be the work of such a perverted creature, a serial killer who delighted in murdering women of the street? From the *Causes Célèbres*, he quoted the case of a debauched French Baron, a 'demon of the grossest and most unaccountable sensuality', who had murdered several young women and drunk their blood, before being apprehended and executed.[8]

There was no reaction to this challenge, either from the police or from the newspaper journalists, perhaps because the exposure of the Cavendish letter as a falsification rendered part of its reasoning obsolete. This is a pity because the theory proposed has many things speaking in its favour. The cunning with which the murder was committed, the calm demeanour of the killer, the absence of a sound when the murder was committed, and his stealthy escape from the house puzzled Inspector Field very much. It was like it had all been premeditated and carefully planned, and as if the Foreigner had killed before. Was the Waterloo Road Horror the work of a serial killer, and was Eliza Grimwood perhaps not his first victim?

13

THE FREDERICK STREET MURDER, THE WESTWOOD MYSTERY, AND SOME SUSPECTS

In the 1830s, there was no such thing as a serial killer. Murder always had a motive, it was thought, and the concept of some person committing murder for the mere pleasure of it was unheard of. Yet it is inexplicable that no police detective connected the murder of Eliza Grimwood with the Frederick Street murder of 1837, since there are striking parallels with regard to the lack of an obvious motive, the modus operandi, and the social status of the victim.

The two murder victims even shared the same first name. Early in the morning of 9 May 1837, at the King's Arms public house in No. 19 Frederick Street, the body of 21-year-old barmaid Eliza Davies was found in the landing outside her bedroom.[1] Her throat had been cut with great violence, without any of the people resident at the pub hearing anything. Mr George Wadley, her employer and the proprietor of the King's Arms, thought the killer was an 'ill-looking fellow' who used to come into the pub early in the morning asking for a knife to cut his bread.[2] He had once quarrelled with Eliza Davies, after she had refused him a pint of beer on credit, and skulked out saying he would 'do for her'. This man, who had been a steady customer

THE ASSASSIN SEIZED THE POOR GIRL BY HER BACK HAIR AND CUT HER THROAT FROM EAR TO EAR.

The murder of Eliza Davies. A fanciful drawing from the *Illustrated Police News* of 22 December 1888.

at the pub for at least three weeks, was described as an ugly, scruffy-looking foreigner, about 40 years old. The pot boys Benjamin Bunn and Alfred Hitchcox had both seen him more than once, as had Frederick Russell, one of the pub regulars. Significantly, he had failed to make his daily visit to the pub on 10 May, something that convinced Mr Wadley of his guilt.

Several witnesses came forth saying that Eliza Davies had been seen with a foreign-looking man, although their descriptions diverged wildly. One man was certain that he had been French and about 45 years old, answering to the name of M. Entre or André, another that he was a young, well-dressed Frenchman who seemed to be her boyfriend, a third that he was an Italian and possibly named Zucchelli. Inspector William Aggs and Constable Henry Pegler, who were in charge of the case, assumed that all these sightings concerned the same person, and also identical with the scruffy-looking foreigner described by Mr Wadley. The latter individual had been described as wearing a dark coat, Scotch plaid waistcoat and fustian trousers. A butcher named Mr Malpas had seen a man wearing a dark coat and fustian trousers standing at York Square not far from the King's Arms. He was looking very melancholy, not answering the butcher's observation that if he wanted a drink, he would be lucky to find a public house open at twenty to six in the morning. Inspector Aggs made up his mind that this was the murderer lurking outside the pub. Still smarting over the slight at not being trusted with credit, this villainous foreigner had sneaked into the pub just after Eliza Davies had unlocked the doors, cut her throat, and disappeared without trace. Through the newspapers, handbills and word-of-mouth, there was a nationwide alert for the murderer: a foreign-looking man between 20 and 40 years old, dressed in a dark coat, fustian trousers, and possibly a Scotch plaid waistcoat.

Since the Frederick Street murder was widely publicised, the result of issuing this vague description can easily be imagined. There were citizens' arrests of suspicious-looking men all over London. One suspect was taken into custody in Great Marylebone Street, another near Fitzroy Market, a third in Islington and a fourth in Greenwich. Inspector Aggs and Constable Pegler were continually on the move, racing through London in their hansom cabs to confront a series of scruffy-looking individuals who had had the misfortune of wearing dark coats and fustian trousers. When a man arrested in Beckenham, Kent, was taken to the Marylebone Street police office in a hackney coach, the vehicle was pursued by a considerable mob, and the suspect would have been lynched had not some sturdy policemen protected him. He turned out to be a young vagabond who had been loitering about, reluctant to give an account of himself when challenged by an officious amateur detective. As soon as he had been disposed of, another man was brought up: a young street beggar who had been taken in the Rose and Crown public house. He had been unwise enough to boast that he had spent time in both Maidstone and Lewisham jails, and that he would have been transported if he had had his due. When the young jailbird fell asleep after having swigged heartily from his beer glass, the landlord ran outdoors, found a policeman and explained that the murderer of Eliza Davies was sleeping in his pub. But again, there was no evidence against him, and the pot-boy Hitchcox could not identify him as the suspect.

In the meantime, the body of young Eliza Davies had been laid out, in the clubroom of the public house. Two surgeons declared themselves convinced

Sketch of ELIZA DAVIES as she lay on the Mattress after the Murder.

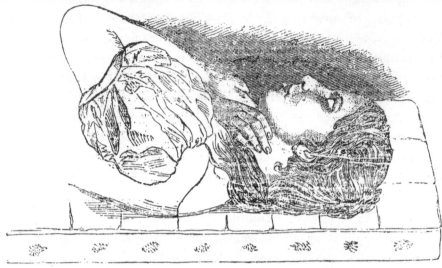

A sketch of Eliza Davies done after her death by some enterprising journalist, from the *Weekly Chronicle* of 21 May 1837.

that she had been murdered: there was no possibility she could have committed suicide, due to the extreme force with which her throat had been cut. When a busybody wrote to *The Times*, suggesting that the 'medical gentlemen' should determine whether or not she had been pregnant, the doctors declared themselves confident that was not the case. How they could be so sure is a mystery, since according to the newspapers, there was no autopsy. Although several surgeons offered their own services, and many gentlemen wanted to be spectators, Mr Wadley declined all offers. Probably for religious reasons, he wanted to keep the body intact: it was shrouded, placed in a handsome coffin covered with black cloth, and interred before 'an immense assemblage of persons' on 15 May 1837.[3]

We know very little about Eliza Davies, except that she was a native of Glamorgan and orphaned at an early age. A pamphlet approvingly describes her as 'a fine young woman', adding that she was much esteemed for her civility. Barmaids were considered sexually 'easy' at the time, and not a few of them were part-time prostitutes. She was a pretty young girl, popular among the pub customers, and would have had many chances for illicit affairs. Although Mrs Berry, wife of the former proprietor of the King's

Arms, told a reporter that Eliza Davies had been a quiet, obedient girl who had always behaved with proper decorum, respect for the dead and concern about the pub's reputation may well have induced her to twist the truth a bit. It is notable that Eliza's savings bank receipt book was found to contain nearly £23, surely more money than most 21-year-old barmaids possessed at the time.

The murder mania spread further afield. A young Italian was apprehended in Bath, a Dutchman in Hull, and a foreign-looking labouring man in Colnbrook, near Windsor. When Inspector Aggs was interviewed by a reporter from *The Times*, at his temporary headquarters at the King's Arms, he said that he and Pegler had travelled nearly 100 miles in the previous twenty-four hours. There had been many anonymous letters, 'to which much importance is attached'. The interview was concluded in the following dramatic manner:

> A messenger has just now arrived in breathless haste at the King's Arms bringing with him a letter addressed to Inspector Aggs, who immediately got into a cab with Pegler, and ordered the driver to go on with all possible speed. The vehicle proceeded up Tottenham-court-road, and it is understood that a person strongly suspected of being the murderer was to be met with at a public house in the vicinity of Whitechapel church.[4]

★ ★ ★

After another couple of weeks dashing around London interviewing dodgy foreigners with dark coats and fustian trousers, Inspector Aggs started using his brain, an organ he seems to have left unconsulted since the start of this dismal wild goose chase. Was it really likely that a foreign tramp or labourer would murder someone just for being refused beer on credit? Instead, the inspector was beginning to suspect the young Frenchman or Italian who had been seen with Eliza Davies at the pub, but this character was never tracked down.

Just like in the Grimwood case, the Frederick Street murder had some dramatic late-stage developments. In late July, there was sensation when the police claimed to have arrested an accomplice to the Frederick Street murderer. It was an old gypsy woman who went under the name Amelia Smith, although she sometimes used the name Taylor; she lived at No. 25 Charles Street, Drury Lane. At an early stage, a mysterious letter had been found in a drawer in the bedroom of Eliza Davies, beginning with the words, 'Young Woman – You are born under tow plannets, Mars and Venus. The worst of your troubles is past under your first plannet, but the second denots of good fortune in all your undertakings ...' The letter went on to predict, very wrongly as it would turn out, that Eliza would marry a man with a dark complexion, and that she would have six children.[5] The letter clearly indicated that Eliza had been interested in some variety of fortune telling, and the old crone Amelia Smith had been observed by the pot-boy Hitchcox skulking about the King's Arms. Eliza had told the cook that she had told her fortune for a shilling. Police Constable Roderick apprehended the gypsy fortune teller in York Square, but when brought before the sitting magistrate at the Marylebone Street police office, the old crone gave nothing away: she was not in the habit of telling fortunes, although she admitted having drunk beer at the pub. Hitchcox said that Eliza had been dissatisfied by the old woman's soothsaying, since some events she had predicted did not happen, and this, Inspector Aggs speculated, would have given the gypsy fortune teller a motive for murdering her. Aggs seemed quite astonished that the magistrate did not at all share his suspicions, and Amelia Smith was set free.[6]

In December 1837, when the police were searching for a young Frenchman or Italian rather than some scruffy tramp, a well-dressed young man who called himself Lascerti got off the Bath coach in Devizes. At the principal inn in town, he seemed to have overheard some people at the next table discussing the Frederick Street murder. The Italian promptly walked out, leaving behind a hat in a box, marked 'Perring, Strand' and a handkerchief with the initials J.H. When there was a rumour that Lascerti had been arrested and brought back to London, there was much excitement in the Regent's Park area: a crowd of 700 people gathered near the King's Arms to find out the latest news. But a messenger brought back the bad news that although the indefatigable Inspector Aggs and Constable Pedler were at that moment racing down to Devizes, Lascerti was still at liberty.[7]

The newspapers were now wholly critical of Inspector Aggs and his handling of the case. Nor were his superiors particularly bonhomous. When Aggs put in a bill for £10 13s 6½d for travel and subsistence for himself, Constable Pegler, and witnesses, the Commissioners of Police refused to pay it in full, since they deplored his bungling of the case. Yet Aggs kept his position within the police, and was several times employed on following up various loose leads in the Eliza Davies case. In 1841, the prisoner David Venables accused another criminal, Henry McCane, of the Frederick Street murder. He had asked Venables to sharpen a knife with a grinder, and then suddenly and motivelessly walked into the King's Arms, seized hold of Eliza Davies and cut her throat. Venables had seen him exit the public house, still carrying the bloody knife. The police did not believe him, since the murder had been committed with a kitchen knife, which had been left behind on the bar.[8] In April 1845, a young drunk named Walter Chambers actually confessed that he had cut the throat of Eliza Davies, threatening the barmaid at the King's Arms that: 'I'll jump over the counter and serve you the same!'

When facing the Marylebone magistrates, Chambers had sobered up; it had all been a joke, and he had got into trouble due to his own foolishness. He certainly did not seem like a calculating murderer, and the ever-present Inspector Aggs added that he did not at all resemble the main suspect. Chambers was discharged. A great crowd had congregated, and they were all very keen to see the self-accused murderer as he was taken away.[9]

As late as 1848, there was further sensational news. A young man told Inspector John Tedman that at the time of the Frederick Street murder, he had been a servant in a house not far from the King's Arms. A man named Holland, the brother of the housekeeper, was a frequent visitor to this house, and also a regular at the King's Arms. After the murder, the servants thought his clothes so closely resembled those of the main suspect, that they had a collection to raise sufficient money to buy him a new pair of trousers! This was thought a very good lead, but as the police were out searching for the elusive Holland, better was to come. A man named Alfred Gee claimed to have seen a foreign-looking young man running out of the pub at 6 o'clock on the morning of the murder, pausing to wash the blood from his hands in the gutter. When asked why he had not informed the police of this vital sighting eleven years earlier, Gee responded that he had told his master at the time, and that this gentleman had informed the magistrate at the Marylebone Lane police office, but he had not been taken seriously.

The now retired Inspector Aggs admitted that he had indeed heard this evidence before, but paid little attention to it, since the man had not worn a scruffy dark coat and fustian trousers! But Inspector Tedman tracked down Holland to Southampton and had Gee travel there to try to identify him. But Gee was not certain Holland was the man he had seen, and there the matter would rest, forever.[10]

The investigation of the murder of Eliza Davies makes for dismal reading. Inspector Aggs acted with great determination, but with little judgement. Led on by the foolish Mr Wadley, he made up his mind too soon about the scruffy foreigner in the pub, and once the description had been posted, there was no way back, except to travel all over London searching for this protean pseudo-suspect. It is particularly blameworthy that the police did not investigate Eliza Davies's personal life properly. Surely, it is more likely that someone she knew grabbed her in the landing or stairs, than that some nameless intruder murdered her for no motive and no profit at all.

Agreeing with these deductions, crime writer Joan Lock proposed George Wadley himself as an obvious suspect. Might he have had an affair with the barmaid, or killed her on being rebuffed in his advances?[11] But Mr Wadley was a respectable young man with no previous criminal conviction. He was popular in the neighbourhood and did much to aid the hunt for the murderer, posting a £50 reward himself. There was a Mrs Wadley sleeping in the same bed; how would her husband escape out of it and kill his paramour, and then return to the marital bed without the wife noticing anything untoward? George Wadley had a long and prosperous career as the landlord of various public houses in London and had at least seven children with his two wives; he was still alive in comfortable retirement as late as 1891. Instead, it would seem reasonable to suggest that the murder was most probably committed by a man who had been invited by Eliza to spend the night with her. This individual was most probably her boyfriend, the dapper-looking, French-speaking young foreigner who had been seen speaking with her in the pub skittle alley.

There are obvious similarities between the murders of Eliza Davies and Eliza Grimwood. Both women were killed by a strong man who cut her throat with a formidable and very sharp instrument. The killer was able to murder both victims without them making any noise, and in spite of the ferocity of the attacks, he avoided getting his clothes stained with blood.

The reliable descriptions of the culprit have many similarities: young, well-dressed, foreign-looking, capable of speaking French and possibly also Italian, but also making use of English without a pronounced accent.

★ ★ ★

In June 1839, a year after Eliza Grimwood had been murdered, there was another high-profile murder case in London. Mr Robert Westwood was a successful watchmaker who had been in business at Princes Street, Soho Square, for several decades. He had invented a new kind of eight-day watch that became highly sought after; in consequence, Mr Westwood became very wealthy indeed. But it does not appear as if this accumulation of money made Mr Westwood's life particularly happy. He had married a much older woman, for money it was alleged; there was no love lost between them and they were constantly at loggerheads.

Mr Westwood did not trust banks and kept all his money and property back home. This was known to the criminal fraternity, with the inevitable results.

THE UNFORTUNATE VICTIM WAS LYING ACROSS THE FLOOR PARTLY BURNT AND HIS THROAT DREADFULLY CUT.

The discovery of the murder of Mr Westwood, from the *Illustrated Police News* of 12 January 1889.

Once, three men broke into the house, knocked Mr Westwood down and tied him to the bedpost, before carrying off a number of valuable watches. In 1822, when Mr and Mrs Westwood were at church, burglars broke into his house and stole money and watches worth £2,000. A young man named William Reading had been observed loitering in the churchyard next to Mr Westwood's shop; when arrested, he was found to carry six gold sovereigns, two of which the watchmaker identified as his property, since he had marked them with his special mark. Reading was urged to name his accomplices and tell where the stolen goods were kept, but he did neither. After Reading had been executed, some of the stolen property was recovered from various Jewish receivers of stolen goods; again, Mr Westwood's habit of marking his sovereigns stood him in good stead.

This surreptitious thieving and ill-treatment from his fellow humans seems to have permanently soured Mr Westwood's character. He became increasingly morose, suspicious and paranoid. A scruffy, unkempt-looking old fellow, he always slept downstairs, next door to the room where his precious watches were kept, armed with a brace of loaded pistols. Mr Westwood beat and ill-treated his wife, bullied and shouted at his workmen, and annoyed his lodgers with his constant penny-pinching. This real-life Ebenezer Scrooge feuded with business rivals, quarrelled with his neighbours and mistreated his customers. One sea captain complained about a watch he had purchased and had it snatched out of his hand, thrown on the floor, and stamped upon. A young man who was also dissatisfied with his timepiece was evicted from the premises at pistol point.

Just after midnight on 3 June 1839, smoke was seen billowing out from Mr Westwood's house. The police were quickly on the scene and extinguished the blaze, which originated in the downstairs room where Mr Westwood kept guard over his treasures. On the floor was Westwood's mangled corpse: his throat had been cut with great force, and his clothes had been set on fire.[12] Near the body was a heavy sash-weight with hairs stuck to it; this was probably the weapon used to knock Westwood down. The police also found a curious apron with large pockets, which no one in the house had seen before. Mr Westwood's foreman counted the watches, finding that over eighty of them were missing. A young man had seen two foreign-looking men emerging from the premises shortly after midnight;

Mr Owen sees the two murderers leaving Mr Westwood's shop, from the *Illustrated Police News* of 20 February 1904.

both were wearing dark frock coats, and one of them was younger and taller than the other. Not unreasonably, the police believed that these two were the murderers, particularly since it would have been difficult for just one man to murder Mr Westwood, set the house on fire and steal the watches.

Inspector Nicholas Pearce, who was put in charge of the Westwood murder investigation, had no shortage of suspects. There were no obvious signs of a burglary, so it seemed as if the murderers had either sneaked into the house unnoticed during the evening, quite possibly possessing a key to the premises, or that they had been let in by one of the inhabitants of the house. Mrs Westwood told the police that she suspected two former lodgers, William and Caroline Stevenson, who had been evicted from the house just ten days earlier. Mr Westwood had originally been quite pleased with the Stevensons, since the man was young and healthy and thus useful to defend the premises against burglars. But after Mrs Westwood had objected to the number and assortment of Mrs Stevenson's male visitors, as well as to her 'free and easy' manner, the irascible watchmaker had evicted his lodgers, on the spot. There was an angry scene, in which Mrs Stevenson scratched her husband's face when he refused to defend her honour. Mrs Westwood claimed that the lodgers had promised to 'do for' their former landlord when leaving the premises. But the two Stevensons turned out to have a reasonably solid alibi. A writer in *The Times* instead favoured Mrs Westwood herself as a suspect, or perhaps rather instigator of the murder, since she was more than 80 years old. Not long before the murder, she had appealed

The discovery of the murder of Mr Westwood, from the *Illustrated Police News* of 13 February 1904.

to the Marlborough Street magistrates to restrain her husband's violence against her.

Inspector Pearce built up a long list of all Mr Westwood's enemies: business rivals, people he had annoyed or insulted, workmen he had sacked, or customers who had complained of faulty watches. Westwood had for some time been receiving anonymous threatening letters, but their sender was never traced. It had never been ascertained exactly how many watches had really been stolen; the police clearly mistrusted the allegation that over eighty timepieces had been taken by the murderers, but they had no means of proving otherwise. They approached a wide network of jewellers, watchmakers and pawnbrokers with a makeshift list of the stolen watches, but not a single one was recovered. This led the police to presume that the stolen watches had been taken abroad. Suspicion briefly fell on a watchmaker named William Campion, who had been sacked by Westwood four years earlier. Now, he had great difficulty getting another job and blamed Westwood for his downfall; he had been heard saying that 'some day he'd be damned if he did not cut his bloody throat!' But Campion had an alibi for the time of the murder.

Another worthwhile lead concerned the family and friends of William Reading, the young man who had been hanged on Westwood's evidence for the 1822 burglary. Inspector Pearce and his men managed to track down some of Reading's former associates. One of them, a certain George Redgrave, supposed to be a burglar, had been seen with new clothes after the murder. Reading's brother was watched by constables for some time without anything suspicious coming to light.

A further clue concerned a paperhanger named Nicholas Carron, who had lived only two doors from the Westwoods in Princes Street. He was a foreign-looking cove, the son of a Swiss workman who had moved to London. Carron knew the watchmaker's premises well, having decorated them not long before. After the murder, he shaved his whiskers and left London in disguise, leaving his wife and children behind. The police first thought he had left London to escape his many creditors, but an anonymous letter from America claimed that Carron had come to New York, that he was spending money freely and that he was sending for his family. When an ex-housekeeper of Carron's, whom he had thrown out after she had become pregnant by him, was tracked down, she claimed to have seen the sash-weight and paperhanger's apron found at the murder scene in Carron's possession.

This same woman also claimed that Carron had ideas above his station in life. He spent money freely and was notoriously unfaithful to his wife. He had used to spend much time with a prostitute in Waterloo Road; in fact, she was one of the main reasons he was so severely out of pocket at the time. Inspector Pearce, who was quite impressed by this evidence against the absconded paperhanger, persuaded an ex-policeman named Cartwright to cross the Atlantic to try to find him. But the ending of this unconventional murder investigation was a farcical one. Cartwright, who was clearly an unscrupulous character, had had time to assess the situation, and to make plans accordingly. Clearly, the promise of a small reward from his former employers in London was nothing compared to what could be accomplished if he joined forces with the murderer. Cartwright told Carron all about Inspector Pearce's plot, and it would appear as if the two divided the loot and lived happily ever after. The murder of Mr Westwood would remain unsolved.[13]

There were vague rumours already at the time that there was a link between the Grimwood and Westwood murders, mainly due to the obvious similarities in the crimes. In 1840, there was a claim by a man in Hull that he knew that Eliza Grimwood and Mr Westwood had been murdered by the same man, but nothing came of this.[14] Crime writer Joan Lock rightly criticised this lack of imagination from the police, particularly since the modus operandi of the two murders were very similar, and since Carron had a link to a prostitute in Waterloo Road.[15]

★ ★ ★

At this stage of the book, I would suspect that most readers agree with me (and with Inspector Field) that the Foreigner was the guilty man. In an attempt to learn more about his identity, it is worthwhile to use a strategy well known to the 'Ripperologists' and have a look at some of the convicted killers of women of the time, to see if any promising leads might be forthcoming. As we have seen, we also have three unsolved London murders in the years 1837, 1838 and 1839, those of Eliza Davies, Eliza Grimwood and Robert Westwood, with vague rumours linking these three crimes. Was a serial killer at large in London in the late 1830s, and did he claim more victims than three?

One of the criminal sensations of 1839, nearly rivalling the murder of Mr Westwood, was the 'Cadogan Place murder'.[16] In the Chelsea house of the magistrate Henry Edgell, a young under-housemaid named Elizabeth Paynton was found dead on 17 May, with her throat dreadfully cut. Since the only person supposed to be with her in the house at the time of the murder, the young footman William Henry Marchant, was nowhere to be found, he immediately became the prime suspect. Two days later, Marchant gave himself up to a police inspector in Hounslow and confessed to the murder. He was in a dreadful state of anxiety, claiming that he could hear the ghost of the murdered girl pursuing him. When tried for the murder, Marchant pleaded guilty. The motive was supposed to be unrequited love, since the other servants said that, although Marchant had been very partial

The execution of William John Marchant, from a worn old handbill.

to the attractive Elizabeth Paynton, she had been disposed to laugh at him. Marchant was hanged on 8 July. To begin with, Marchant appears a reasonably good suspect. Partial to the ladies, he had killed one of the objects of his desire by cutting her throat, before absconding. None of the contemporary sources states that Marchant was a foreigner, but his name has a French sound to it and he may well have looked foreign.

Importantly, one of the Strand Theatre witnesses thought that the Foreigner looked like a gentleman's servant. But there are also some very strong arguments that seem to free Marchant from any suspicion of being a serial killer. Firstly, the execution of the murder, and the subsequent confession, suggests that Marchant had acted in a sudden rage rather than planning his crime. Secondly, he was only 18 years old when executed, and would thus have been only 17 at the time of the murder of Eliza Grimwood, and 16 at the time Eliza Davies was murdered. Although the witnesses seeing the Foreigner described him as young, none of them thought he seemed like a teenager. A newspaper reporter described Marchant as a 'slight puny youth' who cried incessantly and seemed to be 'in a state of dreadful agitation'. According to one of the witnesses at the inquest on Elizabeth Paynton, Marchant did not use a razor since unlike the bewhiskered Foreigner, he did not need to shave. Clearly, there is no need to consider this suspect further.

A much more sinister and cunning London murderer was apprehended some years later. In April 1842, a Putney coachman named Daniel Good had been accused of stealing a pair of trousers from a pawnbroker. When a police constable named Gardiner came to search the stables of Granard Lodge in Putney

Portrait of Daniel Good.

A drawing of Daniel Good, from *Famous Crimes Past and Present*, Vol. I, No. 8.

DANIEL GOOD,

The supposed Murderer of Jane Jones

From a sketch taken at Bow Street, Thursday, April 21ˢᵗ 1842.

Another drawing of Daniel Good, from Vol. 2 of Percy Fitzgerald's *Chronicles of the Bow Street Police Office*.

Park Lane, where Good was at work, the coachman protested his innocence. When searching the premises, Gardiner found no trousers, but instead an object rather resembling a large, plucked goose. At the same instant, Good dashed out, locking the stable door behind him. After the angry constable had struggled to open the door, he returned to have a closer look at the 'goose'. With considerable dismay, he found that it was a dismembered female torso. It soon became clear that this was part of the body of the washerwoman Jane Sparks, alias Jones, alias Good, who had been cohabiting with the absconded coachman. The motive was presumed to be that the amorous Good had wanted to marry the 16-year-old Susannah Butcher, something that 'Jane Good', as she called herself, of course would not tolerate, with ultimately fatal consequences. With considerable coolness and cunning, Good clandestinely murdered her, dismembered her body, and fed it into the stables fireplace. Had it not been for the unfortunate episode with the stolen trousers, he might well have been successful in destroying the body, and quite possibly getting away with murder.[17]

The police suspected that the absconding Good might be hiding with his first wife, 'Old Molly' Good, who kept a stall in Spitalfields Market. Although some of Jane Good's clothes were found in her wardrobe, there was no sign of the coachman. Not unreasonably, giving Good's farcical escape from the police constable, and the delay in tracking down 'Old Molly' and Good's other contacts in London, the newspapers were full of criticism of the police. *The Times* wrote:

> The conduct of the metropolitan police in this case, as in those of the unfortunate Eliza Grimwood, Lord William Russell, and others, is marked by a looseness and want of decision which proves that unless a decided change is made in the present system, it is idle to expect that it can be an efficient detective force, and that the most desperate offender may escape with impunity.

After several weeks on the run, Daniel Good was caught in Tonbridge by a former policeman. He was speedily tried and executed, but the criticism did not abate. *The Times* wrote that the result of the cases, 'of Eliza Davies, the barmaid in Frederick-street, Regent's-park; of Richard Westwood, the

The end of Daniel Good, from the *Curiosities of Street Literature* (London 1871), sheet 195.

watchmaker in Princes-street; and of Eliza Grimwood, in the Waterloo-road, the perpetrators of which still remained undiscovered', showed the incompetence of the police just as clearly as the farcical hunt for Daniel Good, who had been caught more or less by chance. The result of this mounting criticism was the foundation of the Detective Branch of the Metropolitan Police, a team of eight crack officers led by Inspector Nicholas Pearce, which would assist in cases of serious crime and improve communication between the nine police divisions.

Is there any reason to suspect Daniel Good was involved in the murder of Eliza Grimwood? After all, he had a very bad reputation already before the murder of Jane Good, he was searching for female company in far from salubrious circumstances, and he was capable of murdering a woman in a brutal manner. Interestingly, there was once a newspaper story that Good may have been involved in the murder of Eliza Davies, although no evidence in favour of this was forthcoming.[18] A drawing of him in the dock shows that he had dark hair and bushy whiskers. But this drawing, and the description of Good on one of the police reward posters, describe Good as a thin, wiry Irishman, about 46 years old, with a dark sallow complexion and long thin features, and bald on the top of his head. He was just 5ft 6in tall. This description does not agree with what we know about the Foreigner, with regard to age, height or looks. Moreover, Good was a penniless coachman and petty thief, and hardly the kind of person who could afford the company of Eliza Grimwood. And would several witnesses believe an Irishman to be French or Italian, when they had seen him close up and heard him speak? Although Good initially seemed a good suspect, there are too many discrepancies between him and the young, relatively tall, dapper-looking 'Foreigner'.

★★★

On the night of 29 April 1844, the wife of one of the toll-keepers on Battersea Bridge saw a woman come up to the toll house, saying that she had been stabbed. Indeed, she had a dreadful gash in the right side of the neck, extending from the windpipe to the right ear. Before she expired, she gave her name as Sarah McFarlane, a widow living in Bridge Road, Battersea. When asked who had stabbed her, she said, 'Dalmas'. It soon turned out that she was referring to Auguste Dalmas, a Frenchman who had been cohabiting with her for some time. Once he had been a respectable married man with three grown-up daughters, but after the death of his wife he had become very melancholic, losing interest in his work in a chemicals factory and falling into debt. The acquaintance with Mrs McFarlane had not lifted his depressed spirits for very long and it seemed to the police as if the Frenchman had 'settled' a quarrel with his paramour by stabbing her hard in the neck before absconding. Just like in the case of Daniel Good, posters describing Dalmas went up all over London, but the Frenchman remained in hiding for several days. The newspapers were scenting another police failure, hinting that the Dalmas case would be 'added to those of Eliza Davies,

Mr. Shepherd, Eliza Grimwood, and Mr. Westwood, for the cold-blooded murder of whom not a single individual has been brought to justice'. But it was not long before the sad, friendless Frenchman was discovered, trying to secure a bed in a dismal lodging-house. He was convicted for the murder and sentenced to death, but was reprieved due to symptoms of insanity and instead transported for life.[19]

So here at last we have a real 'Foreigner', a Frenchman who had been living in London for twenty years and who spoke very good English. At the time of the murder of Eliza Grimwood, he was living in Battersea not far away. He came from the South of France, may well have been able to speak Italian, and looked very swarthy, with dark hair. But once more there are some serious problems with this suspect. Firstly, he was about 50 years old when arrested, and thus at least 45 back in 1838, which seems too old to fit with the descriptions of the Foreigner, particularly since Dalmas was not a handsome sight – bald-headed and with a large scar on his forehead. The murder of Mrs McFarlane seems to have been an act of desperation from a man who had become increasingly deranged after the death of his wife early in 1843. Before this time, Dalmas had been the perfect citizen, people testified, honest and hard-working, and the author of a book on chemistry. Again, Dalmas does not fit the profile left by Eliza Grimwood's murderer.

The take-home message from this section of the book is that out of these rather 'promising' murderers of women from 1839 to 1844, all three can be ruled out, with certainty, of being the Foreigner who murdered Eliza Grimwood in 1838; nor is there anything to suggest that any of them had any involvement in the murders of Eliza Davies or Mr Westwood. Their age and general appearance were wholly inconsistent with that of the Foreigner, who was after all seen by a number of independent witnesses, who provided similar descriptions of him.

THE MAIN SUSPECT

Lord William Russell was born in 1767, the son of Francis Russell, the Marquess of Tavistock, and the grandson of John Russell, the fourth Duke of Bedford.[1] His father had died young, from the fall off a spirited horse, and his mother had also expired soon after, allegedly from a broken heart. Lord William was educated at Westminster School, where he did not shine; he never attended any university. Like many members of his distinguished family, Lord William took up politics, and he was elected as a Whig Member of Parliament for Surrey in 1789. The same year, he married Lady Charlotte

Villiers, the eldest daughter of the Earl of Jersey; the marriage was a happy one, and produced seven children. When Lady Charlotte died prematurely in 1808, Lord William mourned her bitterly, and he made a habit of always carrying a gold locket containing a curl of her hair.[2]

Lord William Russell in middle age.

Lord William Russell's two elder brothers succeeded as the fifth and sixth Dukes of Bedford, and his nephew Lord John Russell became a distinguished politician. Although Lord William was an ardent Whig himself and sat in Parliament for many years, his political colleagues unflatteringly described him as a 'zero' and 'an accomplished driveller'. It was even commented that in spite of his many years in the Commons, he 'never discovered any particular aptitude for business, nor did he often appear in debate'. Lord William dabbled in art and sculpture, and assisted his brother in building up his famous collection at Woburn Abbey. A painting of Lord William in middle age shows a distinguished-looking gentleman, dressed in fashionable attire. He spent much time abroad, travelling aimlessly around Italy and Switzerland. His nephew and namesake, whom he joined in Florence in 1822, wrote that 'He appears such an unhappy wandering spirit that I was glad to offer him a home, but he is too restless to remain in it & wanders about from tavern to tavern without knowing why or wherefore. I quite pity him'.[3]

In the late 1830s, when his daughters were married and his surviving sons settled in life, Lord William took up residence at No. 14 Norfolk Street near Park Lane. This street had been laid out in the 1750s, and all its houses had been occupied by 1761. The houses on the west side were grander than those on the east, and had short gardens extending to Park Lane. Lord William's house on the east side of Norfolk Street was a tall and narrow terraced Georgian town house with a lower ground floor and four upper floors. The kitchen, scullery and butler's pantry were on the lower ground floor, and the dining room on the ground floor. Lord William had his drawing room and writing room on the first floor and his bedroom and dressing room on the second. The third floor housed the servants' bedrooms.

PORTRAIT OF LORD WILLIAM RUSSELL, *Engraved specially for Cleave's Penny Gazette of Variety,*

Lord William Russell in old age, from *Cleave's Penny Gazette* of 16 May 1840.

LORD WILLIAM RUSSELL'S HOUSE,
No. 14; NORFOLK STREET, PARK LANE, LONDON.
His Lordship's Bed-room was on the Second-floor, fronting the street.

Lord William Russell's house, No. 14 Norfolk Street, not far from Park Lane. From the *Penny Satirist* of 16 May 1840.

In 1840, when Lord William Russell was 73 years old, he remained in reasonable health, although hampered by asthma, deafness and a serious rupture that forced him to wear a truss day and night. A drawing of him shows an eccentric-looking, bald-headed, edentulous old cove. Although fully compos mentis, his habits were decidedly whimsical. For unknown reasons, he liked to put his watch in his mouth, and once, when he had lost his timepiece, some person suggested that he must have swallowed it by mistake. In 1840, the Duchess of Bedford described him as 'Old William, who chatters more and more to himself every day'. Lord William had a large white sheepdog, of which he was very fond; he commissioned several paintings of his faithful canine companion, and exhibited them in the house. The elderly nobleman daily exercised this formidable animal in Hyde Park nearby; the dog did not live in the house at Norfolk Street, but was kennelled in the Ham Yard mews behind the property. There were two women servants employed at No. 14 Norfolk Street: the cook Mary Hannel and the housemaid Sarah Mancer. There had also been a footman named James Ellis, but he had left in late March 1840, to enter the service of the Earl of Mansfield. Lord William decided that the 24-year-old Swiss valet François Benjamin Courvoisier should become his successor, with a salary of £45 per annum.

★ ★ ★

François Benjamin Courvoisier was born in 1816, in the small Swiss village of Mont-la-Ville, where he had been educated at the local school before becoming a labourer at his father Abraham's small farm. He had a sister, who went to live in Paris. He had come to London in early 1836, to join his uncle Mr L. Courvoisier, who had worked as the butler to a wealthy baronet, named in a newspaper as Sir George Beaumont, for not less than eighteen years. Since Courvoisier could speak no English at all, the only employment his uncle could help him secure was that of hotel servant at the French-speaking Hotel du Port de Dieppe, kept by Messrs Piolaine and Vincent, and situated at No. 2 Leicester Place, near Leicester Square. After about a month, he moved to a larger and more respectable hotel, the Hotel Bristol in Jermyn Street. Courvoisier learnt English with alacrity, and later in 1836 his uncle managed to get him a post as footman to Lady Julia

Lockwood. He stayed there for seven months, before becoming second footman to the wealthy Dover banker Mr John Minet Fector MP. He was based at Mr Fector's London town house in Park Lane, but occasionally accompanied his master to his country residence at Kearsney Abbey near Dover, and to his Scottish country estate. Although strictly supervised by Mr Fector's butler, Courvoisier took every opportunity to enjoy the London nightlife; he had ideas above his station in life and was very fond of the ladies. At Mr Fector's Scottish estate, he once visited a wedding in Thornhill, where his dancing aptitude was much admired.[4] Although he looked older than his age (journalists presumed him to be 30 years old in 1840, rather than just 24), he was far from ugly, in spite of a low and receding brow, and keen always to be dapperly dressed. He spoke excellent English, with the French accent still audible.

The reason Courvoisier left Mr Fector's large and wealthy household, and joined the elderly misanthrope Lord William Russell's frugal abode in Norfolk Street instead, may well have been that Mr Fector's butler had disapproved of his partying habits in London's low life, and his partiality to young ladies of dubious virtue. Perhaps he reasoned that in a smaller household, where he was the only manservant, routines would be slacker, giving him more time for his nocturnal revels. Still, it must be remarked that neither Lady Julia Lockwood nor Mr Fector had any complaints about Courvoisier's conduct: they thought him a good and attentive servant without any tendencies to laziness or dishonesty, and gave him excellent references. But the cantankerous Lord William Russell soon found faults with Courvoisier: he was slothful, unpunctual and generally unreliable, and this earned him more than one tongue-lashing from his elderly employer. Once, when Lord William had visited Kew, a gold locket had been lost, and Courvoisier had been blamed for not taking proper care of it.

On the morning of 5 May 1840, Lord William Russell had his breakfast and attended to his correspondence, before giving Courvoisier a number of messages. The elderly nobleman left the house on foot at half past twelve, walking with the aid of a stick. One of his messages was to have the bell-wire in his bedroom tightened, and this was done by an upholsterer, with good success. In the afternoon, the footman Henry Carr, in the employ of Mr Fector in Park Lane nearby, came calling to see his former colleague Courvoisier.

The Swiss valet was pleased to see him, and invited him in to have tea with the other servants in the household; they had quite a jolly time, until the coachman William York, who lived in the coach-house in the mews behind No. 14 Norfolk Street, and who took care of Lord William's dog, came calling at a quarter past five. With a start, Courvoisier remembered that one of Lord William's orders had been to send York to pick him up from Brooks's Club at five o'clock in the brougham!

York dashed off in the brougham, but when he reached Brooks's, it turned out that Lord William had already left the premises. Back at No. 14 Norfolk Street, Courvoisier bragged to the two female servants that he would still be able to extricate himself from the situation, since his elderly employer's memory was quite defective, and he would not remember at what time he had asked to be picked up at his club. But when Lord William arrived home in a hansom cab, his memory turned out to be in good working order, and he treated the scapegrace Courvoisier to another well-deserved tongue-lashing.

After the brougham debacle, Lord William's day returned to its usual routine: he sat down to dinner at seven o'clock, and was waited upon by Courvoisier, and then he went up to his drawing-room. York came to collect the dog at nine, and an hour later Lord William rang for his China tea. Mary Hannel went out in the evening, but Courvoisier and Sarah Mancer remained at No. 14 Norfolk Street and had their evening supper together. The Swiss valet was in a gloomy frame of mind: he regretted that he had ever entered Lord William's service, since his lordship was always so very cross and peevish. He quite startled his fellow servant when he angrily exclaimed, 'Billy is a rum old chap. If I had half his money, I would not remain long in England!' When Mary Hannel returned home later in the evening, Courvoisier offered to go out and fetch her a tankard of beer for her belated supper. This offer surprised both his fellow servants, since although the young Swiss enjoyed quite a decent salary, he was normally disposed to spend it entirely on his own amusements in London low life. The thirsty Mary Hannel swigged hard at the tankard of beer, and Sarah Mancer also had a small glass, after drinking which she felt quite drowsy. Still, she was able to prepare Lord William's bedroom for the night, and light the fire in the hearth. His lordship went to bed not long after, followed by his two tired female domestics. The stage had been set, and the opportunistic killer had his sights set on his elderly victim. Without his faithful canine companion, the feeble old Lord William lay in his bed alone and unprotected, while his two female servants slept soundly in their beds on the floor above. The spectre of murder, late of Frederick Street, Wellington Terrace and Princes Street, was once more on the prowl, and death would be the result of its nocturnal visitation to the unsuspecting household at No. 14 Norfolk Street.

* * *

On Wednesday 6 May 1840, Sarah Mancer woke up at six o'clock, got dressed and headed downstairs; the cook Mary Hannel, who had swigged hard from the (adulterated?) beer the evening before, slept deeply and could not be roused. When Sarah went downstairs, she saw that the door to Lord William's writing room was wide open, and that the room itself was in much disorder, like it had been searched by an intruder intent on plunder. Lord

MURDER OF LORD WILLIAM RUSSELL.

The Valet and the Housemaid discovering the Murdered Body of their Master.

The discovery of the murder of Lord William Russell, from *Cleave's Penny Gazette* of 16 May 1840.

William's Davenport writing table had been knocked over, and wads of letters and documents protruded from its drawers; even more correspondence was strewn on the floor. Lord William's bunch of keys, which he never allowed to leave his keeping, lay on the hearth rug, and a screwdriver was on the seat of a chair. Suspecting that the house had been burgled during the night, Sarah Mancer continued downstairs. At the front door, which was unchained and unbolted, lay a pile of articles purloined from the house: Lord William's large blue evening cloak, his gold-mounted opera glasses, his silver trinket box, and his gold pencil case, among other small gold or silver articles tied up in a napkin. The door to the ground-floor dining room was ajar, and the floor was scattered with silver forks and spoons. Sarah dashed upstairs and did her best to rouse the drowsy Mary Hannel. She then knocked on Courvoisier's door, and although the Swiss valet was normally very fond of his morning's sleep, he promptly answered the door fully dressed. She asked him if he knew of anything being the matter last night, as she expressed it, and he answered in the negative. When she explained that the silver and other valuables were strewn about, and that the house might well have been burgled, he went downstairs with her, and into the butler's pantry, exclaiming, 'My God, some one has been robbing us!' Sarah urged him, 'For God's sake let us go and see where his lordship is!' and they went up to the bedroom. When Courvoisier opened the shutters to the middle one of the three windows to the street, Sarah could see that the bed and pillows were full of blood, and she called out, 'My lord!' but Lord William did not stir. Not daring to examine the situation any further, she gave a scream and ran out of the room and upstairs to her own bedroom, then downstairs again and out into the street, where she frantically rang the bell at No. 22 and No. 23 Norfolk Street opposite. She managed to tell the other servants answering the door that the household at No. 14 had been burgled, that her master was lying still in his bloodstained bed and that he had almost certainly been murdered.

The Norfolk Street servants promptly sent for the police and a doctor. When Sarah Mancer returned into the house, she was surprised to find Courvoisier sitting on a chair in the dining room, scribbling on a small piece of paper. When she asked him, 'What the devil do you sit here for, why don't you go out and see for some one, or a doctor?' he calmly answered that he was writing to Lord William's son in Cheshunt Place. The doctor and the

The entrance of the Policeman and the Housemaid, on the Discovery of the Murder of Lord William Russell.

DISCOVERY OF THE MURDER OF LORD WILLIAM RUSSELL, AT HIS RESIDENCE, IN NORFOLK PLACE, PARK LANE.

Lord William Russell discovered to be Murdered.

Three other views of the discovery of the murder, from the *Penny Satirist* of 16 May 1840, the *Sunday Times and People's Police Gazette* of 17 May 1840, and an unknown newspaper.

police constable inspected Lord William's bedroom, and found him stone dead in his blood-soaked bed, with his throat cut with great violence. This was clearly a case of murder, and as soon as Inspector John Tedman, of the 'D' or Marylebone Division of the New Police, had arrived, the police took possession of the murder house. They found a gloomy-looking Courvoisier skulking in the pantry, moaning that as a result of the murder, he would lose both his place and his character.

Courvoisier told Inspector Tedman that No. 14 Norfolk Street must have been broken into from the rear yard. He showed the policemen some modest damage to the rear door, the top bolt of which was hanging by only one screw. Inspector Tedman thought that the damage to the door and the doorpost did not correspond, however, and all the screws were very rusty and brittle. The other doors to the house showed no signs of having been tampered with. If Courvoisier was right, then the intruder or intruders must have managed to scale the high wall to the rear yard, although the whitewashing showed no marks at all, before making use of a ladder to descend, and break open the wooden basement door instead of the glass-panelled one up the steps.

Inspector Tedman was surprised that the drawing room, which was full of valuables, remained entirely untouched, and also that many objects of value had simply been left behind in the hall, something no experienced burglar would ever have done. Courvoisier admitted that the screwdriver found on a chair in Lord William's writing room was his own, and that it normally belonged in a toolbox kept in the pantry. When Lord William's body was inspected, the Swiss valet appeared calm and collected, as if seeing mangled bodies and blood-spattered rooms was something he did at regular intervals. Inspector Tedman speculated that Lord William had been attacked and murdered when he was still asleep in bed. The washstand in his bedroom was entirely clean, indicating that the killer had not cleaned himself in this room; nor was any basin full of bloodstained water found elsewhere in the murder house. Having recovered from her early morning hysterics, Sarah Mancer gave clear and accurate answers to Inspector Tedman's questions about her observations, and she generally gave a good impression. Nor did the still drowsy Mary Hannel appear to have anything to hide. Tedman cautioned all three domestics at No. 14 Norfolk Street that they must not leave the premises, speak to any person, or do any cleaning or sweeping inside the house.

Two scenes from the early investigation of the murder of Lord William Russell, from the *Sunday Times and People's Police Gazette* of 24 May 1840.

At this early stage of the murder investigation, the police could discern three different scenarios when it came to the planning and perpetration of the crime: either one or two inexperienced burglars had broken into the house, having chosen it more or less at random, and panicked and fled after murdering Lord William; or a burglar turned murderer had been let into the house by one of the servants; or the murder was an 'inside job' committed by Courvoisier. Still, it spoke in the Swiss valet's favour that his demeanour after murder had been very cool and confident, and that his clothes were not at all stained with blood.

★ ★ ★

For several reasons, it was considered desirable to hold the coroner's inquest on Lord William Russell immediately, on the evening of 6 May, the same day the murder had been discovered. Firstly, the influential Russell family wanted to scotch the persistent rumours that Lord William had committed suicide; secondly, Lord William's son was keen to have the body removed to his own house to make preparations for the funeral; thirdly, it was considered a good idea to get the inquest out of the way to allow the police to proceed with their investigations. Accordingly, Mr Thomas Higgs, the Deputy Coroner for Westminster, opened the inquest at half past five, at the City of Norwich Arms public house in Norfolk Street. The Marquess of Normanby and several others of high degree were present as spectators. The coroner and the fifteen jurymen saw the body and inspected every room in the murder house. Mr Henry Elsgood, surgeon, of No. 91 Park Street, and his colleague Mr J. Nursey, of Cleveland Row, testified that this was definitely a case of murder. Firstly, Lord William Russell's throat had been cut with great force; secondly, the murder weapon was nowhere to be found; thirdly, the killer had covered Lord William's face with a towel after the deed. The Constable John Baldwin testified that in spite of the damage to the lower-ground-floor back door of No. 14 Norfolk Street, there was nothing to suggest that an intruder had forced an entrance that way.

When Courvoisier's box had been ransacked, a purse containing a £5 note and six sovereigns had been found, but as cool as a cucumber, the Swiss valet had said that he had once given Lord William five sovereigns for the note. Courvoisier was himself the next witness. Repeating his earlier testimony to the police with calmness and authority, he gave a very good impression, particularly since the helpful Mr Fector had given him an excellent character before the opening of the inquest. After Sarah Mancer had briefly given evidence about her observations the morning after the murder, Mr Higgs asked the foreman of the jury whether he wished any other witnesses to be called. Being no close student of the case, the foreman answered in the negative, and the jury returned a verdict of murder against some person or persons unknown. The coroner agreed with this verdict, commenting that it would allay idle public speculation, and discredit false rumours about the cause of Lord William's death.

A few of the London papers, like *The Standard* and the *Morning Post*, managed to provide a brief outline of the murder of Lord William Russell already in their late editions of 6 May, giving the bare facts of the tragedy and pointing out that the police had taken possession of the murder house.[5] On 7 and 8 May, all the London newspapers featured the murder of Lord William Russell.[6] The venerable age of the deceased nobleman, his great name and influential family, and the ferocity of the mysterious deed, all contributed to great public excitement. The papers gave a full account of the inquest, adding that Lord William's funeral was scheduled for Tuesday 12 May. The murdered nobleman's eldest son Lieutenant-Colonel Francis Russell had died unmarried in 1837, and his younger brother Commander John Russell had also predeceased his father, but one son and two married daughters

THE POLICEMAN SHEWING COURVOSIER, THE ARTICLES FOUND IN THE PANTRY.

DISCOVERY OF LORD W. RUSSELL'S PURSE IN THE PANTRY OF HIS VALET

CORRECT PORTRAIT OF LORD RUSSELL.

FUNERAL OF LORD RUSSELL.

Four scenes from the investigation of the murder of Lord William Russell, from the *Sunday Times and People's Police Gazette* of 24 May 1840.

were still alive. The newspapers pointed out that the police investigation of the murder was in good hands, the commissioners Richard Mayne and Colonel Rowan personally having inspected the murder house. As a result of contradictory police bulletins from the inventories of the missing articles in the murder house, there were various contradictory articles about the items stolen. The newspapers vaguely supported the burglary hypothesis, although false rumours had been circulating that Courvoisier had already been arrested. After denying these rumours, the *Morning Post* issued a description of him:

'The valet is a young man, apparently about 25 years of age, having very dark hair and eyes, brown complexion, and regular handsome features.'[7] *The Times* pointed out that this was the second dreadful murder taking place in the district within a short period: the similarities between the unsolved slaying of Mr Westwood in 1839 and the current Norfolk Street outrage were only too obvious, and the newspaper hoped that the exertions of the New Police in capturing the murderer would be more successful in the present case.[8]

★ ★ ★

On 8, 9 and 10 May, Norfolk Street was crowded with well-dressed people, a great portion of whom were female, who had come to see the murder house.[9] There was much speculation what was going on inside, and whether Courvoisier would be arrested. There was a government reward of £200 for the apprehension of the murderer, which was matched with another £200 from the Russell family. The police had received a letter from a certain 'W.B.', stating that he had murdered Lord William and then left for the Continent, but they did not attach much value to this communication, since they knew that practical jokers were in the habit of sending such letters in cases of much-publicised London murders.[10] Inspectors Pearce and Tedman had tracked down Henry Carr, whom they suspected of being Courvoisier's accomplice, but he managed to convince them that he had nothing to do with the murder. Nor was there anything to suggest that a proper burglary had taken place, and the police were becoming convinced that Courvoisier was the guilty man, possibly with an outside accomplice. Importantly, two bank notes, a Waterloo medal and some gold sovereigns were found hidden in the scullery, where Courvoisier would have had the opportunity to deposit them. With his habitual coolness, the Swiss valet denied any knowledge of these objects, but the police thought he was lying; why, if there had been an outside accomplice, would this individual not have absconded with the gold coins and bank notes? Late in the evening of 10 May, Courvoisier was clandestinely arrested and taken to the Bow Street police station, where he was charged with murder and locked up in the cells.

On 11 May, Courvoisier was examined in the station house at Bow Street. Mr Hobler, the solicitor for the police commissioners, attended to

FRANCOIS BENJAMIN COURVOISIER,
{*Valet to, and Charged with the Murder of the Late Lord* WILLIAM RUSSELL

Francois Benjamin Courvoisier,

SENTENCED TO DEATH ON THE 20TH OF JUNE, 1840,

FOR THE MURDER OF HIS MASTER, LORD WILLIAM RUSSELL.

Three drawings of a dark-haired, villainous-looking Courvoisier, from the *Penny Satirist* of 23 May 1840, *Cleave's Penny Gazette* of 27 June 1840, and Major Arthur Griffiths' *Chronicles of Newgate*.

prosecute, and the solicitor Mr Flower, of Hatton Garden, represented the prisoner. Inspector Pearce gave evidence about the finding of Lord William's mangled body, the verdict of the coroner's inquest, and the important find of the valuables hidden away in the scullery. A chisel found in a box in the butler's pantry, which Courvoisier admitted belonged to him, corresponded to the marks on the plate drawer, and the screwdriver found on a chair also appeared to have been used when breaking into Lord William's plate cupboard. Questioned by Mr Flower, Inspector Pearce had to admit that several people had been in the house at the time he had found the stolen goods in the scullery. The prisoner was remanded in custody for three days, and sent to the New Prison, Tothill Fields.

The funeral of Lord William Russell took place on 12 May just as planned: his lordship's remains were put to rest in the Russell family mausoleum at Chenies Church, Buckinghamshire. His only surviving son Mr William Russell was in attendance, as were his two daughters, many other Russells of high degree, and a great many other members of the nobility and gentry. The police were represented by Inspector Tedman and Sergeant Smith, both appropriately attired in deep mourning, and a troop of local constables. Performing the ceremony, the Rev. Mr Bowers struck his head hard against a projecting stone when descending into the vault, and received a severe contusion to the forehead, but this did not prevent him from conducting the remainder of the funeral in a becoming and solemn manner.[11]

As for the prisoner Courvoisier, further examinations at Bow Street followed on 14, 23 and 27 May, and the available evidence was thoroughly sifted. Fourteen silver spoons and forks with the Russell family crest, some French gold coins, and a gold ear trumpet, were still missing from Lord William's effects, and the police had been searching the murder house to find out if Courvoisier had been hiding these valuables on the premises, or whether they had been carried off by an accomplice. Defended by Mr Flower, Courvoisier seemed as calm and collected as ever, and he made no admission of guilt. There was nothing to suggest that his clothes had been stained with blood, and the murder weapon was nowhere to be found. There was newspaper speculation that Courvoisier might have thrown the murder weapon into the back garden of another house, from his third-floor bedroom window, but the police retorted that all gardens had been searched without anything interesting being found. On 29 May, Courvoisier was committed to Newgate, awaiting trial at the Old Bailey for murdering Lord William Russell. Many people still believed that he was innocent: Sir George Beaumont contributed £50 to his defence, and a subscription was raised among the foreign servants of London. John Minet Fector also contributed to Courvoisier's defence, and promised to take him back as a footman after he had been acquitted.

★ ★ ★

Awaiting trial, Courvoisier was consoled by the Swiss clergyman Charles Baup, of the French Protestant Church in London, who had been asked to intervene by the prisoner's grieving parents back in Switzerland, since they had heard that he would stand trial for murder in London and risked being hanged.[12] Like everyone else, Baup found the Swiss valet a very cool customer, who gave nothing away and maintained an admirable composure throughout his ordeal. The experienced Mr John Adolphus was retained for the prosecution, and after he had consulted with his two juniors Bodkin and Chambers, and inspected the murder house, he wrote in his diary, 'I have not the slightest doubt of the wretch's guilt, but many are of the opinion that the Jury will not convict on circumstantial evidence, and I am far from being sure that they are mistaken.'[13] Courvoisier was defended by the eloquent Irish barrister Charles Phillips, who was known for his unconventional tactics: from his diary, it is clear that Mr Adolphus was more than a little concerned what antics his opponent would be up to in court.

When the trial of François Benjamin Courvoisier, for the murder of Lord William Russell, commenced on 18 June, before Chief Justice Sir Nicholas Tindale and Baron Parke, the court was crowded with people of nobility and distinction.[14] The Duke of Sussex was present, as were the Duke of Bedford and Marquis Saldanha, the Portuguese Ambassador. Mr Adolphus opened proceedings with a lengthy speech, going through the case from beginning to end, and presenting a mass of circumstantial evidence against Courvoisier. The Swiss valet had been discontented with his situation, angry with his master and envious of his wealth. There was no evidence that the house had been burgled in the first place, and surely, if burglars had broken into the house, they would have taken all the available valuables with them, and not left banknotes, gold and silver behind. A rush light in Lord William's room had been lit by Sarah Mancer, and later extinguished by the murderer; experiments showed that it had been burning for an hour and a half, indicating that the murder had taken place close to midnight. The house had been searched by some person who had a good idea where the valuables were stored, and who but Courvoisier would have had anything to gain from hiding the bank notes and gold coins in the scullery? Pointing out Courvoisier's Swiss descent, he pontificated that foreigners believe that English noblemen carry vast sums of gold with them, and that with foreigners murder was often a prelude to

Courvoisier on trial, from the *Penny Satirist* of 27 June 1840.

robbery, for they imagined that if they had murdered the victim, there would be no testimony against them.

Sarah Mancer was the first witness. She described feeling very tired after drinking the beer that Courvoisier had fetched for her, and suspected that something noxious had been put in it. When she gave the alarm in the street after Lord William had been discovered, she had said that his lordship had been murdered. Charles Phillips did his best to confound her: had she not testified, at the inquest, that she had just seen that there was blood on the pillow? Mary Hannel, the cook, was the next witness: she had also felt very tired and sleepy after drinking the beer, although she had to admit that it had had no unpleasant taste. When cross-examined, Constable John Baldwin had to admit that at the inquest he had testified that the back door had been forced from the outside, although he objected that he had later found that he was mistaken. Baldwin was harshly treated by Mr Phillips, who forced him to admit that he had read about the £400 reward posted and that he thought this a great amount of money.

The following day, the audacious Charles Phillips did his best to harry the policemen, implying that they had decided to 'frame' Courvoisier to get their hands on the reward. Inspector Tedman had to admit that there were marks on the back door of the house that had not been there when he first examined it. Courvoisier had seemed very calm and collected throughout his ordeal, almost as if he had committed murder before, and was confident that he would get off scot-free. Fourteen silver forks and spoons, a gold ear-trumpet, and some minor articles were still missing from the house. Inspector Pearce admitted that he had made some marks on the back door of the house, while carrying out some experiments. When the bank notes and gold coins had been found in the scullery, he had shown them to Courvoisier and exclaimed, 'Can you look me in the face and say you know nothing about these things?' in order to force an admission, although he denied doing so in order to stake a claim for the reward. This concluded the case for the prosecution.

Lady Julia Lockwood and Mr Fector both testified that whilst in their employ, Courvoisier had been a harmless and inoffensive young man, on good terms with his colleagues, and a quiet and efficient servant. The proprietor and waiter at the Hotel Bristol in Jermyn Street also had nothing but good to say about the prisoner's character. Mr Adolphus appears to have been rather worried that there would not be sufficient evidence to get Courvoisier convicted for murder. In the evening of 19 June he went for a consultation with the Attorney-General, to discuss the prosecution of Edward Oxford, who had taken a shot at Queen Victoria as she came past him in her carriage. As he emerged from this meeting, he was informed that there had been important developments in the Courvoisier case. Madame Charlotte Piolaine, the manageress of the Hotel du Port de Dieppe in Leicester Place, had come to the police to tell them that six weeks earlier, a young man known to her as 'Jean', who had once worked at the hotel, had come to deposit a parcel with her. Her cousin Joseph Vincent had read about the trial of Courvoisier in the newspaper, and the missing forks and spoons in particular, and he had started to suspect that 'Jean' was identical to the Swiss valet, and that the surprisingly heavy parcel contained the stolen goods. Vincent and Madame Piolaine took the parcel to a solicitor, where it was opened and found to contain the stolen forks, spoons and ear-trumpet, wrapped up with a jacket and a pair of stockings. The police took Madame Piolaine to Newgate, where she at once identified Courvoisier as the man who had given her the parcel.[15]

On 20 June, the third and final day of the trial, Charlotte Piolaine was the first witness. When Courvoisier saw her in court, he went deathly pale and trembled like a leaf. Although Mr Phillips tried to confound Madame Piolaine as best he could, implying that the Hotel du Port de Dieppe was a gambling-den and a hideout for thieves, she confidently described how 'Jean' had asked her to keep a parcel for him, and she identified the prisoner in the dock as that very man. Joseph Vincent and the solicitor Richard Cumming, who had opened the parcel, gave corroborative evidence. Two witnesses identified the ear-trumpet as that of Lord William, and the spoons and forks had the Russell crest. The jacket matched one worn by Courvoisier while in the service of Mr Fector, and a washerwoman identified the stockings as belonging to the prisoner. The print-seller Mr Molteno identified the paper the parcel was wrapped up with as that he himself had used to pack up a print that Lord William had purchased.

The appearance of the last-minute witness Madame Piolaine was a hard blow to Charles Phillips, but although he must have realised that all was lost for his client, he made an eloquent three-hour speech, pointing out the docile and law-abiding nature of the Swiss, and describing Courvoisier as a friendless young man in a hostile foreign country, surrounded by crooked policemen who wanted to 'frame' him for the murder and divide the reward money over his coffin. If Madame Piolaine's evidence was at all true, it was conclusive of robbery rather than of murder. Chief Justice Tindale summed up the case in an even-handed manner, warning the jury not to be misled by the exhortations of the legal counsel on either side: he left it to them to decide whether the murder and the robbery had been perpetrated by different men, and whether there had been a burglary at all. After the recovery of the ear-trumpet and the spoons and forks, there was nothing to suggest that thieves had removed any property from the murder house, however. The jury was out for an hour and twenty-five minutes before returning a verdict of guilty, and Chief Justice Tindale sentenced Courvoisier to death.

As Courvoisier languished in the condemned cell in Newgate, he tried a final roll of the dice to save himself from the gallows. On 22 June, he wrote a full confession, saying that he had read a very wicked book about a profligate young man of good family, who made a jolly life for himself by thieving and living off his wits. Courvoisier had decided to follow in the footsteps of the hero of this book, but as he was stealing Lord William's property, the elderly nobleman caught him in the act and threatened to dismiss him without a character. The Swiss valet thought the only way to save himself was to murder Lord William. But although Courvoisier later 'improved on' his confession by stating that he had been led astray after pilfering some wine and drinking it, he was not believed. The murder had been premeditated, and had been committed with impressive coolness and cunning; the story of Lord William going back to bed after confronting a thief in his own house did not appear particularly credible.[16] The motive for the Swiss valet to be telling sob-stories about being led astray by a wicked book, and being drunk from drinking wine when he committed the murder, was of course that he was hoping for a late reprieve.

★ ★ ★

On 24 June, *The Times* newspaper had quite an extraordinary story to tell, one that was spread to the other London newspapers the following day. It deserves to be given in full:

> A circumstance has just been communicated to us which, were it not for the confidence we have every reason to place in our informant, we should consider wholly incredible. He assures us, upon authority in such a case is unquestionable, that the miscreant who is now in Newgate under sentence of death for the murder of Lord William Russell has confessed that he is also guilty of the murder of Eliza Grimwood, an unfortunate woman, who, as it will be remembered, was found about two years since in a house in the Waterloo-road under circumstances which left no doubt that a murder had been committed, although the utmost ingenuity of the police could never discover a clue by which the criminal could be traced.
>
> It appeared at the time, from what meagre evidence could be procured, that the crime had probably been committed by a foreigner; but the absence of any apparent motive, or of any article of property by which the murderer could be identified, rendered it, as in the late melancholy occasion, impossible until now to connect any person with the crime.

> We give this information as we have heard it, but we are further informed that means have been taken to prevent this confession from being made known to the public, and that the most strict injunctions have been laid on all persons admitted to the prisoner to preserve reserved the most scrupulous silence upon the subject.[17]

The Times journalist deplored the excessive secrecy with regard to Courvoisier's confession to the murder of Eliza Grimwood: surely, more action should have been taken, and his statements should have been compared with the evidence given at the coroner's inquest on Eliza Grimwood. With regard to the motive for the authorities in trying to suppress Courvoisier's confession, the newspaper speculated that they wanted to avoid public excitement ahead of the execution. Then as well as now, *The Times* was considered a very reliable newspaper, and the story of Courvoisier confessing to the murder of Eliza Grimwood was widely reported in the press, from the London papers to the provincial ones, not excluding even the Dublin *Freeman's Journal*. A writer in the *Globe* declared himself wholly unconvinced, however, accusing the venerable *Times* of publishing 'a mischievous string of monstrous falsehoods, for which there is not, and never was, the slightest ground'. Nor did a *Standard* journalist believe in the story of Courvoisier's confession, claiming:

> There is no foundation whatever for the story of Courvoisier's having confessed himself the murderer of Eliza Grimwood, given in a respected morning contemporary. So far our authority, which is the best. For ourselves we may add, that the murderer of Eliza Grimwood is, we believe, perfectly well known to be a detestable miscreant who, in this country, moved in a much higher rank than Courvoisier, and is now supposed to be somewhere in Italy, of which he is a native.[18]

On 25 June, *The Times* unexpectedly retracted its report of Courvoisier confessing to the murder of Eliza Grimwood. The rumour had been circulated through town on Monday and Tuesday (22 and 23 June), and *The Times* had 'our information from a source on which we were disposed to place full reliance', but nevertheless the story had proved not to be true.[19] The other

London newspapers crowed at this lapse of judgement, and subsequent eating of humble pie, from the normally so reliable *Times*.[20] To rub salt into the wounds, the *Era* published what was supposed to be a conversation between Sheriff Evans and Courvoisier in Newgate. The Sheriff said: 'I am most anxious to know whether there is any foundation in the report which has got abroad that you had something to do with the death of Eliza Grimwood, who was murdered in the Waterloo-road. Have you anything to say upon that subject?' In response Courvoisier assured him that 'he knew nothing in the world about that or any other murder, except the murder of Lord William Russell. He knew that he must die, and if he had committed any other dreadful offence, he would not have hesitated to mention the fact to the Sheriff.'[21] Thus, after a few days of exultation that one of London's modern murder mysteries had been solved after more than two years had gone by, the enthusiasm about the newspaper story of Courvoisier's confession to the murder of Eliza Grimwood quickly petered out.

In spite of the retraction from *The Times*, there is reason not to dismiss the story of Courvoisier adding other murders to his confession, but changing his mind when facing Sheriff Evans. In 2006, I purchased a copy of an old crime book, *Guilty or Not Guilty* by Guy Logan. The book had pasted in a dedication from Logan to a certain Peter Farrin, with a signature that matches that on a photograph of Logan in his book *Dramas of the Dock*. Interestingly, the book also turned out to contain a typewritten note on yellowing paper.[22] This 'Logan Memorandum' is reproduced in full in this book, along with the photograph and dedication; the two first sections are those of interest:

> The house in Wellington Terrace where Eliza Grimwood was murdered in
> -38, is the twelfth house from the bridge. The late George R. Sims told me,
> that when Courvoisier was in Newgate, he wanted to confess to two murders
> of unfortunate young women, but his uncle persuaded him to remain silent.

This statement would seem to confirm the *Times* report of Courvoisier's confession to the murder of Eliza Grimwood. Importantly, London only had two unsolved murders of young women in the relevant period of time: those of Eliza Davis in 1837 and Eliza Grimwood in 1838. The reader should note that when questioned by Sheriff Evans, Courvoisier

A signed photograph of Guy Logan, from his book *Dramas of the Dock*, the dedication to Peter Farrin, and the entire 'Logan Memorandum'.

The house in Wellington Terrace where Eliza Grimwood was murdered in -38, is the twelfth house from the bridge.
The late George R. Sims told me, that when Courvoisier was in Newgate, he wanted to confess to two murders of unfortunate young women, but his uncle persuaded him to remain silent.
A saddler and harness maker set up in business in the shop where the Darbys had been butchered.
The houses in Burton Crescent, Euston Square and Great Coram Street can be visited in twenty minutes time.

spoke of more than one murder, without being prompted to do so by the sheriff's question.

Guy Logan was a distinguished historian of crime, who took particular interest in London houses where celebrated murders had taken place. He was the author of seven valuable true crime books, published between 1928 and 1935.[23] There is no doubt that he took an interest in the murder of Eliza Grimwood, and he several times mentioned it in his writings. In 1903, when he was active as a journalist at the old magazine *Famous Crimes Past & Present*, he provided an answer to a correspondent: 'Eliza Grimwood was murdered at 11, Wellington Terrace, Waterloo Road. These houses were only built in 1818. We shall give an account of this crime.'[24] This account of 'The Shocking Murder of Eliza Grimwood' was published five months later. Guy Logan found it curious that several people had been sleeping upstairs when the murder was committed: 'Our readers will remember that never a sound was heard as Jack the Ripper despatched his victims. It was from the same cause. The sudden slash of the knife and – silence.'[25] Logan gave an account of the murder, the Cavendish letter, the time-waster M'Millan, and the hatred and prejudice against Hubbard; he wrongly claimed that the latter had sought refuge in America. In 1905, Guy Logan again referred to the murder house at No. 12 Wellington Terrace, assuring his readers that in spite of the renumbering of the houses in Waterloo Road, it was still standing.[26] In his 1929 book *Guilty or Not Guilty*, Logan returns to the Grimwood mystery in a chapter about unsolved London murders of women:

[Eliza] was well known in that always doubtful neighbourhood, and the driver of a hackney coach was found who was able to identify her as a 'fare' he had picked up in the Strand on the night of the crime. She was accompanied by a man, and he drove them to the end of Waterloo Bridge on the Surrey side. The next morning the girl was found dead in her bedroom, with a fearful gash in her throat. The man had coolly stayed to wash his hands, had thrown the bed-clothes over the body, and calmly walked out of the place. Not a sound had been heard in the night, and no clue of any kind was left behind.[27]

This short account of the crime is likely to be the reason the 'Logan Memorandum' was put inside this very book.

George R. Sims was a well-known author, playwright and poet, remembered for 'Christmas Day in the Workhouse' and other overblown ballads.[28] Sims also took a serious interest in the criminal history of the metropolis; he expired in 1922, implying that the memorandum was written between that year and 1939, when the Grimwood murder house was pulled down. Most probably, it was written in the late 1920s, when Logan was active researching his books. It may be objected that there is no direct evidence as to his authorship of the memorandum, and that it could have been written by Farrin or by some other person. Guy Logan did eventually write about Courvoisier in his 1935 book *Wilful Murder*, but infuriatingly, he mentions nothing about the crucial information from Sims.[29] Still, there is good reason to presume that Logan *did* write the memorandum. The third section has the text, 'A saddler and harness maker set up in business where the Darbys had been butchered'. This refers to the murder of the Darby family (husband, wife and baby) by Edgar Edwards in the shop at No. 22 Wyndham Road, Camberwell. Guy Logan wrote about this case in one of his other books, stating that the shop 'had a very desolate look when I passed it some months afterwards, but, on going that way again two or three years later, I found

that a saddler and harness maker had set up in business there'.[30] This similarity would seem to prove that the memorandum was indeed written by Guy Logan.

George R. Sims was exceedingly popular in his own lifetime, and people likened him to Charles Dickens for his social conscience,

A postcard showing George R. Sims.

and his obvious sympathy for London's poor. When Sims joined the *Referee* newspaper in 1877, he assumed the pen name 'Dagonet' and wrote a weekly 'Mustard and Cress' column, which would continue for forty-five years until Sims died in harness. His punning and laborious wit, and frequent 'lapses into poetry', appealed to the literary taste of his contemporaries, and the 'Dagonet' column became enormously popular and did much to keep his name in the public eye. Sims also became known for his overblown and ultra-sentimental ballads like 'Christmas Eve in the Workhouse' and 'Billy's Rose', which were fashionable recital pieces in Victorian times. His plays, *The Lights of London* in particular, were equally popular, and provided Sims with a generous income, most of which he spent on gambling and high living. When liver trouble forced the hard-drinking Sims to take to the lemonade bottle, the ballads ceased completely, and the remainder of his output also became less sprightly.

George R. Sims was something of a snob, who liked to hobnob with those of high rank in society. He took a strong interest in London crimes and criminals, and built up his own criminal museum, containing objects like the knocker from Thurtell and Probert's murder cottage in Elstree, a kitchen chair from Mrs Pearcey's murder house, the hanging beam of old Newgate, a 'Jack the Ripper' letter, and various relics of the murderers Percy Lefroy Mapleton, Henry Wainwright, Herbert Bennett and James Canham Read. He belonged to the select Crimes Club, to which Guy Logan, who was a penny-a-line journalist connected with lowly publications like the *Illustrated Police News* and *Famous Crimes Past & Present*, could not aspire to obtain membership. Nevertheless, there are indications that the two men, who were united by their strong interest in London's criminal history, met more than once. In the 'Jack the Ripper' chapter in his 1928 book *Masters of Crime*, Guy Logan wrote that 'the late George R. Sims was fond of declaring that, in the end, the murderer's identity was known to the police'.[31] It would have been perfectly in character for the two men to have met and discussed famous Victorian criminal cases, like the murders of Eliza Grimwood and Lord William Russell. Where Sims had obtained the information about Courvoisier confessing to the murders of Eliza Davies and Eliza Grimwood cannot be ascertained. I have read quite a few of his 'Dagonet' columns in the *Referee*, but although Sims frequently discussed contemporary and historical London crimes, I found no evidence that he ever mentioned Courvoisier or Eliza Grimwood. The Courvoisier police file makes it clear that both before and after his conviction for murder, Courvoisier kept in touch with his uncle Mr L. Courvoisier, butler to Sir George Beaumont. Letters in the police file indicate that while languishing in the death cell in Newgate, Courvoisier was visited both by his uncle and by the clergyman Baup.[32] In a sudden fit of despondency, did the Ripper of Waterloo Road for once lose his cool, and make a reference to the full extent of his crimes, only for his horrified uncle, who did not want a serial killer in the family, to persuade him to keep quiet and deny everything when he was questioned by Sheriff Evans?

★ ★ ★

Apart from the newspaper report of his confession, and the 'Logan Memorandum', what evidence is there in favour of François Benjamin Courvoisier being the murderer of Eliza Grimwood, or even a serial killer with at least three or four victims?

Firstly, it is notable that he perfectly fits the description of the Foreigner who accompanied Eliza back to Waterloo Road, with regard to stature, build, and general appearance. Four witnesses stated that the Foreigner was between 5ft 7in and 5ft 8in tall; Courvoisier was stated to have been 5ft 7in in height. The seven witnesses who saw the Foreigner with Eliza described him as young, dark-haired and dapperly dressed; he spoke good English, with the French accent still clearly audible. Courvoisier came from Mont-la-Ville in the Canton du Vaud near Lausanne, a French-speaking part of Switzerland; two newspaper accounts agree that he also knew Italian, which had been his second language back in Switzerland.[33] One witness who saw him with Eliza, namely the waitress Charlotte Parker, thought he looked like a respectable gentleman's servant.[34] It is true that the old crime writer Yseult Bridges, who published a lengthy essay on the murder of Lord William Russell, described Courvoisier as having abundant straw-coloured hair, but here she was certainly mistaken: the contemporary press descriptions of him, the multiple likenesses of him, and his death mask at Madame Tussauds, all depict him with very dark brown hair.[35] Courvoisier's appearance and clothing is fully consistent with the witness observations of the Foreigner, on every point. He also fits the description of the young Frenchman who was the 'boyfriend' seen with Eliza Davies, and we may also speculate that he was one of the two murderers of Mr Westwood, seen fleetingly while making his escape with his countryman Carron. As we know, there were contemporary rumours that Eliza Grimwood and Mr Westwood had been murdered by the same man. The modus operandi was the same in all four cases of murder: Eliza Davies, Eliza Grimwood, Mr Westwood and Lord William Russell had all had their throats cut with great force.

In 1838 as well as now, French-speaking people were known for their reluctance to learn foreign languages. Since the options to learn English back in France or Switzerland were limited for all but the wealthy, the Foreigner must have been a resident of Britain, most probably London, for some time. How many young Frenchmen were there in London who could speak Italian, and also knew fluent English, and who perfectly matched the description of the Foreigner? Certainly not very many. The better class of London Frenchman was represented by those connected with the French Embassy, and a smattering of businessmen involved in the wine and grocery trades; these individuals could usually speak good English. At the lower end of the social spectrum, there were quite a few restaurant cooks and waiters, hotel servants of every degree, as well as a variety of mariners; these men were usually well-nigh monoglot. As a French-speaking gentleman's valet with five years of experience in various London households, and a great fondness for nocturnal amusements with the ladies, Courvoisier fits the profile of the Foreigner to perfection. In 1875, Laura Cecilia, Countess of Antrim, told Colonel Harold Malet that sometime in the late 1830s, Courvoisier had come home in the early hours of the morning, panting and bedraggled, and it was suspected that he had committed a murder or a highway robbery.[36]

We may also speculate about Eliza Grimwood's cryptic remark to her friend at the Strand Theatre, overheard by *The Times* reporter John Sharp: 'I am going out with ... He is here.' This sentence makes no sense whatsoever, but what if Eliza, who spoke no or little French, had in fact said, 'I am going out with Courvoisier', pronouncing his name 'Coor-voos-hier' like an English speaker would? Then there is the matter of the statement of

Catherine Edwin, namely that she thought the name of the Foreigner was very similar to that of one of the men who had taken a shot at the King of France. The chief conspirator in the attempt to assassinate King Louis Philippe in 1835 was Giuseppe Marco Fieschi, who was caught, tried and guillotined. Now compare the names, as pronounced by an English speaker: 'Fi-e-schi' and 'Coor-voos-hier'. Courvoisier was in London at the time of all four murders, and while the three convicted killers of women discussed in Chapter 13 could be excluded as the murderer of Eliza Grimwood, with the greatest of ease in all cases, there is nothing whatsoever to exclude Courvoisier as a suspect. It may be objected that it is uncommon for a serial killer to murder young women for the sake of perverted pleasure, and wealthy men for the purpose of gain, but then we have the talented Richard Brinkley, who murdered his prostitute girlfriends for kicks, before forging the will of an old lady, murdering her and trying to poison the person who witnessed the will but accidentally murdering two other people. The opportunist serial killer, who kills both for pleasure and for profit, may well be a rare phenomenon, but he does exist.[37]

In his confessions, Courvoisier never explained how he could avoid getting his clothes bloodstained while murdering Lord William. After all, the murder room was a dreadful sight, and liberally sprinkled with gore. It was considered surprising that there were no bloodstains in the remainder of the house, nor any bloody fingermarks on the doors. In his confession, Courvoisier just said that when he cut Lord William's throat, he had turned up the coat- and shirtsleeves of his right hand. This was manifestly impossible, however, and did not satisfy the curious, since the blood spatter was so very extensive, and would have deluged the remainder of his clothes. Later, before his execution, when he was again asked how he had avoided getting his clothes stained with blood, he delivered the same unsatisfactory explanation. According to John Adolphus, when Sheriff Evans once more asked Courvoisier the same question before he was taken to the scaffold, the murderer explained that he had committed the murder in a state of nudity.[38] This remarkable statement was never mentioned in any contemporary newspaper, and may well be untrue.

A story has been stewing for a long time that a profligate young lord, or possibly a general, had been visiting a lady in the house opposite Lord

William's residence. On the evening of the murder, he had seen a young man escalating the stairs with a lighted candle at No. 14 Norfolk Street. When he read about the murder in the newspapers, he realised that he had seen the murderer, but to protect the honour of his Norfolk Street lady friend, he initially did nothing at all. When one of the housemaids became a suspect, Lord X went to see his solicitor, since he alone knew that Courvoisier was the guilty man, but the solicitor advised him to wait a little. Not long after, Courvoisier was discovered to have pawned some of the stolen goods, and Lord X could remain silent.[39] Initially, this story seems to provide a neat explanation of what had happened, but it has multiple drawbacks. Firstly, neither housemaid at No. 14 Norfolk Street was ever a suspect; secondly, Courvoisier had never pawned any valuables from the household. Thirdly, there is nothing to suggest that the murderer had washed inside the murder room. A naked man descending the stairs dripping with blood would surely have left bloodstaining on the stairs. Fourthly, the murder house had no bathroom or bathtub. How was the wretched man supposed to get clean after committing the murder, with the use of only a primitive sink and a jug of water, without leaving any bloodstaining behind?

The police inventory of Courvoisier's wearing apparel shows that the Norfolk Street murderer was the owner of a mackintosh.[40] I would suggest that he wore this garment over his clothes while committing the murder, just like the murderer of Eliza Grimwood was presumed to have done. By removing this garment after the crime, and putting it in a bag, he would have avoided any substantial bloodstaining to his clothes. When Courvoisier's box was searched after the murder, nothing suspicious was found, but when Inspector Tedman searched it a second time several days later, he found a pair of white gloves, a silk handkerchief and a false shirt front, all with slight bloodstaining. During the trial, the audacious Charles Phillips tried to insinuate that the police had planted this false evidence to inculpate Courvoisier, but rightly, he was not believed. I would suggest that these garments were some of those worn by the murderer underneath his mackintosh, and that the story of Courvoisier committing the murder in the nude is a falsehood. One can only speculate why he did not want the real story behind the crime to become public knowledge; was it because he knew that the murderer of Eliza Grimwood had been clearly seen to carry a mackintosh on a perfectly fine summer day, or because the Ripper of Waterloo Road had made use of the same stratagem to avoid bloodstaining to his clothes during all four of his crimes?

15

THE BEAUTIFUL CORPSE

In the eighteenth century, criminals in general and murderers in particular fell into three categories. A few murderers were popular characters, working-class heroes who stood up against the authorities: the highwayman Dick Turpin, the protagonist of many a story and legend, stands out among them. In reality, Turpin was quite a cowardly character who shot down the Epping Forest keeper Thomas Morris in cold blood.[1] The highwayman Claude Duval and the daring jailbreaker Jack Sheppard were also the subject of legend and admiration.

Another minority of murderers were regarded with pity and compassion, none more than the apprentice George Barnwell, who became corrupted after an affair with a prostitute and was lured into stealing from and in the end murdering his uncle. There is nothing to suggest that the sentimental story of George Barnwell has any truth to it, or that the man ever existed, however.[2] The schoolmaster and scholar Eugene Aram, who murdered his friend Daniel Clark in 1744, and disposed of his remains in a cave in Knaresborough, was also viewed with interest and some degree of sympathy. Although goods belonging to Clark were found in Aram's garden, there was not enough evidence for him to be tried for murder, although there was much local gossip about him. On being set at liberty, Aram left his wife and got a job as a schoolmaster in London. When Clark's remains were found inside the cave in 1758, Aram was arrested and tried for his murder; after

Published by the Navarre Society London

RICHARD TURPIN *Shooting a Man near his Cave on Epping Forest.*

Dick Turpin murdering Thomas Morris, from Vol. 3 of the *Complete Newgate Calendar.*

The Murder committed by Eugene Aram.

Eugene Aram murdering Mr Clark, from Vol. 2 of Wilkinson's *Newgate Calendar*.

being found guilty, he was hanged at Tyburn. The sad fate of the scholar turned murderer has been told and retold over the years, and it inspired Thomas Hood's poem 'The Dream of Eugene Aram'.[3]

The vast majority of eighteenth-century murderers, however, were viewed simply as inhuman monsters; they could not count upon any sympathy whatsoever, and the cautionary tales of their exploits were told in a variety of *Newgate Calendars*. Charles Drew, who murdered his father in 1740, and Matthew Henderson, who murdered Lady Dalrymple in 1746, were typical *Newgate Calendar* villains, as were that mariticidal trio, Mary Aubrey, Catherine Hayes and Amy Hutchinson, and the sadistic Elizabeth Brownrigg, who murdered one of her servant girls in 1767.[4]

★ ★ ★

In early nineteenth-century London, literacy was increasing, and there was a vigorous newspaper press, catering to readers who were often keen to read about the latest criminal news. At this time, several factors contributed in

Engraved for The Malefactor's Register.

W. Grainger, in et fc.

CHARLES DREW *shooting his own* FATHER, *at Long-Melford, in Suffolk.*

Charles Drew guns down his father, from Vol. 3 of the *Malefactor's Register.*

making a 'media murder'. Firstly, the general gruesomeness of the crime or crimes, and the number of victims: having a mass murderer on the loose in the metropolis was a media sensation of the highest order. This was never more apparent than in the Ratcliffe Highway murders of 1811, where an unknown assassin went into a draper's shop and murdered the entire Marr family: husband, wife and son, and a young apprentice lad as well. Hundreds of people came to see the murder house, and outside it was such a throng of spectators that Ratcliffe Highway became well-nigh impassable. Twelve days later, Mr and Mrs Williamson were murdered at their tavern, the King's Arms in New Gravel Lane. A man named John Williams was arrested for the murders, and he later committed suicide in prison. Not only were the Ratcliffe Highway murders featured in the newspapers, but there were prints showing Marr's shop, the King's Arms murder pub, and the procession taking the body of Williams through the Wapping streets to a suicide's grave at the crossroads. The reason the Ratcliffe Highway became one of the earliest media murders was simply that the East End people were frightened of being murdered themselves.[5]

Other Victorian serial killers, like the Rugeley poisoner Dr William Palmer and the Northern Borgia Mary Ann Cotton, who poisoned three of her husbands and eleven of her thirteen children with arsenic, also became criminal celebrities, as did the baby-farmers Amelia Sachs and Annie Walters. Another element influencing the media popularity of recent murders were if some person of high rank

Mary Aubrey murdering her husband, from Vol. 2 of Wilkinson's *Newgate Calendar*.

had been involved, like the eighteenth-century murderer Earl Ferrers, the murder victims Sir Theodosius Broughton and Lady Dalrymple, and for that matter Lord William Russell himself. The Radlett murder of 1823 was another 'media murder' of its time: the gambler John Thurtell and his cronies Hunt and Probert had invited the wealthy solicitor Mr William Weare, to whom Thurtell owed £300, for a weekend of gambling at Probert's country cottage. On the way there, Thurtell shot Weare in the face with a pistol, and

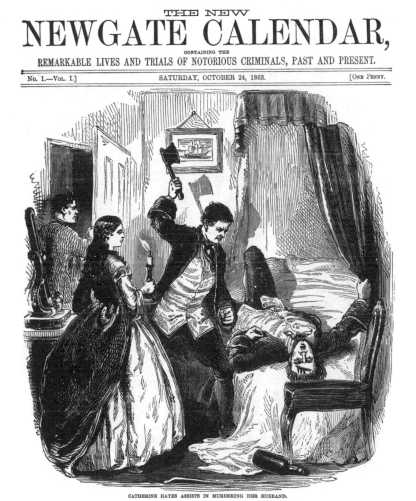

The mariticidal Catherine Hayes, from the first volume of the *New Newgate Calendar* (London 1863).

then finished him off with a knife and the pistol butt. The corpse was thrown into a pond, and the three miscreants went on to amuse themselves in the cottage all evening, eating, drinking and carousing. In the end, Thurtell was hanged, Hunt was transported to Australia, and Probert, who had given evidence against the other two, was later executed for another crime. Thurtell's wax effigy was exhibited at Madame Tussauds for 150 years, and a mug with his portrait enjoyed good sales. The murder of William Weare owed some of its fame to being a cold-blooded and premeditated act, but more to the constant immorality of the murderous trio, who liked prizefighting, gambling, partying and bad company.

The execution of Catherine Hayes, from the first volume of the *New Newgate Calendar* (London 1863).

Murderesses were viewed with particular revulsion, the aforementioned husband-killers and baby-farmers in particular. In 1849, the married couple Frederick and Marie Manning murdered the moneylender Patrick O'Connor, stole his money and railway shares, and disposed of his remains underneath the kitchen floor. There was widespread public interest in this murderous couple, who were eventually captured, tried and convicted for the murder. Marie Manning was a native of Switzerland and, just like Courvoisier, she had entered service as a domestic servant; she equalled her countryman with regard to amorality and cunning, and many people found it equally revolting and fascinating that a woman had taken an active part in a premeditated murder plot for profit.[6]

Matthew Henderson murdering Lady Dalrymple, from the first volume of the *New Newgate Calendar* (London 1863).

Another, more obscure cultural motif that could make an early Victorian media murder was that of the 'beautiful female murder victim'. As outlined by the American scholar Daniel A. Cohen, there was an unwholesome public interest, on both sides of the Atlantic, in cases of women being murdered by men for sexual motives.[7] The typical scenario was that a young and attractive unmarried woman was murdered by a young unmarried man, in the context of a romantic encounter gone wrong; the murder victim had a sexual 'past' and her seduction or 'fall' was directly related to her murder. There was typically more than a hint of necrophilia,

MARIA MARTEN.—(FROM A PORTRAIT PUBLISHED AT THE TIME OF THE TRIAL.)

Maria Marten and the cottage where she lived, from the *Romance of Crime* (London 1860).

THE COTTAGE OF THE MARTENS AT POLSTEAD.

with graphic and salacious descriptions of the victim's corpse. Dr Cohen attempted to link the cult of the beautiful female murder victim to medieval court romances, but not with much success, and I would be disposed to suggest that this particular cult began around the year 1800, and enjoyed its culmination from 1820 until 1840. As judged from the sometimes unwholesome interest in Mary Kelly, the fifth and youngest victim of Jack the Ripper, and the Black Dahlia mystery in the United States, remnants of it flourished well into modern times, and it may well still be influencing tabloid journalism today.

Corder wooing Maria Marten, from the first volume of the *New Newgate Calendar* (London 1863).

Maria Marten, who was murdered in the Red Barn at Polstead, Suffolk, in 1828, was an early and prominent English 'beautiful female murder victim'.[8] Maria was born in the year 1801, the daughter of a mole-catcher who lived in a cottage in the village of Polstead. A good-looking, dark-haired wench, she was seduced by Thomas Corder, the son of a wealthy local farmer, already in her teens, and she gave birth to a child that died young. Maria then had an affair with the well-to-do yeoman farmer Peter Matthews, and gave birth to yet another child. Matthews did not want to marry Maria, but at least he paid her some maintenance money for his son. The feckless Maria went on to enjoy other village intrigues, to the embarrassment of her father and stepmother, who wanted to see her married and settled down. In 1826, Maria met William Corder, the younger brother of Thomas, who had been her first lover. William was a short, ugly young man wearing a strange, over-large cap, but Maria was impressed with his wealthy family, and willingly became his mistress. They had yet another child, and when it died at the age of four weeks, Corder took the body away and buried it in secret. He assured Maria's father and stepmother that he still wanted to marry her, but in reality, he was getting tired of his mistress and wanted to get rid of her. In the end, he lured her to go to the Red Barn in Polstead, and here he shot and stabbed her to death and buried the body in a shallow grave. But although Corder assured Maria's father and stepmother that she was still alive and well, and lodging with his friends in Ipswich, they were getting increasingly apprehensive. In the end, the stepmother, who may well have known more about proceedings than she wanted people to believe, told a story that she had dreamt of Maria being murdered and buried at the Red Barn. Excavations proved this story to be nothing but the truth. Corder, who had absconded to London and married a woman who taught at a school in Ealing, was arrested, tried and convicted of murder, and hanged at Bury St Edmonds in front of a great crowd of people. More than 1 million execution broadsides, priced at a penny each, were sold to the populace.

There was immediate interest in the Red Barn Murder, and Londoners made excursions to Polstead to see the Marten family's cottage, Corder's house and the Red Barn itself. Maria's gravestone at Polstead cemetery was eventually chipped away to nothing by souvenir hunters, and the planks

Corder and Maria Marten bury their infant, from the first volume of the *New Newgate Calendar* (London 1863).

of the Red Barn itself were made into memorabilia toothpicks and paper-weights, until it eventually burnt down in 1842. Corder had been dissected after the execution, and his skin had been tanned and used to bind a book about his trial. His mounted skeleton was used, for many years, to teach the nurses anatomy at the West Suffolk Hospital.[9] His clothes, and the rope used to hang him, were also put on exhibition. In the popular retellings of the Red Barn Murder, the blackguard Corder was transformed into a wicked squire, capable of any crime, and intent on seducing the innocent village beauty Maria. Her somewhat colourful past, with three bastard children all

THE RED BARN AT POLSTEAD.—(FROM AN ORIGINAL SKETCH.)

INTERIOR OF THE RED BARN.—(FROM AN ORIGINAL SKETCH.)

The Red Barn and its interior, from the *Romance of Crime*.

with different fathers, was only hinted at. Corder's constant immorality did not need to be exaggerated: there were rumours that he had murdered his own child with Maria to get rid of an encumbrance, that he had enjoyed an affair also with Maria's stepmother, who was just one year older than her, and that he consorted with cattle-rustlers and stole pigs from other Polstead farms just for the fun of it. After murdering Maria and absconding to London, Corder had advertised for a wife in the *Morning Herald* and *The Sunday Times*, getting no fewer than ninety-eight replies from various metropolitan 'lonely hearts'. From this harem of candidates he chose Miss Mary Moore, whom he married in Holborn; they were teaching at a school in Brentford at the time of his arrest. There was a series of Staffordshire pottery figures of Maria Marten, William Corder, and the Red Barn, and the Victoria & Albert Museum has a set of marionette puppets used to re-enact the Red Barn Murder before an enthusiastic audience. There were several fictional and semi-fictional accounts of the Red Barn Murder, and a play based on the case was the most frequently performed in Victorian times. There was also a 1935 melodrama starring Tod Slaughter as Corder, and a 1980 BBC drama based on the case.

As we know, there was an invented link between the murders of Maria Marten and Eliza Grimwood from an early time, since it was claimed that 'at the period of the murder of Maria Martin, by Corder, Eliza Grimwood was at that particular time on a visit to a friend's house in the immediate vicinity, and that she was the first person who entered the Red Barn where the murder was committed, and beheld the mangled corpse of the ill-fated girl'.[10] This is clearly untrue, since we know that Corder buried Maria underneath the floor of the barn, and that she was eventually dug up by her father after her stepmother's extraordinary dream. But there are many other parallels between the murders of Maria Marten and Eliza Grimwood, since both were variations on the theme of the 'beautiful female murder victim'. There was intense public interest not only in the murder of Eliza Grimwood, but also in her past life, and her 'fall' from respectable womanhood into becoming a common prostitute, 'available' to any paying customer, just like Maria Marten had been 'kept' by Corder and her previous string of lovers. In the public mind, Hubbard was of course the obvious murderer: a detestable prostitute's bully, as bad as Corder, and capable of murder and any

The murder of Maria Marten in the Red Barn, from the first volume of the *New Newgate Calendar* (London 1863).

Mrs Marten's extraordinary dream, from the first volume of the *New Newgate Calendar* (London 1863).

other crime. The newspaper coverage of the Grimwood mystery was equal to that in the Red Barn case, with some very dubious additions, like publishing a picture of Eliza's stays, and dwelling at length on the necrophiliac horrors of the autopsy findings. The number of handbills on the Grimwood case is said to have exceeded all precedents. A crowd kept vigil outside the murder house, and then we have the matter of the bizarre auction arranged by the brothers Grimwood, selling Eliza's belongings for very good prices to a throng of the curious, and the exhibition of Eliza's dog in a public house. Moreover, there were two illustrated novels about the Grimwood mystery, published in 1841 and 1864.

★ ★ ★

In October 1841, an illustrated novel about the murder of Eliza Grimwood was advertised in the *Penny Satirist* newspaper. To stir up interest, the first part of *Eliza Grimwood, A Domestic Legend of the Waterloo Road* was given away to every purchaser of that newspaper. The second part would contain the wrappers and frontispiece.[11] As is usual for a 'penny dreadful', not many copies remain of this rare novel, which is adorned with some distinctively amateurish drawings of the main characters.[12] It is a strange mixture of fact and fiction, beginning with the quotes:

'Out damned spot!' – *Lady Macbeth*

'Who murdered Eliza Grimwood?' – *Popular Question*

In this novel, Eliza Grimwood is the orphaned daughter of a brave sergeant major, who perished in the wars against Napoleon, and his Spanish wife. She is brought up by her paternal grandparents in the countryside. But her uncle Jacob Grimwood wants to prevent her from getting her inheritance. He plots with villainous nobleman the Earl of Rakemore, his sister Lady Mary Johnstone and a vicious hag named Mrs Bruin to achieve her downfall. Eliza's simple-minded friend Kate Elmore overhears the earl speaking to Mrs Bruin and kills the latter in self-defence, but goes mad from the shock and is abducted by Lady Mary. The wicked earl is thus free to seduce Eliza, only to cast her aside as soon as she is pregnant.

Poor Eliza has to leave her bucolic idyll and go to London, where she has an abortion. Contemplating suicide, she walks out onto Waterloo

GRATIS! GRATIS!! GRATIS!!!

WITH THIS WEEK'S

PENNY SATIRIST, is Given to every Purchaser, the First Number of

ELIZA GRIMWOOD,

A DOMESTIC LEGEND OF THE WATERLOO ROAD

A Work of Thrilling Interest;

Written by an Author of great eminence; in which are developed the personal misfortunes, virtues, and vices of many individuals of certain classes, now, and recently living in London.

The Cottage Fireside, with peace and happiness blessed — Youth and Beauty with innocence adorned—The Possession of Wealth and evil-directed Passions combined—The Snares of the evil designer laid—The hope of the Aged broken—Virtue preserved, and virtue lost—The Destroyer triumphant, and the Sufferer oppressed—The Poor avenged, and the Rich laid low—Criminals on the Bench, and justice prevented—Judges in jeopardy, and truth triumphant—The meanest poverty and the proudest wealth—Peasant and Peer, Beggar and King!—All are developed in personal and faithful portraitures.

And there is truth in every incident and adventure related : whether these be of lovers, marriages, seductions, desertions, battlefield achievements, youthful indiscretions, boarding-school elopements, hot pursuits, duels, wounds, death, revenge, retaliation, gambling-houses, widows' tears, childrens' cries, virtuous charities, false accusations, police reports, penny-a-liners, London newspapers, and fearful and mysterious crimes : whether the incidents relate to all, or any of these, or other circumstances not mentioned in this catalogue, the Reader will recognize them as realities with which the Public is acquainted.

There are no vulgar prejudices appealed to—nor indelicate scenes opened offensirely to virtuous eyes. The whole is intended to be read by all who value the promotion of virtue and the suppression of crime; but whose knowledge of human nature, and of the various classes of persons in London in particular, is confined to the narrow sphere of their own observation.

The Proprietors of The PENNY SATIRIST had intended to have given also with No. 1, of ELIZA GRIMWOOD, an Emblematical Wrapper, and a highly-finished Frontispiece Plate ; but, in consequence of a slight indisposition of their Artist, these Embellishments were not finished in time to be published with No. 1; however, the purchasers of

No. 2, will be presented, Gratis, with both WRAPPER & FRONTISPIECE !

Office, 18, Duke-street, Lincoln's-inn-fields, London.

An advertisement for the penny dreadful *Eliza Grimwood, A Domestic Legend of the Waterloo Road*, from the *Penny Satirist*, 16 October 1841.

ELIZA CONSENTS TO ENTER THE EARL'S CARRIAGE.

Eliza Grimwood enters the Earl's carriage. An illustration from the penny dreadful *Eliza Grimwood, A Domestic Legend of the Waterloo Road*, like the following one.

Bridge, but instead she actually saves another desperate female who tries to jump off the bridge. Eliza is employed as a servant by the intended suicide victim's grateful family and for a while things are looking brighter, but soon the earl reappears, seduces her again and lures her into a false marriage. Thus, in this bizarre novel, 'the Countess' is a countess for real, or at least so she thinks.

The author then appears to entirely run out of ideas. Eliza is left behind, installed in the earl's cosy Baker Street love-nest, as the action instead follows the earl's hirelings Davidson and Croker. They drink and revel, Davidson shoots a man in a duel, and the corpse is clandestinely buried. Myriad other obscure characters are introduced: the jovial Mother Royster, the penniless journalist George Augustus Crowe, the amorous Squire Greville, and the mysterious Rachel Elliott, who is followed everywhere by a huge Newfoundland dog.

DAVIDSON, THE EARL AND ELIZA; THE FALSE MARRIAGE.

The false marriage between the Earl and Eliza.

Eventually, after not less than 130 pages have been spent on the antics of these secondary characters, the wicked earl reappears. He wants to marry the wealthy Ellen Daleford and orders Davidson and the equally wicked Bow Street policeman Bob Badger to abduct her. But Rachel Elliott sets her Newfoundland dog on the two villains and Badger is torn to pieces by the infuriated animal, before Davidson shoots the dog and kidnaps Ellen Daleford. Davidson then visits Eliza Grimwood and tells her the truth about her 'marriage'. Poor Eliza again sinks low, and she has to enter a brothel. In a quick tying together of the story, Eliza one day recognises Davidson when he is fleeing from the police, and to keep her quiet, he murders her. The book ends with some newspaper articles being reproduced, to support the mock-authenticity of the murder.

Eliza Grimwood, A Domestic Legend of the Waterloo Road is a very odd book indeed. Its author did not lack talent, and some of the descriptions of the seamier side of London were clearly done from life. In his *Fiction for the Working Man 1830–1850*, Louis James even calls it the outstanding book among the various novels of the time dealing with particular crimes and criminals.[13] Still, the untidy structure of the plot would suggest that either the author was incorporating some other material written earlier into the story, or perhaps rather that there was more than one author, with one 'penny-a-line' hack writer taking over the manuscript started by another colleague and turning a gothic romance into a study of London low life.

A later historian has wrongly claimed that Hubbard fled the country and that it was the unpopular Duke of Cumberland who was lampooned as Eliza's murderer, instead of his Teutonic equal the Duke of Brunswick.[14]

★ ★ ★

The second novel about the murder of Eliza Grimwood appeared as late as 1864. As far as can be ascertained, *Eliza Grimwood, or the Mystery of Crime* was never published in book form, only as penny parts of the *New Newgate Calendar*.[15] Its anonymous author had some knowledge of the murder case, but clearly also an overactive imagination, and a predilection for the cheap gothic novels of the time. Its full-page illustrations in the *New Newgate Calendar* are quite attractive.

In this novel, innocent young Eliza Grimwood grows up in the Kent countryside. She has two admirers: her cousin Tom Hubbard and the wealthy young squire Lionel Faversham. Since Hubbard is a sinister-looking creature, Eliza prefers the young squire, and she is seduced by him. As the novel expresses it 'from the day she yielded her honour to Squire Faversham, her fate was sealed – all was lost'. The enraged Hubbard tries to stab Lionel, but the squire is saved by his Newfoundland dog. Lionel is a caddish fellow, however: he deserts poor Eliza and goes to Vienna for some 'fun' with the ladies. Having recovered from the dog bites, the sinister Hubbard plans to murder his faithless cousin by a ruined mill, but she is saved by Rattling Rob, 'the Idiot of the Mill'. Eliza travels to London, where she is reunited with Lionel and installed as his mistress. But a vicious libertine, Captain Desborough,

The timorous young Eliza Grimwood leaves her parental home to meet her seducer at an old mill. A fanciful illustration taken from the *New Newgate Chronicle* (London 1863), like the following five.

Eliza is confronted by the jealous Hubbard, who threatens to murder her.

sends his burglar friend Jem the Duffer to murder Lionel and abduct Eliza. The amorous captain tries to seduce Eliza, but rather understandably, she wants nothing to do with him. He then instead plans to rape her, but at the critical time, another gang of burglars break into the house. The captain is kidnapped, tortured and killed, and Eliza liberated.

Next, Eliza becomes the mistress of the wealthy banker Marmaduke Stanley, who surrounds her with luxury. But Stanley finds out that she has an affair with the dashing burglar Flash Harry, who had helped to rescue her from Captain Desborough. Stanley tries to murder Harry, but the muscular burglar kills him instead. Eliza joins the gang of burglars and takes part in some of their raids. So does Hubbard, who has come to London to seek his fortune as a burglar. Harry rents a house for Eliza, and for a while they live happily, but the jealous Eliza finds out about his other mistress and betrays

Lionel Faversham is murdered by the burglars.

Captain Desborough, Eliza's next 'protector', is held captive by the burglars Grinder and Gunpowder Bill.

him to the police. She instead moves in with Hubbard in the house in Wellington Terrace. She also becomes a prostitute: 'Lost to all shame, Eliza Grimwood now boldly pursued a life of infamy.' Hubbard, who really loves her, vainly tries to change her ways, but she scoffs and jeers at him, saying, 'the veriest stranger that crosses my path I prefer to you!' In May 1838, the jealous Hubbard often follows her around, so also on that fatal May evening when she meets a foreign-looking man and brings him back to the house in Wellington Terrace. In this version of the tale, the Foreigner leaves without incident. The jealous Hubbard comes sneaking into Eliza's bedroom, seizes her and cuts her throat with great violence. Nobody in the house hears Eliza's feeble cry for help.

Due to the extreme scarcity of the 1863–64 *New Newgate Calendar, Eliza Grimwood, or the Mystery of Crime* has eluded the interest of the literary

The sad end of Captain Desborough.

Eliza Grimwood and her burglar friends are nearly captured by the Bow Street police.

historians; it has not been appreciated that the murder of Eliza Grimwood inspired not just one but two novels. *Eliza Grimwood, or the Mystery of Crime* makes rather more sense than its chaotic predecessor, although the novel is a typical 'penny dreadful' of the time, full of murder and bloodshed. Both novels highlight the 'fall' of Eliza when she was seduced by the Earl of Rakemore or by Squire Faversham; this makes her an outcast from decent womanhood, but also makes her interesting and sexually 'available' to the lustful male characters in the novels. In *Eliza Grimwood, A Domestic Legend of the Waterloo Road*, the heroine is just a cardboard gothic heroine, wandering from peril unto peril, whereas in *Eliza Grimwood, or the Mystery of Crime*, she is more spirited, taking part in burglaries for the fun of it, choosing her male companions from her own will – preferring Flash Harry to Marmaduke Stanley, for example – and choosing prostitution in Waterloo Road instead of monogamy with the creature Hubbard. Neither novel has any valuable insights with regard to the identity of the perpetrator of the murder of Eliza Grimwood. There is nothing to suggest that Eliza possessed any dangerous knowledge about any burglar or other miscreant. Nor is there any evidence that Hubbard showed any jealousy towards Eliza, or that he was following her around or spying on her.

★ ★ ★

In the 1830s, 23-year-old Helen Jewett was an upmarket young prostitute in New York City. She was based at a brothel at No. 41 Thomas Street, but still had freedom to choose her clients herself, and to keep a healthy proportion of her earnings. In the early hours of 10 April 1836, Helen was found murdered in her room. She had been struck several heavy blows to the head with a hatchet, and the murderer had then set fire to her bed. The brothel madam had seen a man she knew as Frank Rivers in Helen's room, and he was tracked down and arrested. His real name was Richard Robinson, and he was just 19 years old, but still a steady customer of Helen's. No immediate motive for him to murder her could be discerned, and he protested his innocence with impressive candour. There was immediate media interest in the murder of Helen Jewett. She had been a well-known New York prostitute, and the street was thronged with people gawping at the murder house.[16]

The murder of Helen Jewett.

James Gordon Bennett, the editor of the *New York Herald*, published a breathless and salacious report of his alleged visit to the murder room: 'The perfect figure – the exquisite limbs – the fine face – the beautiful bust – all, all surpassed in every respect the Venus de Medicis … For a few moments I was lost in admiration at this extraordinary sight – a beautiful female corpse – that surpassed the finest statues of antiquity.'

There was fascination with the previous career of Helen Jewett: she had run away from home in her teens, 'fallen' after being seduced by some local Lothario, and gone on to become a prostitute in Boston and New York. James Gordon Bennett and the *New York Herald* argued in favour of Robinson's innocence, even suggesting that the police and the brothel madam were deliberately trying to falsify a solution to the murder. In contrast, many working-class people believed that Robinson was the guilty man, a vampire preying on the vulnerable Helen Jewett, who in the end had mur-

Helen Jewett and the suspect Robinson.

dered her for the perverted pleasure of it. But when Robinson was on trial for murder, the witnesses from the brothel were not believed, and he walked free as a result. There was outrage among the common people of New York, who believed that Robinson had used the money of his wealthy relatives to purchase an acquittal. Robinson changed his name to Parmelly and moved away from New York; he died from a fever in Louisville, Kentucky, in August 1855. The old murder house at No. 41 Thomas Street, New York, stood as late as 1899, which is admirable considering the transatlantic fascination with wrecking balls and newly constructed tall buildings.[17]

In July 1841, 21-year-old New York cigar shop assistant Mary Cecilia Rogers told her boyfriend that she would be away for a few days, visiting her aunt and some other family members. Three days later, her corpse was found floating in the Hudson River at Hoboken. There was bruising and swelling to the throat, indicating murder.

Mary had been born in Connecticut in or around 1820, but her father had died in a steamboat explosion, and a few years later her mother moved to New York City and opened a boarding house. At the age of just 17, Mary got a job as a sales assistant at Mr John Anderson's Tobacco Emporium at No. 319 Broadway. Her charm and youthful good looks made her very popular

CONFESSION

OF THE

AWFUL AND BLOODY TRANSACTIONS

IN THE LIFE OF

CHARLES WALLACE,

THE

FIEND-LIKE MURDERER OF MISS MARY ROGERS,

THE BEAUTIFUL CIGAR GIRL OF BROADWAY, NEW YORK, WHOSE
FATE HAS FOR SEVERAL YEARS BEEN WRAPT IN
THE MOST PROFOUND MYSTERY.

MISS MARY ROGERS.

TOGETHER WITH A THRILLING NARRATIVE OF

THE BROWN MURDERESS! EMELINE MORERE!!

WHO, AT THE INSTIGATION OF WALLACE, ASSASSINATED HER MASTER AND MISTRESS,
AND THEIR FOUR HELPLESS CHILDREN, WITH AN AXE; FOR WHICH ATROCIOUS
ACT THEY WERE BURNED ALIVE BY A MOB OF INFURIATED LYNCH-
ERS, ON THE BANKS OF THE MISSISSIPPI, ON THE 11TH DAY
OF AUGUST, 1850. FROM HIS OWN MEMORANDA,

Given at the Burning Stake, to the Rev. HENRY TRACY.

NEW ORLEANS:
PUBLISHED BY E. E. BARCLAY & CO.
1851.

The title page of a pamphlet on the murder of Mary Rogers.

among those who frequented the cigar shop, and she was a valuable asset to Mr Anderson, since she drew customers from both near and far. In 1838, Mary had gone missing for a few days, and there were rumours that she had committed suicide or undergone an abortion, but she was soon back at the Tobacco Emporium safe and well.

Three years later , the brutality of the killing, the youth and beauty of the victim, and her previous notoriety among the New York low life, made sure that the slaying of the 'beautiful cigar girl' became yet another 'media murder'. There were divergent hypotheses concerning who was responsible. Some commentators suspected that she had died from a botched abortion, quite possibly at an establishment run by a certain Madame Restell, and that her body had later been dumped into the river; this hardly explains the bruising to the throat and the other indications that she was murdered, however. Her boyfriend Daniel Payne was suspected by some, and he later committed suicide under dismal circumstances, but he had a modestly solid alibi. Others pointed the finger at the young midshipman Philip Spencer, who was later hanged for setting up a mutiny. Her jilted suitor Alfred Crommelin and her employer John Anderson were other suspects. The author Daniel Stashower brought forward the hypothesis that Mary Rogers had indeed arranged to have another abortion, but that she had died as a result of the abortionist's clumsiness, and since Mary was so very well known in New York, it was decided to fake a murder to lead suspicions away from the feticidal bungler. There was as much speculation about the unsolved murder of Mary Rogers as there

Another pamphlet about the murder of Mary Rogers.

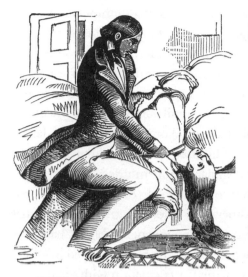

THE BOSTON TRAGEDY.

TIRRELL MURDERING MARY ANN BICKFORD.

PRICE 12 1-2 CENTS.

HIGHLY INTERESTING WORK.

LIFE AND CORRESPONDENCE
OF THE LATE
MARIA A. BICKFORD.

The above portrait was drawn from a daguerreotype miniature, taken from the trunk of Mrs. B. by Coroner Pratt, on the morning of the murder, and engraved expressly for this work by Brown & Worcester, eminent artists of this city. The fac simile of the superb satin dress which she wore is executed with remarkable fidelity. This dress is reported to have cost $100, and was presented to her by Albert J. Tirrell.

The murder of Mary Bickford.

One of the pamphlets about the life and murder of Mary Bickford.

had been in London about the case of Eliza Grimwood; the murder inspired several pamphlets, and also Poe's *The Mystery of Marie Rogêt*, a fictionalised version of the case in which Marie is found dead in the Seine.[10]

In October 1845, 21-year-old Mary Bickford was found murdered in a disreputable boarding house in Cedar Lane, Boston. The killer had cut her throat, before setting fire to the room and absconding down the stairs. Mary Bickford had deserted her husband in Bath, Maine, and gone to Massachusetts with her lover, who soon deserted her. She fell low for a while, as a prostitute in a Boston brothel, before she met the giddy young reveller Albert Tirrell, who set her up as his mistress. Together, they squandered Tirrell's substantial inheritance, living in various hotels and boarding houses, and drinking and partying to excess. In spite of her obvious moral shortcomings, Mary was young and attractive, with dark hair and regular features. Tirrell was infatuated with her, although he suspected that she might well have been unfaithful to him more than once. There was immediate newspaper fascination with the murder of the beautiful Mary Bickford: although she had been leading a vicious life, she was depicted as a fallen woman and a sentimental murder victim; an unsophisticated country girl who had been lured into adultery after her marriage.[19] Tirrell was tried for the murder, but due to the lack of motive, eyewitnesses and conclusive evidence, and the exhortations of a high-quality legal team, he was acquitted. There were several books and pamphlets about the Bickford case, as well as an illustrated biography of the heroine herself, detailing her downfall that would one day lead to murder. As for Tirrell, he eked out the remainder of his life in obscurity, dying in 1880.

Thus we have a cluster of five very similar 'media murders' of young and attractive women from 1828 until 1845, on either side of the Atlantic. Three of the victims were prostitutes, the other two 'fallen' women with a sexual 'past'. In each and every case there was much newspaper publicity, handbills and pamphlets, as well as illustrated biographies of the five murdered heroines, often with fictional content. There was particular fascination with the murder victim's initial 'fall' from chastity, and this event was viewed as the prelude to licentiousness, depravity and murder. There was also a very unwholesome tendency to contrast the good looks of the 'beautiful female murder victim' during life, with the violated but still perversely attractive corpse after the murder had been committed. In each of the five cases, there is a male predator, known to the murder victim, and the murder takes place in a setting of a sexual encounter gone wrong. William Corder was the only murderer to pay the ultimate penalty for his crime. The 'stage villains' in the Grimwood, Jewett and Bickford cases escaped scot-free, and in the Rogers case, no main suspect was ever identified. It is not immediately obvious what sociological event triggered this perverted cult of the 'beautiful female murder victim' that flourished from the 1820s until the 1840s. It may well have played a part that among respectable people of this period, prostitutes were no longer viewed as lewd and wicked women, but as 'fallen women' and victims of society. Once they had been chaste and virginal 'ideal women', before they were led astray by wicked men; this drawn-out process of female corruption, leading to promiscuity, perversion and violent premature death, fascinated many people at the time. The cult of the 'beautiful female murder victim' abated as abruptly as it had begun: the unsolved murders of three London prostitutes – Emma

Jackson, Harriet Buswell and Annie Yates – in 1863, 1871 and 1884, were the topic of a good deal of newspaper interest, mostly realistic with regard to the circumstances and sordidity of the crimes, but without any unwholesome fascination with the private lives of the murder victims, or any voyeuristic interest in the appearance of their mangled bodies after the murderous events.[20]

★ ★ ★

His biographers agree that Charles Dickens was not infrequently inspired by real-life crimes and criminals when inventing characters for his novels. The clearest example of this is the wicked governess Madame Hortense in *Bleak House*, who was clearly based on the aforementioned murderess Marie Manning. It is also obvious that the murder of the swindler Montague Tigg in *Martin Chuzzlewit* was influenced by the 1823 murder of the gambler William Weare by Thurtell and Hunt. There has been speculation that the finding of poison by Jonas Chuzzlewit was inspired by a similar incident in the case against suspected murderess Christina Gilmour. Julius Slinkton in *Hunted Down* has features of the poisoners William Palmer and Thomas Griffith Wainewright, and the villain of *Little Dorrit*, the Frenchman Rigaud, rather resembles the double murderer Pierre François Lacenaire, who was guillotined in 1836. The fraudster Mr Mardle in the same book may well have been partially based on James Sadleir, a Member of Parliament who defrauded a bank where he was a director.[21]

BILL SYKES.
"DO YOU HEAR ME CALL" COME ERE"
CRIED SYKES TO THE DOG"

A ruffian-looking actor playing the part of 'Bill Sykes', from an old postcard

Since he lived in London in 1838, and was a keen observer of true crime, Charles Dickens must have been well aware of the murder of Eliza Grimwood. Indeed, he several times alluded to her in his published writings. In an article in his magazine *Household Words*, he wrote that the father of 'the King of the Bill-stickers' was buried by the murdered Eliza Grimwood, in the Waterloo Road. Then again, as we know, he spoke to Inspector Field in 1850, and retold the story of the lavender-coloured gloves as the second of his Three Detective Anecdotes. For quite some time, there has been speculation among Dickensians whether one of the most powerful scenes in his fiction, the brutal murder of Nancy by her villainous paramour Bill Sikes in *Oliver Twist*, might have been influenced by the murder of Eliza Grimwood.[22] Dickens was active writing this novel, in monthly instalments, for the periodical *Bentley's Miscellany*, at the very time Eliza was murdered. As we know, the popular newspapers and prints represented Eliza as a downtrodden prostitute and Hubbard as a criminal bully, the very counterparts of Nancy and Sikes. There was also a tradition that a young man wanted to rescue Eliza from her life of vice, just like Maylie did Nancy, only to be thwarted by the murderous Hubbard (or by 'Don Whiskerando' in another version).

"HE MOVED, BACKWARD, TOWARDS THE DOOR: DRAGGING THE DOG WITH HIM."

Sikes murdering Nancy in *Oliver Twist*.

Just as the newspapers debated the significance of the presence of blood-stains on Hubbard's clothes, and his bloody shoes, Sikes took care to wash after the murder, and his dog's feet were bloody. Every reader of *Oliver Twist* will remember how Sikes is pursued by the image of Nancy's eyes and that he yells, 'The eyes again,' just before falling to his death. When Harriet Chaplin gave evidence, she untruthfully claimed that Eliza had still been alive when Hubbard had found her, and that he had seen her eyes move: 'I tell you that her eyes were open; she looked at me, and I never shall forget the look she gave me!'

There are also some key differences between the murder of Eliza Grimwood and the fictional murder of Nancy in *Oliver Twist*, however. Firstly, it is entirely wrong to claim that Dickens was 'obsessed' with the Grimwood murder, and that it sent him into an early grave; nor was Eliza half-dressed in bed when she was murdered, and there is nothing to suggest that she was forced to her knees, as claimed in an inaccurate newspaper article.[23] It is questionable whether Hubbard should be described as a common pimp, since he had steady employment and lacked previous criminal convictions; he was definitely not a hardened robber of Sikes' calibre, although the biased public prints represented him as such. Furthermore, Nancy was a poor and downtrodden prostitute, whereas Eliza was relatively wealthy and independent, and able to prostitute herself if and when she wanted to. There was a dog present at both murders, although there is a discrepancy between Eliza's timid little spaniel, the dog that did not bark in the night, and Sikes's ugly cur that he later attempts to destroy. With regard to the modus operandi of the murders, Eliza had her throat cut, and was stabbed and 'ripped', whereas Nancy was beaten to death with a pistol-butt and a cudgel. Nancy pleaded with Sikes, begging him to spare her; Eliza, overcome by the sudden murderous intent of the Ripper of Waterloo Road, uttered no such exhortations, but died swiftly and silently. Sikes fled in horror after his crime, whereas Hubbard remained at No. 12 Wellington Terrace, and calmly asserted his innocence throughout his ordeal. The situation would appear to be that although Dickens was inspired by the murder of Eliza Grimwood when he described the murderous end of the relationship between Sikes and Nancy, he made use of his novelist's imagination to change many of the circumstances, and adapt them to the plot of *Oliver Twist*.

16

GOING TO SEE
A MAN HANGED

Young people, I pray give attention
And to my tale of woe lend an ear
Ah me! My sinful heart 'tis breaking
My God forgive thee, François Courvoisier!¹

After the shenanigans about his two confessions, François Benjamin
Courvoisier lived quietly in the Newgate condemned cell, awaiting his
execution, which had been fixed for 6 July. His cell was large and airy, and
furnished with a bed and a table and chairs. Since the authorities were fearful that the prisoner might commit suicide, he was watched night and day
by two turnkeys. Courvoisier slept soundly, but he seemed very depressed
and despondent during the daytime. Once, he made a half-hearted attempt
to destroy himself by cramming a towel down his throat, but the turnkeys
swiftly pulled it out. Courvoisier suffered ill effects from his rash action.²

★★★

Historical mysteries have a perpetual fascination: many of us are fond of
reading new books about, for example, the identity of Jack the Ripper or
the truth about the Man in the Iron Mask, in the vain hope of finding some
vital clue that will finally solve the conundrum. The concept of a historical

Courvoisier in the condemned cell, from the *Sunday Times and People's Police Gazette* of 5 July 1840.

mystery is that of an important past event that has been disputed for some considerable period of time, but still remains unsolved. A characteristic of many famous historical mysteries is that there are large quantities of contradictory evidence, giving rise to a multitude of theories, although it remains unlikely that a final, universally accepted solution will ever be found.[3] One important type of historical mystery is that of disputed identity: either a mysterious foundling is discovered, or a claimant asserts his right to some high title or usurps the identity of some famous or wealthy person presumed to have been deceased. A second type, exemplified by the case of Eliza Grimwood, is the unsolved murder mystery; then there are sundry other mysteries, involving robbers and other criminals, political shenanigans, and various other matters outside the scope of this book.

In 1828, a mysterious boy came walking into Nuremberg: he appeared to be quite half-witted, but still had aspirations to join the local cavalry regiment as a trooper. He gave his name as Kaspar Hauser. Since he seemed entirely incapable of looking after himself, he was imprisoned in the Luginsland Tower, where he sat on the floor of his cell and played with a wooden horse. One day, Kaspar was able to tell his life story: he had spent his entire youth in a small dungeon, without knowledge that there were other people in the world. His jailer had then taught him to write his name and to speak a few words, before he was taught to walk and set on his way to Nuremberg. Many people believed this fantastic story, and Kaspar was well taken care of. There were dark rumours that he was the Crown Prince of Baden, stolen away by a wicked countess at the age of 2, with an ailing child substituted in the royal cot. After Kaspar died mysteriously in 1833, under circumstances suggestive of murder, the speculation about his true identity continued, and many books were written with various suggestions. In 1996, mitochondrial DNA from the bloodstain on Kaspar's underpants was compared with samples from descendants of the House of Baden; they did not match. Thus the specific question 'Was Kaspar Hauser the Crown Prince of Baden?' can be answered in the negative, whereas the open question 'Who was Kaspar Hauser?' remains open for debate. Myself, I rather tend to believe that he was a poor simpleton taught to become a professional beggar through telling heart-rending stories about how he had been abandoned and mistreated.[4]

DNA technology has been used, with considerable success, in many a contemporary case of murder, and an example of its successful use in an older murder mystery is provided by the so-called A6 Murder of 1962. James Hanratty was convicted of the murder of Michael Gregsten, sentenced to death and executed, but debate concerning his guilt continued until 2002, when DNA evidence conclusively proved that he was the guilty man. In that case, the specific question 'Did Hanratty murder Michael Gregsten?' could be answered in the affirmative. Attempts to make use of DNA technology to solve the mystery of Jack the Ripper have proven wholly unsuccessful, however, mainly due to the considerable amount of wishful thinking involved, and the dubious origins of the material tested. The attempt by

Patricia Cornwell to make a case against Walter Sickert based on analysis of various letters sent to the police by Jack the Ripper was scuppered by the fact that the letters were most probably sent by hoaxers rather than the Whitechapel Murderer himself. The recent investigation by Russell Edwards and Jari Louhelainen, using analysis of stains on a very loosely authenticated shawl supposed by some to have belonged to the Ripper victim Catherine Eddowes to incriminate the established suspect Aaron Kosminski, also proved to be substantially flawed.[5]

In the case of Eliza Grimwood, there is of course no option of making use of DNA analysis. This raises the question of whether it is at all possible to solve a murder mystery dating back to 1838 making use of deductive reasoning alone. When visiting London to put the finishing touches to this book, I went to the British Museum to reacquaint myself with the Rosetta Stone, the inscribed boulder with text in Greek, hieroglyphs and demotic Egyptian, found by the French at Rosetta near Alexandria in Egypt during Napoleon's campaign in 1799. After the French defeat in Egypt, the stone became spoils of war, and it was taken to the British Museum in 1803. It was instrumental for the celebrated linguist Jean-François Champollion to decipher the hieroglyphs in 1822, through years of painstaking analysis. But can there be a Rosetta stone to translate the hieroglyphs of 1838 into plain English nearly 180 years after the event?

★ ★ ★

> I was brought up by honest Parents
> In Switzerland I first drew my breath
> And now, for the horrid crime of Murder
> I am deem'd to meet an ignominious death.

Courvoisier's honest parents back in Switzerland made no attempt to come and see their unhappy son in the condemned cell, nor did his sister who lived in Paris, but his uncle L. Courvoisier paid him several visits. The wretched convict was also regularly visited by the Swiss clergyman Baup and by the Rev. Mr Carver, the Newgate chaplain.[6] In the days preceding his execution, Courvoisier frequently gave way to paroxysms of the utmost grief

The face of the Foreigner? A close-up view of Courvoisier's death mask, reproduced by permission of Madame Tussauds Archives.

and despair. He barely slept at night, and ate next to nothing. In vain did the wretched convict scan the pages of the French Bible he had been given, in search of some much-needed spiritual succour, but he found no apocryphical prophet with aberrant views on the ultimate fate of murderers, no eccentric anchorite who made confused predictions about the afterlife of various criminal elements, no fallen angel in disguise who could present him with a post-apocalyptic free pardon: for him, there was no hope.

★★★

A kind of old-fashioned novel readers
Demanded 'mysteries' and had to be titillated
With titles like:
'The Mystery of Castleford'
'The Nightingales Mystery'
And others of that ilk.

But why in such a hurry? Why so impatient?
Just give yourselves time, and Time itself will obscure
Even the simplest and most obvious actions!
Never a day without an ambiguity![7]

Thus wrote the distinguished Swedish poet and philosopher, the late Professor Lars Gustafsson, and his meaning is clear: the investigation of historical mysteries is in vain, since the sheer passage of time creates its own mysteries:

In the novels there was always a Detective,
A man from London, in a checkered suit,
And buttoned-up yellow boots
With traces of clay from the bed of roses.
He always first investigated 'the motives'.

But why in such a hurry! Why so impatient?
Just give yourself time, and Time itself will create motives
Even for the most marvellous actions.
The motives breed themselves, as we well know!

In Professor Gustafsson's novel *The Tennis Players*, the same theme recurs.[8] The novel's narrator, a Swedish academic teaching literary history at a Texan university, and lecturing about Strindberg's Inferno crisis, is challenged by a PhD student who has discovered the memoirs of a Polish anarchist, describing how a gang of foreign nihilists had tried to gas Strindberg with chloroform at the Hotel Orfila in Paris, to be able to steal his alchemical formula for making gold. They optimistically planned to make use of this recipe to dump the market with gold French francs, to make the world's financial markets crash and start an international revolution. Thus Strindberg's Inferno crisis was nothing but fact and actuality: he was really persecuted by a gang of mysterious strangers who lived in the room above his at the hotel, and who tried to bore holes in the roof to gas the tormented Swede. Teaming up with a computer expert from the US Air Force, the narrator makes plans to digitise both Strindberg's own account and the memoirs of the Polish anarchist, using a powerful Air Force computer to construct the true and final account of the Inferno crisis. Initially they make good progress, but the computer expert is sacked from the US Air Force before he is able to combine the two books, leaving the silent underground supercomputer to ponder the insoluble mystery of Strindberg's experiences at the Hotel Orfila, in perpetuity.

★ ★ ★

For a whole week I planned the murder
It engaged my mind by day and night
I felt no remorse, but, like a demon
It seemed to me a source of great delight

On Sunday 6 July, the Rev. Mr Carver preached the condemned sermon to Courvoisier, in the chapel of Newgate. The sheriffs, who had received many applications for admission to the chapel, decided to open the gallery, which had been closed since the execution of the forger Henry Fauntleroy in 1824. Lord Adolphus Fitzclarence, Lord Coventry, Lord Alfred Paget, and others of rank and distinction purchased tickets to see the dejected Courvoisier escorted into the chapel by the turnkeys. He sat on a bench before the pulpit, and never once raised his eyes during the sermon. When he had been taken back to the condemned cell, there was a visit from the Swiss Consul, who handed him a letter from his mother. Courvoisier wept bitterly as his thoughts went to his disgraced parents back home in Switzerland, but he managed to regain his composure to write a few lines in reply.[9]

★★★

Lars Gustafsson represents a philosophical school of what we can call historiographical negativism: the thoughts and actions of past generations are naturally obfuscated by the passage of time, and the analysis of historical conundrums, like the example of Strindberg's Inferno crisis, is in vain even with the most sophisticated technological tools. For an example of the diametrically opposite view, one needs look no further than the present-day amateur criminologists making use of various Internet resources to bring forward a novel 'solution' to the mystery of Jack the Ripper. Such an armchair detective of the computer age would not need any reference library, nor would there be any need for travel or other exertions, with Google Books and other online literary archives just a click away. As for original newspaper material, the British Newspaper Archive and other capacious online repositories are readily available to subscribers.[10] There are several Internet bulletin boards where Ripper enthusiasts can debate their most recent discoveries. As shown by the present-day deluge of privately published books, often of an execrable quality, historical research is easier than it has ever been and is available to a much wider class of people than the traditional university scholars. It can be a double-edged sword that becoming a published author, through some Internet 'vanity' service, is today within the grasp of any person.

A question of key importance for this book is whether a historical mystery can be solved through deductive reasoning alone. In vain did the learned German scholar Hermann Pies dedicate his life's work to investigating the life and mystery of Kaspar Hauser, only for his theories to be crushed by DNA analysis; in vain did a multitude of French theorists speculating about the fate of the unhappy 'temple child' Louis XVII propose their favourite 'False Dauphins' as the rightful heirs to the French throne; in vain did a variety of transatlantic enthusiasts support the cause of the impostor Anna Anderson, who managed to persuade many people that she was Grand Duchess Anastasia of Russia. As for Britain's national mystery, the identity of the elusive Jack the Ripper, the lucubrations of myriad imaginative theorists have introduced novel and unexpected 'suspects' like Prince Albert Victor, Duke of Clarence and Avondale; Sir William Gull, the eminent physician; Sir John Williams, who founded the National Library of Wales; Lewis Carroll, author of *Alice in Wonderland*; and even the murderess Mary Eleanor Pearcey. Instead of closing in on the elusive Jack, through painstaking analysis of the available evidence, the popular newspaper brand of modern Ripperology has managed to distance itself from the original Whitechapel Murderer, corrupted by greed for money, blatant falsifications and dismal publishing hoaxes.

As for some other celebrated Victorian murder mysteries, the murder of the barrister Charles Bravo in his Balham mansion in 1876 stands out as one of the most famous. The journalist James Ruddick strongly suspected that he was poisoned by his wife Florence, who was actively aided and abetted by her lady companion Mrs Jane Cox, and here I believe he was right, although other authors have held divergent views on the case, some even suspecting suicide.[11] Guy Logan and Jack Smith-Hughes both strongly suspected that, although the shop assistant Augustus Payne stood trial for murdering Mrs Ann Reville in Slough in 1881, the true killer was in fact her husband Hezekiah. I myself am not entirely convinced by their reasoning.[12] Guy Logan also found strong reason to believe that John Lee – also known as 'The Man They Could Not Hang', after his execution was badly botched – was guilty of murdering Miss Keyse at The Glen, Babbacombe, in 1885, and here I believe he was right.[13]

The distinguished crime historian Richard Whittington-Egan took much care to research the Riddle of Birdhurst Rise, the 1928 triple murder of three members of a prominent Croydon family, concluding that the mystery woman Grace Duff had murdered her husband, sister and mother; some later commentators have agreed with his deductions, and pointed his investigation out as a model of its kind; one modern writer has entirely disagreed, however.[14] Mr Whittington-Egan also investigated the mysterious 1945 Lower Quinton 'Murder by Witchcraft' case, along with fellow criminologist Bernard Taylor, presenting solid-looking arguments that the old field labourer Charles Walton was murdered by his employer, the farmer Alfred Potter.[15] In another book, I have taken care to reinvestigate thirteen unsolved late Victorian murder mysteries, making use of the original police files at the National Archives, if extant, as well as a variety of online newspaper databases, and sundry published secondary sources.[16] In one case, the Eltham murder of Jane Maria Clouson in 1871, I was in a position to present novel arguments to the effect that the young man Edmund Pook, who originally stood trial for the murder at the Old Bailey but was acquitted, actually was the guilty man. In five other cases, I was able to identify a main suspect; in three others, it was possible to present arguments against the guilt of the person who had stood accused of the murder at the time; in four instances, mainly murders of prostitutes by elusive late-night 'customers', I had to confess to being wholly clueless.

★ ★ ★

Oft as I lay in my cell lamenting
My wretched situation I deplore
My murdered master appears before me
With his throat all streaming with his gore

That rather disreputable periodical, the *Illustrated Police News*, was fond of depicting the final dream of convicted murderers, with the lurid phantasms of the moribund prisoner in the condemned cell supplied from vivid images of the individual's past crimes.[17] Courvoisier went to bed a few minutes after eleven o'clock on Sunday night, but he woke with a start at midnight and asked the turnkeys what time it was. The condemned man was able to go to sleep again, but the turnkeys heard that he groaned and gnashed his teeth, as if his dreams were far from pleasant ones. Did the spectre of Eliza Grimwood appear to the wretched murderer, to seize hold of the trembling Swiss valet and thrust its bloodstained face into his? Did Lord William Russell come to haunt his former servant, as the writer of the execution poem quoted above speculated, 'his throat all streaming with his gore', presenting a dreadful appearance as he took his cowardly murderer to task? Or did ultimate nocturnal phantasms of the condemned man, for whom there was no hope in this world or the next, involve a foretaste of what horrors awaited him in the afterlife: fearful fiends of nethermost Hell, ever-burning fires, red-hot pokers inserted into various body orifices, and enormous demons farting both day and night, into the sulphuric fumes of the Netherworld?

★★★

The immediate objection from the critical reader of this book would of course be that a murder mystery from 1838, fifty years before the depredations of Jack the Ripper, cannot be particularly easy to solve: surely, the newspaper coverage would have become too dated, the secondary sources on the crime too muddled, and the motives driving people at the time too obscured, for the enigma ever to be made clear? On the contrary, it can be pointed out that the Grimwood case is more recent than the aforementioned Kaspar Hauser mystery, with a margin of less than a decade; the reign of terror of that figure of dread, the London Monster of 1790, and the much-debated scribblings of that pseudonymous man of mystery, 'Junius' of the *Public Advertiser*, long predate it.[18]

The obvious question given the secondary sources about the murder is of course, 'Did Hubbard murder Eliza Grimwood?' I would answer that question firmly in the negative, since the forensic evidence speaks strongly in favour of his innocence. The main argument in favour of his guilt, namely that he was a disreputable bully who was partly 'kept' through Eliza's not inconsiderable earnings, is not in doubt, but Hubbard's actions the days after the murder were not those of a guilty man, and his modest intellect was hardly capable of planning and executing what was in fact a perfect murder. Hubbard withstood two attempts to incriminate him for the murder, by the creature Owen and by the anonymous letter-writer who may well have been young M'Millan, and he remained unshaken by long and gruelling questionings at the inquest and at Union Hall. If we accept that the Foreigner committed the murder, then we have a number of peripheral contemporary suspects, namely young M'Millan himself, Mr Skinner the tobacconist, the French singer Ernest Tondeur, and the unnamed Jew confronted by Inspector Field; all these men are obviously innocent, and have nothing to do with the murder.

The next question is 'Did Courvoisier murder Eliza Grimwood?' I honestly think that he did. Firstly, we have the matter of his (withdrawn) confession, and then the 'Logan Memorandum' suggesting that while in Newgate Courvoisier spoke of murdering two young women of the street: most probably Eliza Davies and Eliza Grimwood. He exactly fits the reliable witness descriptions of 'the Foreigner', with regard to height, hair colour and general appearance, and one of the witnesses thought his dress indicative of that of a respectable gentleman's servant. Just like the Foreigner, Courvoisier could speak both French and Italian, but he also spoke good English, although with the French accent remaining. One witness thought his name similar to that of the French assassin Fieschi, and Eliza may well have spoken the name of her murderer when he came to fetch her at the Strand Theatre, although a witness misheard it as 'He is here'. There were vague contemporary murmurations that Courvoisier had committed murder before he slew Lord William Russell at No. 14 Norfolk Street, and that he had once arrived home in a very dishevelled state, under suspicious circumstances. Then we have the matter of the mackintosh brought by the Foreigner to the murder house at Wellington Terrace, in order to avoid getting his clothes bloodstained; I rather suspect that this was the modus operandi in the murder of Lord William Russell, and perhaps in the murder of Eliza Davies as well.

Was Courvoisier an opportunistic serial killer, the Ripper of Waterloo Road, who occasionally murdered young women for perverted pleasure, and men for the sake of profit? He fits the description of the dapper-looking young 'Frenchman' who had befriended Eliza Davies, but the lack of reliable witness testimony in this obscure murder case, and the incompetent police investigation, renders it impossible to narrow down the search for the Frederick Street murderer. The main suspect in the murder of Mr Westwood was the Swiss Nicholas Carron, but two men were seen leaving the murder house; was the second culprit another Swiss, motivated both by bloodlust and the desire for plunder? There were contemporary rumours that the murders of Eliza Grimwood and Mr Westwood were linked. The situation is that from 1837 until 1839, three unsolved murders with the same modus operandi were committed in central London. During those years, a young man with a liking for London low life, who later showed that he was perfectly capable of planning and executing a near-perfect, premeditated murder, was at large in the metropolis. When analysing the murder of Eliza Grimwood, or for that matter the murder of Lord William Russell, the impression is that both victims were killed, for motives of both bloodlust and plunder, by a person of superior coolness and cunning, who had committed murder before. Gentlemen of the jury, I rest my case!

The church of St John in Waterloo Road took a direct hit from a German bomb in 1940, and the roof and much of the interior was destroyed. After standing open for ten years, it was eventually restored, and today it looks very much like it did when Eliza Grimwood was buried there in 1838. The churchyard has been much altered and no trace remains of Eliza's gravestone. When I visited the churchyard in 2007, it was infested with drunks and vagabonds, who swigged thirstily from their cider bottles or lay comatose on the ground; when I returned in 2015, these undesirables had relocated to some other hangout, and it would appear that Eliza's restless spirit finally had peace. With Thomas Hood, author of 'The Bridge of Sighs', we can exclaim:

One more Unfortunate,
Weary of breath,
Rashly importunate,
Gone to her death!

Take her up tenderly,
Lift her with care;
Fashion'd so slenderly
Young, and so fair!

★ ★ ★

But hark! I hear my death-bell tolling
And to meet my fate I must away
How shall I meet my offended Maker?
How stand before him on the judgement-day?

François Benjamin Courvoisier rose at four o'clock on the morning of the day he was to be executed. He dressed and occupied himself by writing letters in French to various old friends and relatives. He also signed some rather macabre autographs to the sheriffs and turnkeys:

François Benjamin Courvoisier
The 6th of July, 1840
The Day of My Execution.

The Rev. Mr Carver and M. Baup the Swiss clergyman prayed with him, and administered the holy sacrament. When prompted, Courvoisier whispered, in a barely audible voice, that he was fully penitent for the crime he had committed, and that he had confidence in the atonement of the Saviour; his pale, contorted countenance plainly showed the deep anguish of his soul, a journalist assures us. The executioner William Calcraft then pinioned the prisoner and he was led to the scaffold by two turnkeys, Calcraft and Sheriff Wheelton following him and the Rev. Mr Carver reading the burial service as he walked before the condemned man.

The sheriffs had been inundated with requests to see Courvoisier being executed and 600 seats had been taken by the nobility and gentry adjacent to the scaffold itself. In addition, a curious mob had already congregated in front of Newgate the evening before the execution. Boys were advertising seats at the windows of houses facing the scaffold, and good seats were

THE EXECUTION OF FRANÇOIS BENJAMIN COURVOISIER.

The execution of Courvoisier, from the *Sunday Times and People's Police Gazette* of 12 July 1840.

snapped up for as much as five guineas. In one of the houses immediately opposite the drop, the windows were taken out, to offer the execution enthusiasts inside an unimpeded view of proceedings. Soon, every seat at a window facing the scaffold was sold to various middle-class customers, who did not like to mix with the rowdy mob in front of Newgate. Sir W. W. Wynn had hired a room to the south of the drop, at the George public house, with a party of friends, and Lord Alfred Paget and his friends occupied a window at the undertakers next door. Some execution enthusiasts in the mob went home for their night's sleep, but more hardened elements who had secured good vantage points for the cataclysm to come remained there all night, smoking their pipes and telling stories of other criminals they had seen executed. At two o'clock in the morning, the apparatus of death was brought out of the prison yard, and two carpenters worked for more than two hours to fix it to the scaffold, the sound of their hammers ceasing as the bell of St Sepulchre's chimed a quarter past four. The growing mob gave a long yell of triumph.[19]

TRIAL, SENTENCE, CONFESSION, & EXECUTION
OF
F. B. COURVOISIER,
FOR THE
Murder of Lord Wm. Russell.

THE VERDICT.

OLD BAILEY, SATURDAY EVENING,
June 20th, 1840.

After the jury had been absent for an hour and twenty minutes, they returned into court, and the prisoner was again placed at the bar.

The names of the jury were then called over, and the clerk of the court said—"How say you, gentlemen, have you agreed on your verdict? Do you find the prisoner Guilty or Not Guilty of the felony of murder with which he stands charged?"

The foreman of the jury, in a low voice, said—"We find him GUILTY!"

The Clerk of the Court then said: François Benjamin Courvoisier, you have been found Guilty of the wilful murder of William Russell, Esq., commonly called Lord William Russell; what have you to say why the court should not give you sentence to die according to law?

The prisoner made no reply. The usual proclamation for silence was then made.

SENTENCE.

The LORD CHIEF JUSTICE TINDAL, having put on the black cap, said: François Benjamin Courvoisier, you have been found guilty by an intelligent, patient, and impartial jury of the crime of wilful murder. That crime has been established against you, not indeed by the testimony of eye-witnesses as to the fact, but by a chain of circumstances no less unerring, which have left no doubt of your guilt in the minds of the jury, and all those who heard the trial. It is ordained by divine authority that the murderer shall not escape justice, and this ordination has been exemplified in your case, in the course of this trial, by the disclosure of evidence which has brought the facts to bear against you in a conclusive manner. The murder, although committed in the dark and silent hour of night, has nevertheless been brought clearly to light by Divine interposition. The precise motive which induced you to commit this guilty act can only be known to your own conscience; but it now only remains for me to recommend you most earnestly to employ the short time you have to live in prayer and repentance, and in endeavouring to make your peace with that Almighty Being whose law you have broken, and before whom you must shortly appear. The Learned Judge then passed sentence on the prisoner in the usual form.

The court was very much crowded to the last.

THE CONFESSION OF THE CONVICT.

After the Learned Judge had passed sentence on the convict, he was removed from the bar, and immediately made a full confession of his guilt.

THE EXECUTION.

At eight o'clock this morning, Courvoisier ascended the steps leading to the gallows, and advanced, without looking round him, to the centre of the platform, followed by the executioner and the ordinary of the prison, the Rev. Mr Carver. On his appearance a few yells of execration escaped from a portion of the crowd; but the general body of the people, great as must have been their abhorrence of his atrocious crime, remained silent spectators of the scene which was passing before their eyes. The prisoner's manner was marked by an extraordinary appearance of firmness. His step was steady and collected, and his movements free from the slightest agitation or indecision. His countenance indeed was pale, and bore the trace of much dejection, but it was at the same time calm and unmoved. While the executioner was placing him on the drop he slightly moved his hands (which were tied in front of him, and strongly clasped one within the other) up and down two or three times; and this was the only visible symptom of any emotion or mental anguish which the wretched man endured. His face was then covered with the cap, fitting so closely as not to conceal the outlines of his countenance, the noose was then adjusted. During this operation he lifted up his head and raised his hands to his breast, as if in the action of fervent prayer. In a moment the fatal bolt was withdrawn, the drop fell, and in this attitude the murderer perished. He died without any violent struggle. In two minutes after he had fallen his legs were twice slightly convulsed, but no further motion was observable, excepting that his raised arms, gradually losing their vitality, sank down from their own lifeless weight.

After hanging one hour, the body was cut down and removed within the prison.

AFFECTING COPY OF VERSES.

Attention give, both old and young,
    Of high and low degree,
Think while this mournful tale is sung,
    Of my sad misery.
I've slain a master good and kind,
    To me has been a friend,
For which I must my life resign,
    My time is near an end.

Oh hark! what means that dreadful sound?
    It sinks deep in my soul;
It is the bell that sounds my knell,
    How solemn is the toll.
See thousands are assembled
    Around the fatal place,
To gaze on my approaching,
    And witness my disgrace.

There many sympathising hearts,
    Who feel another's woe,
Even now appears in sorrow,
    For my sad overthrow.
Think of the aged man I slew,
    Then pity's at an end,
I robb'd him of property and life,
    And the poor man of a friend.

Let pilfering passions not intrude,
    For to lead you astray,
From step to step it will delude,
    And bring you to dismay.
Think of the wretched Courvoisier,
    Who thus dies on a tree,
A death of shame, I've nought to blame,
    But my own dishonesty.

Mercy on earth I'll not implore,
    To crave it would be vain,
My hands are dyed with human gore,
    None can wash off the stain,
But the merits of a Saviour,
    Whose mercy alone I crave;
Good Christians pray, as thus I die,
    I may his pardon have.

PAUL & Co., Printers, 2, 3, Monmouth, Court, Seven Dials.

The end of Courvoisier, from the *Curiosities of Street Literature* (London 1871), sheet 193.

One of the men in the mob who had congregated to see Courvoisier hanged was Charles Dickens, who was quite disgusted by the ribaldry, drunkenness and debauchery demonstrated by the Newgate mob; another was William Makepeace Thackeray, who had risen at three o'clock in the morning to be able to join the mob in front of Newgate. At its largest, the audience numbered between 12,000 and 15,000 people – a considerable crowd indeed, but a good deal smaller than that which had congregated to see Greenacre done to death. The coarse and common conversation among the elements of the mob, and their loud and heartless laugh, was irksome to the two literary men, who felt that the crowd behaved as if it had congregated to view some passing pageant or travelling fair rather than to see a man hanged. As the bell begun to strike eight, there was a great murmur among the mob, and women and children assailed Thackeray's ears by shricking horridly. As he expressed it in his famous essay 'Going to See a Man Hanged', 'I don't know whether it was the bell I heard, but a dreadful quick, feverish kind of jangling noise mingled with the noise of the people, and lasted for about two minutes. The scaffold stood before us, tenantless and black; the black chain was hanging down ready from the beam. Nobody came. "He has been respited," somebody said; another said, "He has hanged himself in prison."'[20]

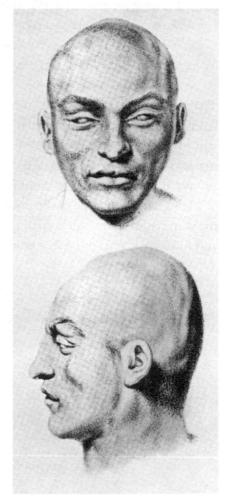

Drawings of a cast of Courvoisier's head, made after the execution.

But in the end, Courvoisier emerged just as planned, and 'a dreadful yell of execration' arose as the condemned man entered the scaffold. As Thackeray expressed it:

> He was dressed in a new black suit, as it seemed, his shirt was open. His arms were tied in front of him. He opened his hands in a helpless kind of way, and clasped them once or twice together. He turned his head here and there, and looked about him for an instant, with a wild, imploring look. His mouth was contracted into a sort of pitiful smile. He went and placed himself at once under the beam, with his face towards St Sepulchre's. The tall, grave man in black twisted him round swiftly in the other direction, and drawing from his pocket a nightcap, pulled it tight over the patient's head and face. I am not ashamed to say that I could look no more, but shut my eyes as the last dreadful act was going on, which sent this wretched, guilty soul into the presence of God.

There was a great roar from the mob as Calcraft swiftly and expertly launched Courvoisier into eternity; the prisoner did not struggle much, and his wicked and profligate life was ended swiftly and effectively. The mystery man François Benjamin Courvoisier took his secrets, of which I suspect there were many, with him to an unmarked grave within the walls of Newgate, later marked with a 'C' in chalk, and pointed out to visitors as the murderous Swiss valet's final resting place. May the London of present and future generations be free of murderers as cruel and cunning as him!

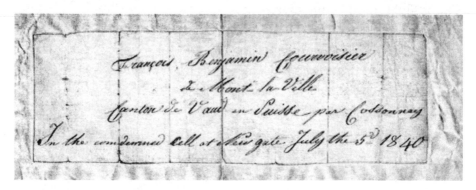

An autograph signed by Courvoisier in the death cell at Newgate.

NOTES

Preface

1. There are copies of this uncommon book at the British Library, at the Bodleian Library, at the Yale University Library and at the University of Kansas Libraries; the Marx Law Library at the University of Cincinnati and the R.G. Menzies Library of the Australian National University have incomplete sets of the penny issues.
2. Work on this book was mainly done at the old Newspaper Library in Colindale, at the British Library, at the National Archives, and at the National Library of Scotland.

Chapter 1

1. Notable biographers of Queen Victoria include L. Strachey, *The Illustrated Queen Victoria* (London 1987), D. Creston, *The Youthful Queen Victoria* (London 1952), E. Longford, *Victoria R.I.* (London 1987), and S. Weintraub, *Victoria* (London 1987).
2. On the media image of the young Queen Victoria, see the articles by J. Plunkett (*Critical Survey* 13 [2001], 7–20 and *Media History* 9 [2003], 3–18), and his book *Queen Victoria, First Media Monarch* (Oxford 2003), 133–9.
3. J. Bondeson, *Queen Victoria's Stalker* (Stroud 2010), P.T. Murphy, *Shooting Victoria* (London 2012).

4. J. Bondeson, *The London Monster* (Stroud 2005), P.D. James & T.A. Critchley, *The Maul and the Pear Tree* (London 1987).

5. C. Reith, *A New Study of Police History* (Edinburgh 1956), 121–245, J. Lock, *Dreadful Deeds and Awful Murders* (Taunton 1990), 7–70, G. Mason, *An Official History of the Metropolitan Police* (London 2004), 9–15, C. Emsley, *Crime and Society in England* (Harlow 2006), 221–52, also the articles by S.H. Palmer (*History Today* 27 [1977], 637–44), P. Lawson (*History Today* 38 [1988], 24–9), R. Paley (*Criminal Justice History* 10 [1989], 95–130) and S. Inwood (*London Journal* 15 [1990], 129–46).

6. On the Donatty murder, see *Annual Register* 1822, 43–5, on the murder of Elizabeth Jeffs, see *Annual Register* 1828, 308–17, and *Illustrated Police Budget* 13 January 1906.

7. C. Reith, *A New Study of Police History* (Edinburgh 1956), 121–245.

8. *The Times* 21, 24 and 25 August 1830, *Morning Post* 30 August and 24 November 1830.

9. J. Lock, *Dreadful Deeds and Awful Murders* (Taunton 1990), 15–24, S. Wise, *The Italian Boy* (London 2005).

10. On the murder of Mr Shepherd, see *The Times* 31 December 1832 and 17 and 19 January 1833, *Morning Chronicle* 18 December 1832, *Hull Packet* 25 December 1832, *Illustrated Police News* 23 and 30 April 1904, and J. Lock, *Dreadful Deeds and Awful Murders* (Taunton 1990), 25–7.

11. On the murder of Catherine Elms, see *The Times* 6, 7 and 11 May 1833, *Morning Chronicle* 7 and 27 May 1833, *The Standard* 6, 7, 11 and 16 May 1833, and *Illustrated Police News* 28 November and 5 December 1903.

12. On the Greenacre case, see C. Pelham, *The Chronicles of Crime*, Vol. 2 (London 1887), 428–53, R.D. Altick, *Victorian Studies in Scarlet* (New York 1970), 37–40, M. Fido, *Murder Guide to London* (London 1986), 163–5, and J. Lock, *Dreadful Deeds and Awful Murders* (Taunton 1990), 28–31.

13. L. Picard, *Victorian London* (London 2005), 255–61, J. White, *London in the 19th Century* (London 2008), 295–321, J. Flanders, *The Victorian City* (London 2012), 393–424.

14. L. Picard, *Victorian London* (London 2005), 255.

15. T. Henderson, *Disorderly Women in Eighteenth-Century London* (Harlow 1999), 52–75.

16. M. Ryan, *Prostitution in London* (London 1839), 88–211.
17. S. Mumm (*Journal of Social History* 29 [1996], 527–46), A.E. Simpson (*Social and Legal Studies* 15 [2006], 363–87).
18. On Waterloo Bridge and its history, see B. Cookson, *Crossing the River* (Edinburgh 2006), 201–21, P. Matthews, *London's Bridges* (Oxford 2008), 109–20, and the papers by E.J. Buckton & H.J. Fereday (*ICE Journal* 3(8) [1936], 472–98) and L.J. Nicoletti (*Literary London* 2(1), March 2004).
19. On the growth of North Lambeth, see Vol. 23 of the *Survey of London*, G. Gibberd, *On Lambeth Marsh* (London 1992) and H. Rennier, *Lambeth Past* (London 2006).
20. *Notes & Queries* 8s. 5 (1894), 316.
21. J. Hawkes (ed.), *The London Journal of Flora Tristan* (London 1984), 81–110.
22. J. White, *London in the 19th Century* (London 2008), 295.

Chapter 2

1. Of the extant short accounts of the murder of Eliza Grimwood, the best are those by W. Long (*Dickensian* 83 [1987], 149–62), J. Lock, *Dreadful Deeds and Awful Murders* (Taunton 1990), 34–9, and J. Oates, *Unsolved Murders in Victorian & Edwardian London* (Barnsley 2007), 13–19. The murder has also been briefly discussed in *Famous Crimes Past and Present* (5(61) [1904], 207–9), G.B.H. Logan, *Guilty or Not Guilty* (London 1928), 261, and R.D. Altick, *Victorian Studies in Scarlet* (New York 1970), 48. The account by B. Cobb, *The First Detectives* (London 1957), 123–42, contains many errors and inventions. In recent years, the Grimwood case has been briefly discussed by M. Spicer (*True Detective*, July 2009, 8–11), R. Crone, *Violent Victorians* (Manchester 2012), 102–4, L. Worsley, *A Very British Murder* (London 2013), 83–4, and J. Adcock (http://john-adcock.blogspot.co.uk/2010/10/who-murdered-eliza-grimwood.html). The case has also been discussed in a modern novel, R. Gowers, *The Twisted Heart* (Edinburgh 2009), albeit without anything new or interesting being deduced.
2. The Strand Theatre was constructed in 1832, at the site of an existing panorama. It was condemned and rebuilt in 1882, and demolished in 1905. Today Aldwych Underground station stands on the site. See the

article by P. Hadley (*London Passenger Transport* 12 [April 1984], 588–93). There does not appear to be any illustration of what it looked like back in 1838, although I found a photograph of it in 1905, just before it was pulled down. J. Oates, *Unsolved Murders in Victorian & Edwardian London* (Barnsley 2007), 14, reproduces a postcard of another Strand Theatre in Aldwych. Constructed in 1905 and also known as the Waldorf Theatre, it is today the Novello Theatre.

Chapter 3

1. The earliest accounts of the murder of Eliza Grimwood were in *The Times*, 28 May 1838, *Morning Post* 28 May 1838 and *Morning Chronicle* 28 May 1838.
2. *Morning Post* 29 May 1838, *Morning Chronicle* 29 May 1838.
3. Old Mother Hubbard, whose cupboard was bare.

Chapter 4

1. These dramatic scenes were detailed in *The Times* 11 August 1835, 8 June 1836 and 14 April 1837, and *Morning Post* 14 April 1837. On the career of Inspector Field, see also P. Collins, *Dickens and Crime* (London 1965), 206–11, and the articles by W. Long (*Dickensian* 83 [1987], 149–62 and *Dickens Quarterly* 30 [2013], 43–54).
2. C. Dickens, Three Detective Anecdotes: 'The Pair of Gloves', originally published in his *Household Words* 1 [1850], 457–60.
3. NA MEPO 3/40.
4. *Ibid.*
5. *The Times* 28 May 1838, *Morning Post* 28 May 1838, *Morning Chronicle* 28 May 1838.
6. These quotes are from *Bell's New Weekly Messenger* 3 June 1838 and *The Globe* 4 June 1838.
7. *Morning Herald* 7 June 1838.

Chapter 5

1. The York Hotel at No. 80 Waterloo Road was a well-known local landmark that stood into the late 1940s before being demolished.
2. The first day of the inquest was described in the *Morning Post* 29 May 1838, *Morning Chronicle* 29 May 1838, *The Standard* 29 May 1838, *The Sunday Times* 3 June 1838, *Weekly Dispatch* 3 June 1838 and *Weekly Chronicle* 3 June 1838.
3. *Weekly Chronicle* 3 June 1838.
4. NA MEPO 3/40.
5. *The Globe* 29 May 1838, *The Times* 30 May 1838, *Jackson's Oxford Journal* 2 June 1838, anonymous article in *Dublin University Magazine* 81 [1873], 273–80.
6. These details, and the Grimwood family tree, are supplied by *The Globe* 29 May 1838 and 18 June 1838, as well as by the 'Grimwood & Grimwade One Name Study' homepage kept by Maggie Driver (http://archive.is/zBEI) and various searches in the FreeBMD and Ancestry databases. There is a discrepancy between Eliza's presumed date of birth, given as 15 December 1807, and her age of death on her death certificate, given as 26 years. Either Eliza had made use of the female prerogative of lying about her age, or the 'Elizabeth Grimwood' born in 1807 died young and another unrecorded 'Eliza' was born in 1812. Eliza had a brother Samuel who died as a teenager in 1815, but her other brothers Thomas, Charles and Richard all married and had families of their own. In 1842, when Richard Grimwood was charged with being drunk and disorderly in Windsor, he presented himself as Eliza's younger brother to gain compassion – see *Windsor and Eton Express* 25 June 1842.
7. Namely *New Newgate Calendar*, Vol. 2 (London 1864), 81–6 and 97–101.
8. *The Observer* 17 June 1838, *Morning Post* 18 June 1838. Eliza had four older sisters, named Frances, Harriett, Sarah and Marianne. The unmarried Charlotte, who died in 1843, is likely to have been the 'cripple', but no sister of hers is recorded to have predeceased her, so the story of the suicide may well be a newspaper invention.
9. *The Observer* 17 June 1838, *Bell's New Weekly Messenger* 24 June 1838.

10. The second day of the inquest was described in the *Morning Post* 1 June 1838, *Morning Chronicle* 1 June 1838, *The Standard* 1 June 1838, *London Dispatch* 3 June 1838, and *The Examiner* 3 June 1838. The strangely named surgeon Mr I'on published an account of the post-mortem appearances in *Lancet* i [1838], 399–400, which was liberally quoted in the daily newspapers – see *The Globe* 31 May 1838 for an example.
11. NA MEPO 3/40.
12. Eliza Grimwood's funeral was described in *Morning Post* 2 June 1838 and *Bell's New Weekly Messenger* 3 June 1838.
13. *The Globe* 2 June 1838.
14. NA MEPO 3/40.
15. H. Mayhew, *London Labour and the London Poor*, Vol. 1 (London 1864).
16. One handbill on the Grimwood murder is kept by the John Johnson collection at the Bodleian Library, and I have another in my collection, both are reproduced in this book. There may well be others in various private collections.

Chapter 6

1. On the capture of Owen, see *The Times* 2 June 1838, *Morning Post* 2 June 1838, and *Morning Chronicle* 2 June 1838.
2. *The Times* 4 June 1838, *The Standard* 4 June 1838, *The Globe* 4 June 1838.

Chapter 7

1. On the third day of the inquest, see *The Times* 5 June 1838, *Morning Post* 5 June 1838, *Morning Chronicle* 5 June 1838, and *The Globe* 5 June 1838.
2. NA MEPO 3/40.

Chapter 8

1. NA MEPO 3/40.
2. *The Globe* 8 June 1838.
3. *The Times* 8 June 1838.
4. NA MEPO 3/40.
5. *The Examiner* 24 June 1838.
6. On the fourth day of the inquest, see *The Times* 9 June 1838, *Morning Post* 9 June 1838, *Morning Chronicle* 9 June 1838, *The Globe* 9 and 10 June 1838, and *Weekly Chronicle* 10 June 1838.

Chapter 9

1. NA MEPO 3/40.
2. *The Standard* 12 June 1838.
3. NA MEPO 3/40.
4. The Cavendish letter is reproduced in *Morning Chronicle* 18 June 1838.
5. On the apprehension of Hubbard, see *Morning Chronicle* 12 June 1838.
6. *Freeman's Journal* 15 June 1838, *York Herald* 16 June 1838.
7. *Morning Post* 12 June 1838.
8. On the examination of Hubbard at Union Hall, see *The Times* 12 June 1838, *Morning Post* 12 June 1838, *Morning Chronicle* 12 June 1838 and *The Globe* 12 June 1838.
9. NA MEPO 3/40.
10. *The Times* 14 June 1838, *The Standard* 14 June 1838, *Morning Post* 15 June 1838, *Morning Chronicle* 15 June 1838, *The Globe* 15 June 1838.
11. Reproduced in *Morning Post* 23 June 1838.
12. On the apprehension of M'Millan, see *The Standard* 15 June 1838.
13. These macabre details are from *The Globe* 14 June 1838 and *The Observer* 18 June 1838, and this scandalous auction is also mentioned by C.E. Pearce, *Unsolved Murder Mysteries* (London 1924), 55.
14. *The Times* 14 June 1838.
15. *The Times* 18 June 1838, *Morning Post* 18 June 1838.
16. NA MEPO 3/40.

17. *The Times* 19 June 1838, *Morning Post* 19 June 1838.
18. *The Times* 20 June 1838, *The Examiner* 24 June 1838.
19. *The Times* 21 June 1838, *The Observer* 24 June 1838.
20. On the Duke of Brunswick, see Anon., *Le Duc de Brunswick* (Paris 1875), O. Böse, *Karl II, Herzog von Braunschweig und Lüneburg* (Braunschweig 1956), *The Mirror*, May 1845, 407–11, and *London Review* July 1863, 62–3.
21. H. Goddard, *Memoirs of a Bow Street Runner* (London 1956), 109–25.
22. *The Standard* 19 and 22 June 1838.

Chapter 10

1. *Morning Post* 23 June 1838.
2. *The Examiner* 24 June 1838, NA MEPO 3/40.
3. *The Observer* 24 June 1838, *Freeman's Journal* 27 June 1838.
4. The *Examiner* 24 June 1838.
5. C. Dickens, Three Detective Anecdotes: 'The Pair of Gloves', originally published in his *Household Words* 1 [1850], 457–60.
6. On Skinner as a murder suspect, see NA MEPO 3/40, W. Long (*Dickensian* 83 [1987], 149–62), *The Times* 4 and 9 July 1838, and *Morning Chronicle* 4 July 1838.
7. *The Times* 4 and 6 July 1838, *Morning Post* 4 July 1838, *The Examiner* 8 July 1838, *London Dispatch* 8 July 1838.
8. NA MEPO 3/40.
9. On the examination of Skinner, see *The Times* 9 July 1838, *Sheffield Independent* 14 July 1838, and *The Champion* 15 July 1838.
10. NA MEPO 3/40.
11. *Household Words* 1 [1850], 457–60.
12. On these transactions, see *The Times* 6 July 1838, *Morning Post* 6 July 1838, and *London Dispatch* 8 July 1838.
13. *Morning Post* 4 July 1838.
14. The sad story of Eliza's little dog is in *Morning Post* 5 July 1838, *Champion* 8 July 1838, and *Bell's New Weekly Messenger* 8 and 15 July 1838.

Chapter 11

1. The 'Golding' and 'Foreign Jew' stories never reached the newspapers, but are in NA MEPO 3/40.
2. *The Standard* 14 and 17 August 1838, *London Dispatch* 19 August 1838.
3. *The Standard* 20 March 1839.
4. *The Times* 1 and 4 April 1839, *Morning Chronicle* 1 April 1839, *The Operative* 7 April 1839.
5. *The Examiner* 25 August 1839.
6. NA HO 44/35, ff 384, 385, 392, 393, 396.
7. On Hill, see *The Times* 25 and 28 August, 8 and 15 September 1845, and *Lloyd's Weekly London Newspaper* 7 September 1845. The original material is kept at NA MEPO 3/40.
8. On the Duke of Brunswick, see Anon., *Le Duc de Brunswick* (Paris 1875) and W.H. Whitehouse, *Charles Duke of Brunswick* (London 1905). On the duke's interest in the murder of Eliza Grimwood, see *The Globe* 19 June 1838 and *The Times* 22 June 1838.
9. On the duke's libel suits and other activities in London, see H. Goddard, *Memoirs of a Bow Street Runner* (London 1956), 109–25, *The Jurist* 10 [1847], 387–9, and *The Times* 25 June 1845, 30 January 1846, 24 April 1846, 1 May 1846, 26 June 1848 and 14 June 1850. The duke later lived in a grand mansion in Paris, where he built a vault for his enormous collection of diamonds, with electric alarms, hidden revolvers and a strong box suspended by four chains. When the vault nevertheless was burgled, and valuable gems stolen, the 'Diamond Duke' was distraught, although the thief was later arrested and most of the loot recovered. He left his fortune to the city of Geneva on the condition that they built him a grandiose memorial monument; it can still be seen at the Quai du Mont-Blanc in that city. The duke's illegitimate offspring were far from pleased with this decision on the part of their eccentric parent, and kept up litigation on the subject as late as the 1930s.
10. On Lunischall, see *The Times* 6, 9 and 12 September 1853.
11. G.A. Sala, *Twice Round the Clock* (London 1862), 242, and *Echoes of Year 1883* (London 1884), 346. Sala had quite a fascination with the Grimwood murder, and also mentioned it in *My Diary in America*, Vol. 2,

13 (London 1865), in his memoirs *The Life and Adventures of George Augustus Sala* (London 1898), 356, in *Belgravia* 23 [1874], 294, and in *Sydney Morning Herald* 29 March 1884. See also J.C. Trewin (ed.), *The Journals of William Charles Macready* (Carbondale IL 2009), 181.

12. *Freeman's Journal* 14 October 1857, *Morning Chronicle* 19 October 1857; see also *Morning Post* 5 November 1857.

13. *York Herald* 28 January 1860.

14. *Morning Post* 11 April 1863, *London Reader*, August 1863, 496. On the murder of Emma Jackson, see J. Bondeson, *Rivals of the Ripper* (Stroud 2016), 31–48.

15. *The Times* 15 December 1863, *Morning Post* 14 December 1863, *The Standard* 15 December 1863.

16. *Freeman's Journal* 23 September 1873.

17. W.F. Peacock, *Who Committed the Great Coram Street Murder?* (London 1873). On the murder of Harriet Buswell, see J. Bondeson, *Rivals of the Ripper* (Stroud 2016), 121–54.

18. *The Standard* 1 April 1869, *Reynolds's Newspaper* 20 October 1878.

19. *Evening Star* 4 March 1876, *Memphis Daily Appeal* 31 July 1881, *New Zealand Herald* 16 March 1929.

20. *Dublin University Magazine* 81 [1873], 273–80.

21. *Daily Telegraph* 6 September 1888, on the Monster see J. Bondeson, *The London Monster* (Stroud 2003).

22. *Irish Times* 9 October 1888.

23. *Essex Herald* 28 September 1838.

24. *Daily News* 18 August 1864.

25. E. O'Donnell, *Confessions of a Ghost-Hunter* (London 1928), 216. On O'Donnell, see R. Whittington-Egan, *The Master Ghost Hunter* (London 2016).

26. *Famous Crimes Past & Present* 10 (125) [1905], 174.

Chapter 12

1. *Household Words* 1 [1850], 457–60.

2. It might of course be speculated that the brothers Grimwood had bribed Owen to perjure himself and that one of them was identical to the man

who had been seen giving Owen money. But Owen certainly seemed crazy enough to have staged the entire thing himself, nor does it make sense for the brothers to hire such a drunken, volatile creature.

3. *Morning Post* 22 and 27 November 1838.
4. *New Newgate Calendar* Vol. 2 (London 1864), 137.
5. *The Times* 28 August 1845. There is no William Hubbard listed as an US immigrant from 1838 until 1848.
6. *Morning Chronicle* 8 March 1841.
7. *The Examiner* 14 March 1841.
8. *The Observer* 17 June 1838.

Chapter 13

1. There are two 'murder broadsides' about the Frederick Street murder. 'Horrid Murder of the Bar-Maid, Hannah Davies' is at the Museum of London (No. A2200), whereas the better-informed 'Another Horrible Murder' is reproduced in the *Curiosities of Street Literature* (London 1871). Much useful original material about the Frederick Street murder is held by the National Archives (MEPO 3/41 and HO 44/30). See also J. Lock, *Dreadful Deeds and Awful Murders* (Taunton 1990), 31–3, J. Oates, *Unsolved Murders in Victorian & Edwardian London* (Barnsley 2007), 8–12, and M. Spicer (*True Detective* December 2011, 54–8). Newspaper sources include *The Times* 11, 13, 15, 16, 19 and 22 May 1837, *Morning Chronicle* 10 and 12 May 1837, and *Weekly Chronicle* 21 May 1837.
2. This public house was at the corner of Frederick Street and Brooke Street off the Hampstead Road, roughly where today Longford Street joins Osnaburgh Place in this vastly changed part of London.
3. *The Times* 15 May 1837.
4. *The Times* 19 May 1837.
5. *Morning Chronicle* 15 May 1837.
6. The tale of the gypsy fortune teller is in the *Morning Post* 27 July 1837 and *London Dispatch* 30 July 1837.
7. *The Times* 27 December 1837, *The Standard* 27 December 1837.
8. MEPO 3/41.

9. *The Times* 28 April 1845, *The Standard* 28 April 1845.

10. MEPO 3/41. The story never reached the newspaper press.

11. J. Lock, *Dreadful Deeds and Awful Murders* (Taunton 1990), 31–3.

12. The police file on the murder of Robert Westwood is MEPO 3/42 at the National Archives. See also J. Lock, *Dreadful Deeds and Awful Murders* (Taunton 1990), 40–50, and J. Oates, *Unsolved Murders in Victorian & Edwardian London* (Barnsley 2007), 20–5. Newspaper sources include *The Times* 5, 6, 8 and 10 June 1839, *Weekly Chronicle* 9 June 1839, *Morning Post* 5, 6 and 8 June 1839, *Morning Chronicle* 8 June 1839, *The Operative* 9 and 16 June 1839.

13. NA MEPO 3/42.

14. NA HO 44/35, ff 384, 385, 392, 393, 396, *The Times* 5 January 1841.

15. J. Lock, *Dreadful Deeds and Awful Murders* (Taunton 1990), 48.

16. On Marchant, see *The Times* 21 May, 22 June and 9 July 1839, *Morning Post* 21 May 1839, *Era* 26 May 1839, and *Morning Chronicle* 20 and 21 May and 2 and 8 July 1839. Later sources include C. Pelham, *Chronicles of Crime* Vol. 2 (London 1887), 478–9, *Complete Newgate Calendar* Vol. 5 (London 1926), 295–6, J. Eddleston, *Foul Deeds in Kensington and Chelsea* (Barnsley 2010), 17–19, and J. Bondeson, *Murder Houses of London* (Stroud 2014), 13–15.

17. On Daniel Good, see F. Tyler, *Gallows Parade* (London 1933), 122–30, M. Fido, *Murder Guide to London* (London 1986), 180–2, and J. Lock, *Dreadful Deeds and Awful Murders* (Taunton 1990), 64–8. The gatehouse of Granard Lodge still stands in Putney Park Lane, but the main house and the stables have been pulled down since they were seen by Guy Logan in 1904, see G. Logan & J. Bondeson, *The True History of Jack the Ripper* (Stroud 2013), 22.

18. *The Times* 25 April 1842.

19. On Dalmas, see *The Times* 1, 2, 3 and 11 May 1844, 24 February 1845, *Morning Post* 1, 2, 6, 7 and 11 May 1844, *Morning Chronicle* 1, 2, 4 and 13 May 1844, and *Lloyd's Weekly Newspaper* 5 May 1844.

Chapter 14

1. The main sources about the murder of Lord William Russell and the trial of Courvoisier are H. Poland, *The Trial of François Benjamin Courvoisier* (London 1917) and Y. Bridges, *Two Studies in Crime* (London 1959), 11–128. There are shorter accounts in the *Legal Review* 11 [1849–50], 376–436, *Law Magazine* NS 26 [1850], 26–36, and *Littell's Living Age* 25 [1850], 289–311. See also A. Griffiths, *The Chronicles of Newgate* (London 1884), 487–91, C. Pelham, *Chronicles of Crime* Vol. 2 (London 1887), 563–83, J.B. Atlay (*Cornhill Magazine* NS 2 [1897], 604–16), R. Storry Deans, *Notable Trials* (London 1906), 260–74, N.W. Sibley, *Criminal Appeal and Evidence* (London 1908), 191–204, C. Kingston, *A Gallery of Rogues* (London 1924), 9–15, and G.B.H. Logan, *Wilful Murder* (London 1935), 58–79. Modern accounts include those by J. Flanders, *The Invention of Murder* (London 2011), 200–8, and M. Knox Beran, *Murder by Candlelight* (New York 2015), 139–81. There is also a good deal of primary material in the National Archives: MEPO 3/44, CRIM 1/1/12 and HO 44/35-37. The Poland book is exceedingly rare, the Bridges book wholly unreliable, and the recent Knox Beran book of an execrable quality, with abundant invented dialogue. The Courvoisier case still awaits its historian.
2. Y. Bridges, *Two Studies in Crime* (London 1959), 13.
3. G. Blakiston, *Lord William Russell and His Wife* (London 1972), 28, 65.
4. There is a biographical sketch of Courvoisier in *Morning Chronicle* 20 May 1840. The story of his dancing at the Scottish wedding was in the *Dumfries Courier*, reproduced in the *Manchester Times* 18 July 1840. An inventory of his clothes in NA MEPO 3/44 shows that this vain and foppish young man possessed six coats, thirteen waistcoats and nine pairs of trousers.
5. *The Standard* 6 May 1840, *Morning Post* 6 May 1840.
6. *The Standard* 7 and 8 May 1840, *Morning Chronicle* 7 and 8 May 1840, *Morning Post* 7 and 8 May 1840.
7. *Morning Post* 8 May 1840.
8. *The Times* 8 May 1840.
9. The murder house at No. 14 Norfolk Street was purchased by the barrister John Ramsden, who lived there until 1851. A number of other householders followed, until the Rev. James Fletcher bought No. 14 in

1868 and lived there well into the 1890s. In 1897, the terrace of houses from No. 12 until No. 19 Norfolk Street was pulled down, and a block of mansion flats erected. Since there was another Norfolk Street in Westminster, from the Strand to the Victorian Embankment, the name was changed to Dunraven Street on 1 July 1939. Dunraven Street still exists, but none of the original houses stand today.

10. *Era* 10 May 1840.

11. *The Standard* 13 May 1840.

12. *Morning Post* 7 July 1840, Y. Bridges, *Two Studies in Crime* (London 1959), 60.

13. E. Henderson, *Recollections of the Public Career and Private Life of the Late John Adolphus* (London 1871), 203–6.

14. On the trial, see Y. Bridges, *Two Studies in Crime* (London 1959), 69–104. Charles Phillips was later criticised over a story that Courvoisier had secretly confessed his guilt to him, although he still demanded to be defended with vigour in court.

15. *Morning Chronicle* 20 June 1840, *Morning Post* 20 June 1840, Y. Bridges, *Two Studies in Crime* (London 1959), 85–8.

16. *Morning Chronicle* 23 June 1840, Y. Bridges, *Two Studies in Crime* (London 1959), 106–10. There was speculation that the naughty book Courvoisier had been inspired by was Harrison Ainsworth's novel *Jack Sheppard*, but the murderer himself claimed it was *A History of the Successful Progress of Criminals*. Here he was taken in a lie, since, according to the Copac and Worldcat databases, no such book exists.

17. *The Times* 24 June 1840.

18. *The Standard* 24 June 1840, *Morning Post* 25 June 1840, *Morning Chronicle* 25 June 1840, *Freeman's Journal* 26 June 1840.

19. *The Times* 25 June 1840.

20. *Morning Post* 25 June 1840, *Morning Chronicle* 25 June 1840, *The Examiner* 28 June 1840, *Blackburn Standard* 1 July 1840.

21. *Era* 28 June 1840.

22. The seller of the book knew nothing of its history, since it had been bought at auction with a parcel of other books.

23. On Logan, see J. Bondeson, Introduction to G. Logan, *The True History of Jack the Ripper* (Stroud 2013), 7–21 and 187–98.

24. *Famous Crimes Past & Present* 3 (37) [1903], 263. He got the number of the house wrong this time.

25. *Famous Crimes Past and Present* 5 (61) [1904], 207–9.

26. *Famous Crimes Past & Present* 10 (125) [1905], 174.

27. G.B.H. Logan, *Guilty or Not Guilty* (London 1929), 261.

28. On Sims, see G.R. Sims, *My Life* (London 1917) and A. Calder-Marshall (ed.), *Prepare to Shed Them Now* (London 1968).

29. G.B.H. Logan, *Wilful Murder* (London 1935), 58–79.

30. G.B.H. Logan, *Verdict and Sentence* (London 1935), 180.

31. G.B.H. Logan, *Masters of Crime* (London 1928), 29.

32. NA MEPO 3/44.

33. *Blackburn Standard* 1 July 1840, *Preston Chronicle* 4 July 1840.

34. Back in 1838, a man's clothing was much more strongly linked to his position in society than it is today, when dukes can dress like dustmen.

35. Yseult Bridges was an old crime writer who liked to think up suitable 'solutions' to historical crimes, and she sometimes made use of her imagination to 'improve on' the facts she possessed. In his *William Roughead's Chronicles of Murder* (Moffat 1991), 204, Richard Whittington-Egan referred to her as 'not the most reliable of authors'. She did not just give Courvoisier straw-coloured hair, but claimed that he was born near Geneva (it was in the Canton du Vaud, and closer to Lausanne). His parents were not 'eminently respectable' but common country people, and he had never received 'an excellent education' but merely attended the village school. He did not run away from home, but was sent to London by his parents in late 1835 to join his uncle. His father Abraham was alive in 1840, so it was also wrong to refer to his mother as being 'widowed'. See Y. Bridges, *Two Studies in Crime* (London 1959), 15–16, 60.

36. H. Malet (*Notes & Queries* 10s. 8 [1907], 408).

37. On Brinkley, see R. Whittington-Egan, *Murder Files* (London 2006), 200–3, and J. Bondeson, *Murder Houses of South London* (Leicester 2015), 264–73.

38. E. Henderson, *Recollections of the Public Career and Private Life of the Late John Adolphus* (London 1871).

39. *John O'London's Weekly* 10 May 1924, Y. Bridges, *Two Studies in Crime* (London 1959), 120–8.

40. NA MEPO 3/44.

Chapter 15

1. On Turpin, see *The Complete Newgate Calendar*, Vol. 3, (London 1926) 88–97, P. Newark, *The Crimson Book of Highwaymen* (London 1979), P. Haining, *The English Highwayman* (London 1991), and J. Sharpe, *Dick Turpin* (London 2004).
2. The Barnwell story is serialised in *New Newgate Calendar* (London 1863).
3. G.T. Wilkinson, *The Newgate Calendar Improved*, Vol. 2 (London 1792), 370–85, E.R. Watson (ed.), *The Trial of Eugene Aram* (Edinburgh 1913), N.J. Tyson, *Eugene Aram* (Hamden CT 1983).
4. *New Newgate Calendar* (London 1863), 1–16.
5. P.D. James & T.A. Critchley, *The Maul and the Pear Tree* (London 1987). Curiously, the early fictional treatment of this case by 'Waters', *Undiscovered Crimes* (London 1862), 255–72, is not mentioned by Baroness James and her cohort. It may be argued that the depredations of the London Monster of 1790 caused a moral panic that equalled the outrage felt at the Ratcliffe Highway murders, but then the Monster never murdered any person.
6. For a discussion of these 'media murders', see the recent works by J. Flanders, *The Invention of Murder* (London 2011) and L. Worsley, *A Very British Murder* (London 2013).
7. D.A. Cohen (*Journal of Social History* 31 (2) [1997], 277–306). See also the papers by S. Chibnall (*Sociological Review Monograph* 29 [1980], 179–217), E.L. O'Brien (*Victorian Literature and Culture* 38 [2000], 15–37), D.A. Cohen (*Proceedings of the American Antiquarian Society* 109 [2001], 51–97) and M.J. Wiener (*Journal of British Studies* 40 [2001], 184–212).
8. On the Red Barn case, see J. & N. Mackenzie, *The Murder of Maria Marten* (New York 1948), D. Gibbs & H. Maltby, *The True Story of Maria Marten* (Ipswich 1949), P. Haining, *Maria Marten* (Plymouth 1992), L. Nessworthy, *Murdering Maria* (Great Yarmouth 2001), S. McCorristine, *William Corder* (London 2014), and P. Maggs, *Murder in the Red Barn* (Chelmsford 2015), articles by E.M. Burrell (*English Illustrated Magazine* 171 [1897], 269–74) and C. Pedley (*Nineteenth-Century Theatre and Film* 31 [2004], 26–38), also *All the Year Round* 19 October 1867, 397–403, *Sunday Times Magazine* 28 May 1967, *Sunday Review* 26 November 2006, and *Murder Most Foul* 82 [2011], 15–21.

9. The skeleton was later handed over to the Hunterian Museum at the Royal College of Surgeons of London, where it was exhibited next to that of the thief-taker Jonathan Wild, but in 2004 it was cremated at the request of Corder's descendants. See *The Times* 18 August 2004, and *Eastern Daily Press* 21 August 2004.

10. *Jackson's Oxford Journal* 2 June 1838.

11. *Penny Satirist*, 16 October 1841.

12. Anon., *Eliza Grimwood, a Domestic Legend of the Waterloo Road* (London 1841). At least three copies of this rare book exist: one is at the British Library, another at the University of Delaware Library, a third was sold by Jarndyce Booksellers in 2002. Louis James misdated this book to 1839, whereas Arthur Edward Waite and Montague Summers misdated it to 1844.

13. L. James, *Fiction for the Working Man 1830–1850* (London 1963), 159–62.

14. I. McCalman, *Radical Underworld* (Cambridge 1988), 227–31. There is a much better informed discussion by J. Adcock on the 'Yesterdays Papers' internet site (http://john-adcock.blogspot.co.uk/2010/10/who-murdered-eliza-grimwood.html), where he makes a good case that the novel was written by the journalist Alexander Somerville.

15. *New Newgate Calendar*, Vol. 2, Nos 53–61, October–December 1864.

16. The standard work on this case is P. Cline Cohen, *The Murder of Helen Jewett* (New York 1998). See also the articles by J.L. Crouthamel (*New York History* 54 [1973], 294–309), P. Cline Cohen (*Legal Studies Forum* 17 (2) [1993], 133–43) and K. Ramsland, 'The Sensational Murder of Helen Jewett' on www.crimelibrary.com.

17. *New York Times* 14 August 1855 and 6 August 1899.

18. Two good recent books on this case, both with bibliographies, are A. Gilman Srebnick, *The Mysterious Death of Mary Rogers* (New York 1995), and D. Stashover, *Edgar Allan Poe and the Murder of Mary Rogers* (Oxford 2006). See also the articles by W.K. Wimsatt (*PMLA* 56 [1941], 230–48), S.C. Worthen (*American Literature* 20 [1948], 305–12), R.P. Benton (*Studies in Short Fiction* 6 [1969], 144–51), and A. Gilman Srebnick (*Legal Studies Forum* 17(2) [1993], 147–65).

19. On the Bickford case, see the papers by B. Hobson (*Boston Bar Journal* 22 [1978], 9–21) and D.A. Cohen (*American Studies* 31(2) [1990], 5–30).

20. These three unsolved murder cases are discussed in J. Bondeson, *Rivals of the Ripper* (Stroud 2016).

21. P.C. Squires (*Criminal Law and Criminology* 29 [1938], 170–201), H.P. Sucksmith (*Dickensian* 71 [1975], 76–83), A. Borowitz, *Blood and Ink* (Kent, OH 2002), 154–7, J. John, *Dickens's Villains* (Oxford 2003), 75–6.

22. C. Dickens, *Oliver Twist* (London 1966), 418–32, 447–53, P. Collins, *Dickens and Crime* (London 1965), 96, H.P. Sucksmith (*Dickensian* 71 [1975], 76–83), W. Long (*Dickensian* 83 [1987], 149–62), see also L. Wolff (*New Literary History* 27 [1996], 227–49), D.C. Archibald in K. Harrison & R. Fantina (Eds), *Victorian Sensations* (Columbus OH 2006), 53–63, and S. Zemka (*Representations* 110 [2010], 29–57).

23. *Daily Mail* 18 April 2009.

Chapter 16

1. From the broadsheet 'Execution of Courvoisier' (British Library shelfmark 1875 D4 (30)).

2. *Morning Post* 23 June 1840, *The Standard* 24 June 1840, *Freeman's Journal* 25 June 1840, *Preston Chronicle* 27 June and 4 July 1840.

3. Popular books on historical mysteries include those by Sir J. Hall, *Four Famous Mysteries* (London 1922) and *The Bravo Mystery* (London 1923), J.G. Lockhart, *Here Are Mysteries* (London 1927), H.T. Wilkins, *Mysteries Solved and Unsolved* (London 1961), and R. Furneaux, *The World's Strangest Mysteries* (London 1961) and *The World's Most Intriguing Mysteries* (London 1965).

4. J. Bondeson, *The Great Pretenders* (New York 2003), 72–126, see also the papers by G.M. Weichhold *et al.* (*International Journal of Legal Medicine* 111 [1998], 287–91) and M. Risse *et al.* (*Archiv für Kriminologie* 216 [2005], 43–53). It is curious that it has later turned out that DNA from the bloodstain on Kaspar's trousers does not match that from hair samples and clothes belonging to him, see B. Brinkmann, Preface to A. von Feuerbach, *Kaspar Hauser* (Leipzig 2006).

5. P. Cornwell, *Portrait of a Killer: Jack the Ripper: Case Closed* (New York 2002), R. Edwards, *Naming Jack the Ripper* (London 2014).

6. *Freeman's Journal* 25 June 1840.

7. L. Gustafsson, *Ur Bild i Bild* (Stockholm 1988), 156–7 (translated from the Swedish by the present author).

8. L. Gustafsson, *Tennisspelarna* (Stockholm 1980).

9. *Morning Chronicle* 6 July 1840.

10. It is curious and noteworthy that much valuable material in this book comes from newspapers not available online, like *The Globe, Weekly Chronicle, Cleave's Penny Gazette* and *Penny Sunday Times*, indicating that the databases for early Victorian newspaper studies are far from comprehensive, and that good old-fashioned research and access to a first-rate newspaper library still play an important part for students of that period.

11. J. Ruddick, *Death at the Priory* (London 2001), J. Bondeson, *Murder Houses of South London* (Leicester 2015), 50–62.

12. G.B.H. Logan, *Guilty or Not Guilty* (London 1929), 163–80, J. Smith-Hughes, *Nine Verdicts on Violence* (London 1956), 1–22.

13. G.B.H. Logan, *Rope, Knife and Chair* (London 1930), 121–37.

14. R. Whittington-Egan, *The Riddle of Birdhurst Rise* (London 1975), see also J.G. Hall & G.D. Smith, *The Croydon Arsenic Mystery* (Chichester 1999), *Master Detective* June 2002, 40–4, and the wholly unconvincing account by D. Janes, *Poisonous Lies* (Stroud 2010).

15. B. Taylor & S. Knight, *Perfect Murder* (London 1987), 241–51.

16. J. Bondeson, *Rivals of the Ripper* (Stroud 2016).

17. For an example, see J. Bondeson, *Murder Houses of South London* (Leicester 2015), 192, on the history of the *Illustrated Police News*, see J. Bondeson, *Strange Victoriana* (Stroud 2016) and *Murderous Victoriana* (forthcoming 2017).

18. J. Bondeson, *The Great Pretenders* (New York 2003), 72–126, J. Bondeson, *The London Monster* (Stroud 2003), A. Frearson (*Journal for Eighteenth-Century Studies* 7 [1984], 211–27). For that matter, the Grimwood case is also predated by the mystery of the location of Major Weir's haunted house in Edinburgh, successfully solved by the present author (*Fortean Times* 311 [2014], 30–6).

19. *The Globe* 7 July 1840.

20. Originally published in *Fraser's Magazine*, July 1840.

INDEX

Index

Macready, William Charles 137
McCane, Henry 167
McFarlane, Sarah 180
Malet, Colonel Harold 210
Malpas, Mr 162
Mancer, Sarah 185, 187–9, 191, 193, 198–9
Manning, Frederick 221
Manning, Marie 221, 245
Mansfield, Earl of 185
Mapleton, Percy Lefroy 208
Marchant, William Henry 175–6
Marr, Timothy 218
Marten, Anne 224, 228
Marten, Maria 7, 68, 222–5, 227–8
Martin, Jem 23
Matthews, Peter 224
Maule, Fox 130
May, James 19–20
Mayhew, Henry 76
Mayne, Richard 16–17, 194
Melbourne, Lord 10–11, 128
M'Millan, Douglas 109
M'Millan, Mr 108–9, 111–12, 117, 154, 206, 258
Molteno, Mr 201
Moore, Mary 227
Morris, Thomas 214–15
Mortimer, Mrs 24

Newland, Samuel 23
Normanby, Marquess of 193
Norris, Mr 18
Norton, Mr 80–1
Nursey, J. 193

O'Connor, Patrick 221
O'Donnell, Elliott 143
Okey, Mr 101, 105
Osborne, William 85
Owen, John 80–3, 87–9, 93–5, 97, 100, 112, 149, 153
Owen, Mr 171
Oxford, Edward 12, 200

Paget, Lord Alfred 254, 261
Palmer, William 218, 245
Palmerston, Lord 137
Parke, Baron 198

Parker, Charlotte 56, 95, 127, 209
Payne, Augustus 255
Payne, Daniel 242
Payne, Elizabeth 69
Paynton, Elizabeth 175–6
Pearce, Inspector Nicholas 171, 173–4, 179, 195–7, 200
Pearcey, Mary Eleanor 208, 255
Peel, Robert 13–16
Pegler, Constable Henry 27, 162–3, 165–7
Pelham, Mr 81, 112, 124, 126
Phibbs, Mr 119
Phillips, Charles 198–9, 200–1, 212
Pies, Hermann 255
Piolaine, Charlotte 185, 200–1
Pook, Edmund 256
Potter, Alfred 256
Powell, Sergeant 52
Price, Sergeant 59, 66, 90, 105, 107, 112
Probert, William 208, 219–20

Read, James Canham 208
Reading, William 170, 173
Redgrave, George 173
Rennie, John 31
Restell, Madame 242
Reville, Ann 255
Reville, Hezekiah 255
Roberts, Mr 130
Robinson, Richard 238–40
Rockall, John 56
Roderick, Constable 166
Rogers, Mary Cecilia 240–2
Rosedale, Mary 58, 90, 95
Rowan, Colonel Charles 16–17, 194
Ruddick, James 255
Russell, Francis 182
Russell, Commander John 194
Russell, John 182
Russell, Lt-Colonel Francis 193
Russell, Lord John 183
Russell, Lord William 178, 182–98, 201–2, 204, 208–12, 219, 257–8, 277
Russell, William 197
Ryan, Dr Michael 30
Ryan, Rebecca 120–2
Ryman, Mr 96–7